The Daily Telegraph
BIG BOOK OF
CRYPTIC
CROSSWORDS
11

The Daily Telegraph

BIG BOOK OF
CRYPTIC
CROSSWORDS
11

PAN BOOKS

First published 2003 by Pan Books

This edition first published 2018 by Pan Books
an imprint of Pan Macmillan, a division of Macmilln Publishers Limited
Pan Macmillan, 20 New Wharf Road, London N1 9RR
Basingstoke and Oxford
Associated companies throughout the world
www.panmacmillan.com

In association with *The Daily Telegraph*

ISBN 978-1-5098-9386-7

A CIP catalogue record for this book is available from
the British Library.

Image-setting and design by Michael Mepham, Frome, Somerset

Visit **www.panmacmillan.com** to read more about all our books and to buy
them. You will also find features, author interviews and news of any author
events, and you can sign up for e-newsletters so that you're always first to hear
about our new releases.

The Puzzles

ACROSS

1 Cricketer with many a hothead in the group (5)
4 In offices press one selection for coffee (8)
10 Problem with medal I'm forging (7)
11 Auditor's complaint? (7)
12 Jack loses his head in church (4)
13 Young leading lady? (5)
14 Born in the Mediterranean? Correct (4)
17 Fatally lose patience when exorcising? (4,2,3,5)
19 Carry out sound alterations in the bell-tower? (4,3,7)
22 Civic head getting a welcome in the grotto (4)
23 One chap accepting military leader from a place in Jordan (5)
24 It is intended to lure one into the club (4)
27 Bright red jalopy I own (7)
28 Brother's top style? (7)
29 Pick out item going round study provided by youth leader (8)
30 After ten years, rotten elm is removed and woody tissue is found (5)

DOWN

1 Raillery is not good in the latter part of one's life (8)
2 Could be late at five past six in Israel (3,4)
3 The man accepting award for an institution (4)
5 Drug pushers who could be stopped by the police (5,9)
6 Man finding gold between the lines (4)
7 Win prosperity (7)
8 Nymph has nothing to study (5)
9 One who believes in self-rule completely disregards convention (3,4,7)
15 Electronic device planted on heartless guy's carriage (5)
16 Penny each possibly? (5)
18 Mother is redrawing the line on the map (8)
20 How poets write upside down (7)
21 Advancing slowly when it isn't steep (7)
22 One caught in the Channel Islands with prickly plants (5)
25 Main point is found in the sports tourer (4)
26 Beast going round New York for some quartz (4)

2

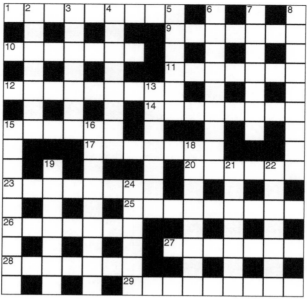

ACROSS

1 Compensates for changes (9)
9 A fall from grace in the Orient appears senseless (7)
10 Parvenu putting a little money into a trust maybe (7)
11 A cash advance could make one representative lie (7)
12 Drags out a few extra words about tractor-production (9)
14 A far from discriminating consumer (8)
15 Ring in to vilify the series (6)
17 Hand over here and now! (7)
20 Quarters many a beast making a getaway (6)
23 Looked around the church and stiffened (8)
25 Fish, or fruit only? (5,4)
26 Size of military body needed to occupy a prison (7)
27 Like a trainee to hold it with just the fingers (7)
28 Nod once perhaps and look the other way (7)
29 A game businessman's aim? (9)

DOWN

2 There's grass to spare possibly (7)
3 A roundabout device, however it's regarded (7)
4 A long but narrow flag for a ship's about right (8)
5 Samuel's holding Sidney up from a wish to hurt (6)
6 Note runs made—or tote buns made? (9)
7 If upset about a domestic pet, will get support (7)
8 Nice teens fashion awareness (9)
13 Superior team's beef (7)
15 A woman's caught on standing (9)
16 Broadcast sport etc absorbing a viewer (9)
18 Taking a relatively favourable attitude (8)
19 Not allowing for that call at the pub (7)
21 Dismiss the person accepting money (7)
22 Get the sack for time on medication? (7)
24 The figure one's repeatedly given (6)

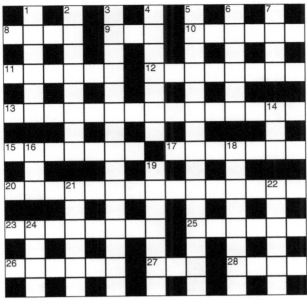

3

ACROSS

8 Ring back for Winnie (4)
9 They are found in the clutch of a radio-van... (3)
10 ...engineers collaborate, in fact (6)
11 Composer to conduct, say? (6)
12 Finally getting rid of the sovereign (8)
13 Traditional sort of assembly has a schedule (15)
15 First-day cover? (7)
17 Tiny piece of insect trapped in tin (7)
20 One may hold surgeries to do with diet (15)
23 Chief looked rather squinty (4-4)
25 Send to Coventry (developed region) (6)
26 Banger unfortunately reverses approaching motorway (6)
27 Silver article displayed by Turkish commander (3)
28 Branch check? (4)

DOWN

1 For a large sum at job-centre, one needs a jacket (6)
2 Slough bad for a malicious woman? (3-5)
3 Breakdown of deliveries (7,8)
4 One could be stuck in a lock on such a bend (7)
5 Describing mathematical function of miracle in grotto, possibly? (15)
6 Package is right in place, being sorted (6)
7 Boy, after midnight, is happy (4)
14 Haggard woman but powerful (3)
16 Foreign aid for the princess in Castle Adamant (3)
18 Ignorance in which Gray's ploughman leaves me? (8)
19 Principal method of making progress (7)
21 Rascal at sea is a foreign sailor (6)
22 A craving is satisfied (6)
24 Ring-tailed yak on its back? Yes, that's fine! (4)

4

ACROSS

7 Try hard to avoid using analgesics (4,5)
8 Is desperate to get American trousers (5)
10 Where a wounded pilot has to be transferred (8)
11 Irritating telephone call around 1.50 (6)
12 Note and second note (4)
13 Move round to dismiss Jack at the wicket (3,5)
15 It is featured in vulgar religious mission (7)
17 Privation clearly seen in Paraguay (7)
20 The drama wasn't bad, to be honest (4,4)
22 Small bird confronts one monkey in S America (4)
25 Tedious rubbish which could ruin the deal (3,3)
26 Took the chair with bias already established (8)
27 Nick is without honour (5)
28 Sang and acted with affectation (3,2,4)

DOWN

1 Sarah's performing in the drawing room (5)
2 Seaweed that is essential for an Australian sheepdog (6)
3 Diet fare served in snack bars (4,4)
4 Some retain a record of correspondence (7)
5 Upsetting misfortune in a tale is likely to be erroneous (8)
6 Rise to meet the challenge (5,2,2)
9 Right to enter objection when describing raw wine (4)
14 Interrogation cell used as a restaurant (5,4)
16 Thank God! (3,5)
18 How the unwary are caught when spring comes (2,3,3)
19 Curiously proud to become a social misfit (4-3)
21 Does it follow John? (4)
23 Bishop in examination of ethnic groups (6)
24 Transport French iron on trains (5)

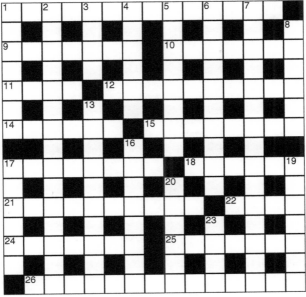

5

ACROSS

1 Something we all have in common (6,8)
9 Last treat for friends at matches (7)
10 Rent row causes a storm (7)
11 Possibly felt that it's not right (4)
12 Dostoievsky's partner in crime (10)
14 Sailor with relevant equipment takes five hundred on the ship (6)
15 Crimes put one's life in jeopardy (8)
17 Bet a long leaping stride is natural to it (8)
18 Slightly deflects the ball and scores (6)
21 Better order meal before I make speech (10)
22 Site in India, grave of Shah Jahan's wife (4)
24 State capital of Natal at variance (7)
25 Swallow one drink that is an aperitif (7)
26 Chatter-box? (9,5)

DOWN

1 Two girls, one on each knee (7)
2 To have to run away from the police is an unexpected occurrence (4,4,3,4)
3 I make an offer in place of a previous quotation (4)
4 Neglect Dad's drink (4,2)
5 Got into a bed made incorrectly (8)
6 Like an astronaut returning—or failing to get lift-off? (5-5)
7 Go under an assumed name (6,9)
8 Sure to change one's ways (6)
13 Genius that outshines all others (10)
16 Near the avenue (8)
17 Is this where the Ark went fast? (6)
19 Not well away from land (7)
20 Saint gets response in church from organ (6)
23 Journey in South Africa (4)

6

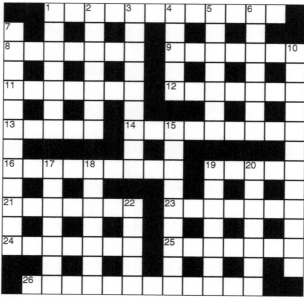

ACROSS

1 You and Eve (6,6)
8 The closest thing to an earnest disposition (7)
9 Alfred II has a following from Lucerne (7)
11 Master who punished boy for an unbelievable lie? (7)
12 Highly abusive letter from a skunk (7)
13 Discover by chance that pop tune is being played (3,2)
14 Oddly enough it means the odds are slim (3,6)
16 Interfere no further with only bird to exist at present (2,3,2,2)
19 How a bird eats large quantities of grain (5)
21 Taken without proof as being a member of a charity board (2,5)
23 Rule broken by a Liberal to form new political grouping (7)
24 Sore back I have proves to be wearing (7)
25 Finish off the rook and you may win it (3,4)
26 Manchester team declares for Uncle Sam (6,6)

DOWN

1 Harbour wine that ships well? (7)
2 Red Indians nip back and enter unnoticed (5,2)
3 A drifter's ultimate financial gain? (3,6)
4 Distribute spare orchard produce (5)
5 Disreputable angle applied to 10 initially (7)
6 Old Mac tells how to avoid sunburn (7)
7 Be aware of the situation particularly in the test match (4,3,5)
10 Lean prisoner rejoined professionals who fly (3,9)
15 Either of us accommodated in tent East of Suez (3,6)
17 Lower way to demonstrate one's unreliability (3,4)
18 One who wants to go places (7)
19 Expression of approval for an archbishop in hell (7)
20 Body armour for objectionable wretch imprisoning terrorists (7)
22 Material running along the border (5)

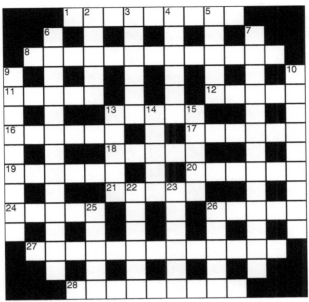

7

ACROSS

1 Bemoaning the faulty alignment (9)
8 Indicator seen in drive (7-6)
11 Some slackness exposed by the cricket team (5)
12 Get to know name of king first (5)
13 Refashioned 'Levi's' can still be worn (5)
16 Record run (6)
17 System used by yours truly does not completely deceive (6)
18 The French hit out using a heavy stick (5)
19 Sea-nymph from Tyneside area has bumpy ride (6)
20 Rogue artist by burn finishes early (6)
21 Little woman in the wood has a twitch (5)
24 Of little folk who are not completely self-indulgent (5)
26 Redhead in hot weather is a card (5)
27 Exploit an opportunity to gain a point on court (4,9)
28 Typist, she is essential to her boss (3,6)

DOWN

2 Join fellow in a dilemma (5)
3 Of interest to consumers? (6)
4 Pretty useless hanger-on? (6)
5 Glen I mistook for another boy (5)
6 One caught fighting... (8,2,3)
7 ...mounted an attack (7,6)
9 Errand-boy creates confusion before turning green (9)
10 I clean out in order to inject (9)
13 Lord taken in by doctor, that's plain (5)
14 Strong fibre cracked tiles (5)
15 Kim's maybe about right to produce an affected smile (5)
22 Suggestion given with a shout of pain that there is an opening in the wall (6)
23 Business concern (6)
25 She's exact about one point (5)
26 Henry goes over the south-eastern port (5)

8

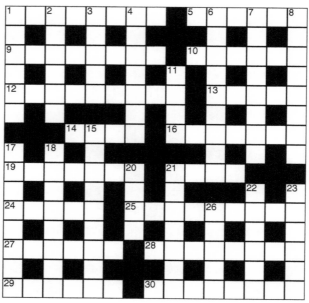

ACROSS

1 The person with a store sticks to new fashion (8)
5 Set heartless fool to study (6)
9 Is rapped for taking a break, and given notice (8)
10 A big noise, a social worker, in Belgium (6)
12 A complaint involving colour (9)
13 Coaches give instruction (5)
14 Equipment kept in storage—a repository (4)
16 Investigate after cheat causes a fight (7)
19 Egghead back from the Orient (7)
21 Getting in the way this month (4)
24 Round some abstract 6 (2,3)
25 Supporters maybe stand around here (9)
27 End up with injuries (6)
28 Repairing 14—time to move out (8)
29 A man given a home by the queen (6)
30 The pursuit of profit (8)

DOWN

1 Pole follows a good man and suffers for it (6)
2 Work on model's face (6)
3 Cut up writer's material and iron (5)
4 Rail over this spy planted in advance (7)
6 Gripes about sound pictures (9)
7 Rose might arrange a date with men (8)
8 Mark will get up in time to set off (8)
11 He's among the richest people in this country (4)
15 Occasions when children may not be choosy (9)
17 Persistent roues let off (8)
18 Criminal dimwits inside (8)
20 Steer straight (4)
21 Popular person, though far from kind (7)
22 A green mould to cause exasperation (6)
23 The appearance of coppers in a group (6)
26 Villain making lament about turn-over (5)

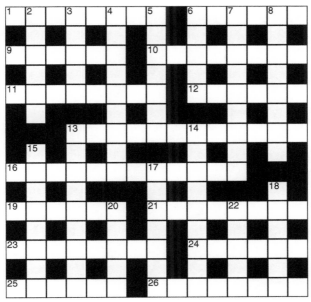

9

ACROSS

1 Spring study makes on knowledgeable (4-4)
6 Somehow, Agatha's without a horror-struck solution! (6)
9 Split stick (6)
10 Was he never an 'in' writer? (8)
11 Mixed choir—it's famous (8)
12 Estate of party chief (6)
13 Late shifts, for example? (5-7)
16 Upsetting ratings, I vote for Dick (12)
19 Ill-fitting insole leaves wound (6)
21 It drains off water when royal egg is cooked (8)
23 Insurance grant for the bedspread (8)
24 Of special architectural interest, is Pisa's tower such a building? (6)
25 Beggarly meals out have yoghurt starter! (6)
26 Cavalier leader of thieves in wrong story? (8)

DOWN

2 Chocolate cake in city study (6)
3 This said, repair is immediate (by a saw) (5)
4 See first at Bath having girth adjusted? It is a plant! (9)
5 Loss of expert around here in France (7)
6 A chief in the lead (5)
7 It shows how far he motored, roughly (9)
8 Guard transported on new line (8)
13 Nine seeds germinating in dearth? (9)
14 Eleventh-hour recovery by the side... (9)
15 ...eleven turning out, taking in work and making a packet (8)
17 Capone, for example, had no name as a popular comedian (7)
18 Tool for taxi-drivers, say? (6)
20 Carolean last words provided for her ongoing sustenance (5)
22 River overlong for this dipper? (5)

10

ACROSS

1 Thoughtful study given incidental regard (11)
10 Allowed to hold Roman coin of the smallest value (5)
11 I shall occupy empty premises despite waver (9)
12 Reference book confirms that the aurochs consumed it (9)
13 Don't let Miss Durie in to play it! (5)
14 French policeman taken to Kansas cinema (6)
16 Cooperate to produce a dramatic dance (4,4)
18 Talks given by Henry Briggs and Tom French (3,1,4)
20 Some minor dictator from Scandinavia (6)
23 Pull up for man at side of road (5)
24 Irritate one president refining oil in Turkey (9)
26 Refusal to go around in California by night (9)
27 Gas a Fellow of the Royal Academy (5)
28 Early contest put disorderly army in peril (11)

DOWN

2 A brave appeal to one of great wisdom (5)
3 Times Educational Supplement suffers a reversal (7)
4 Various people taking the plunge (6)
5 Push the sailor's hammock for a season (4-4)
6 Chest displayed by lofty young male (7)
7 Palm found in employee's apartment (4,2,3,4)
8 Profit declared and denied (8)
9 Memories about Oxford college examinations (13)
15 Case revealing modish attitude of mind (8)
17 Alarming disturbance on the border (8)
19 Money order registered by one on board (7)
21 On receiving small computer, produce circular letter in Greek (7)
22 Look into the winning of every trick in a ski race (6)
25 Where brothers are in command (5)

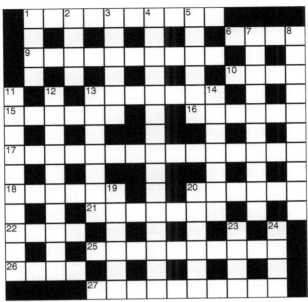

11

ACROSS

1 Uncle who might lend you money (10)
6 Flight, probably rigged (4)
9 Undergo personal participation (10)
10 Ring starts nervous reaction in the ear (4)
13 Ties the rest in knots (7)
15 How's that for charm? (6)
16 See me backing horse entered in Derby, for example (6)
17 A stone's-throw? (7,8)
18 It's capital as a sum resort (6)
20 Unlicensed receivers (6)
21 Dim-sighted King in bed (7)
22 Too many bad workmen tend to blame it (4)
25 Not against change that will prevent the economy from moving (10)
26 Money for one on the staff (4)
27 In a way property is wealth (10)

DOWN

1 Look—here's what we do with the Joneses! (4)
2 Clean the lens, perhaps, for a film effect (4)
3 A gunsmith will add it to his stock (6)
4 Business expenses liable to cause a storm? (8,7)
5 What the unsatisfied audience may shout (6)
7 An impresario may do so without affectation (3,2,2,3)
8 Men creep so to get reward (10)
11 Saw nothing new in an honest feller! (10)
12 He ruins the drink and the game (10)
13 One of rank, perhaps (4-3)
14 Given marks for having been observant (7)
19 Result in changes for part of Ireland (6)
20 Iron man? More deadly, according to Kipling (6)
23 A habit that reveals a lot? (4)
24 Grudging admiration of diplomat who lacks nothing (4)

12

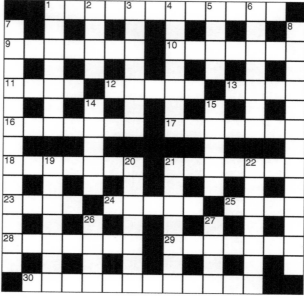

ACROSS

1 Major policy for a minor state (12)
9 True spirit in the heart of a queen (7)
10 Highest army technicians go to dine (7)
11 One looks or looks on (4)
12 Being drunk. And how! (5)
13 Roll—that's what ships do if they roll (4)
16 Suffering from hypothermal exposure, and unconscious (3,4)
17 Storm caused by Strasbourg politician during trial (7)
18 A humpty dumpty backroom boy (7)
21 As a result of being qualified for the next round (7)
23 Jump over a builder's disposal bin (4)
24 Wages paid to prison warder (5)
25 Fit of the sulks displayed by Richard III (4)
28 State of North America attached to the sub-continent (7)
29 Innocent of any cultural attainment? (7)
30 Telephone mix up leads to misunderstanding (7,5)

DOWN

1 Propose dispersing guests around the Grand (7)
2 Riverside where deposits may accumulate (4)
3 Cranky offer which brings nobody any good (3,4)
4 Full understanding is now not far off (7)
5 It crops up in the field of yellow journalism (4)
6 If not too busy you may find it on watch (3,4)
7 How to look smart and urge your case (5,4,4)
8 Didn't start on time so wasn't relieved from duty (4,2,3,4)
14 Frown at a complaining cow (5)
15 Rumba cast a shadow (5)
19 Dutch equivalent of our sovereign given to trade association (7)
20 What autocrats do to their secretaries (7)
21 Famous London street for everyone (3,4)
22 More competent in America are they who take a great interest (7)
26 Bleats from a colonial master (4)
27 Does it teach only 10 letters of the alphabet? (4)

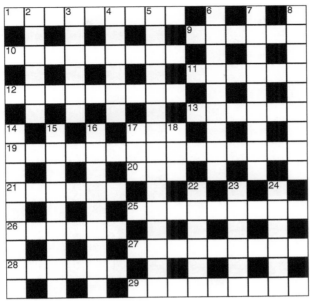

13

ACROSS

1 Roman magistrate in favour of a foreign government agent (9)
9 See nothing in being decrepit (6)
10 A skinhead is bound to find out (9)
11 Vehicle left in the plant (6)
12 No cost at the hostelry on this island (9)
13 Legally bind one to do a favour (6)
17 Some passenger form of transport of old (3)
19 Conditions marionettes have (7,8)
20 Record turned over by youth leader in Strand (3)
21 Materially it holds bits and pieces (3-3)
25 First person in France has short run before arranging meals at a holy place (9)
26 Reduce by removing end of the picture (4,2)
27 Aeroplane prepared three times for member of moneyed social group (3-6)
28 Find a colt kicking about with energy... (6)
29 ...pony? any gee-gee initially cavorting in North Korea (9)

DOWN

2 Is encircled during an insurrection (6)
3 Entry on the right (6)
4 Make known it hasn't been provided by end of day (6)
5 Cure for the world's ills? (9,6)
6 Sweet wobbly food, a vegetable! (9)
7 Is this what one needs eyes in the back of the head for? (9)
8 Votes to finish in a free organisation under the king (9)
14 Right up in the seat with legs wide apart (9)
15 Aroma coming from newspaper in the country (9)
16 At home one day I had some food but was never satisfied (9)
17 Stinger decapitated creeper (3)
18 Home in West Yorkshire (3)
22 Burns, not using the right measure found in the laboratory (6)
23 Result of father's attempt at cooking? (6)
24 it flows always between south and north (6)

14

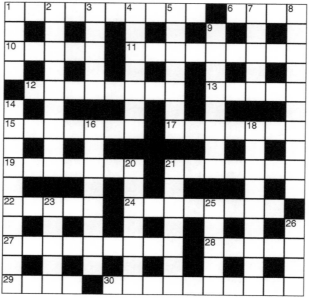

ACROSS

1 A foreigner is done in—an awful discovery (10)
6 Drive, given advance notice (4)
10 Class a high-minded individual held in church (5)
11 Record—it's causing complaint (9)
12 Clears rents, not for the first time (8)
13 Currency that's a little out of the ordinary (5)
15 May be in a bar with a man not allowed alcoholic drink (7)
17 Distinguished, though plainly ineffective (7)
19 Working over fish (7)
21 Finding water running, phoned in really upset (7)
22 Chatter cut short by a minister (5)
24 Many rest badly in any surroundings, showing strain (8)
27 Not polluted, but dull—use in moderation (9)
28 Confused tot left with a key (5)
29 There's still one snowman to be built (4)
30 Fetching sort of dogs (10)

DOWN

1 Well-liked chief—but not for long! (4)
2 See a drop, possibly about 500, which is tough (9)
3 Relative eye-opener in a Mediterranean resort (5)
4 This may well go ahead in America (7)
5 A skilled man's articles about the Right—it's shown as in a muddle (7)
7 Hardly ever converse (5)
8 The underworld charged at random (10)
9 Quietly trade or exchange a hunter (8)
14 Run to earth in the South-east (10)
16 Letters of identification (8)
18 Down town to catch up on popular game (9)
20 Stony, but in great form (7)
21 Some beasts set about police officers and judge (7)
23 Attack, that is lay about a quarter (5)
25 Pomp and display, say (5)
26 The woman having to live on a boat (4)

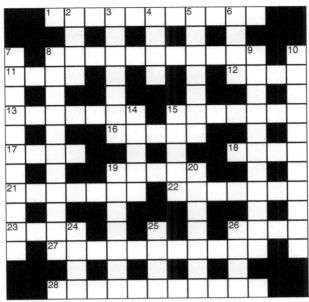

15

ACROSS

1 Wimbledon, for example, popular station (11)
8 Caprine group gathers food all over the place (4,2,5)
11 American bonnet for Robin (4)
12 Tar kept in a cellar? (4)
13 Bunch of ribbons worn as a favour (7)
15 Take on more fellows in a tug, at sea (7)
16 Order from the dictator (5)
17 Remnants of ambition (4)
18 Beginner in mountain district left out (4)
19 Warmish sort of diet includes a pint (5)
21 Without thorns, duramen can be worked (7)
22 Strange dialect associated with river-mouth? (7)
23 Diocese right for this prophet (4)
26 Porgy takes science at university (4)
27 Neck-chop, game and spiced drink (6-5)
28 Shrub that produces light fruit? (11)

DOWN

2 Was in debt for ring, getting married (4)
3 Referee puts me on a diet that is new (7)
4 Crass f-football follower stands on his head (4)
5 Beware!—it may have high tars in it (7)
6 Musical acts in variety (4)
7 Rush to look after sister, possibly (6-5)
8 But does he trade punches? (5-6)
9 Shooting-brake? (6-5)
10 Chest to pose problem? Use this in diagnosis (11)
14 Piped over the border? (5)
15 Bitter cold in dry environment (5)
19 Trial bench for engineers? (4-3)
20 Pluck needed to find treasure in river (7)
24 Fun for students, a kind of Indian music (4)
25 Eyesore you once found on street (4)
26 Mark in saloon on Sunday! (4)

16

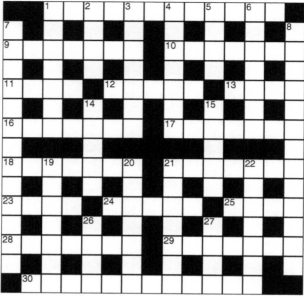

ACROSS

1 I'm so startled when confounded by a poser (7,5)
9 Army men truly needed to get satisfaction (7)
10 Tourist who is heading for a fall (7)
11 One upper-class fool suffering a setback (4)
12 Exhausted writer getting in the way (5)
13 One put in to organise a tumbledown house (4)
16 Last of the wine put down by Fred Astaire? (7)
17 Runs into demure fellow south of London (7)
18 Characteristic otherwise displayed by Judas (7)
21 Plagiarist has advertising material to catalogue (7)
23 Composer dear to the Welsh (4)
24 A little bit of a fight (5)
25 Nothing after 151 is representative of history (4)
28 What the final batsman is given to survive (7)
29 High Priest returns to the house to give praise to God (7)
30 The hit of Paris! (8,4)

DOWN

1 Get Bill twenty-four sheets (7)
2 Neat road-junction on the border (4)
3 Clean son followed by a tiny young dog (5,2)
4 Acts in a fashion which is quite evil (7)
5 Pair heartened by American greeting in America (4)
6 Sovereign has to set out the argument (7)
7 Reprimanded for having one's writings published (7,2,4)
8 Marvellous subject for 'The Racing News' (5,8)
14 What the Palestinians most want to say (5)
15 Rings up small bear of very little brain (5)
19 He sounds like a vinegary old stylite (7)
20 Revised article for public reading (7)
21 Conflicts caused by Conservative whips (7)
22 Staff College needs to accommodate one (7)
26 Large car for the Holy Roman Emperor in 1500 (4)
27 Being written in palindromic form (4)

17

ACROSS

5 Not fit to be a member of the staff (6)

8 Think about as you cut through the outside (4,4)

9 Shows they're the cause of many separations (7)

10 Tries to please and does, perhaps, when young (5)

11 Drink and be demoted (4,1,4)

13 Trickles and spots the paper lining (8)

14 Lots and lots of chips? (6)

17 Sanction the small supplement (3)

19 The name of the game (3)

20 Try to win a home—timbered (6)

23 Where every round is close (8)

26 High-class way of saying "main attraction" (3,6)

28 Jack-fish, we're told (5)

29 For looting in the store, convict (7)

30 Bars intended for the bedroom window (8)

31 Ask the sea to recede as well (6)

DOWN

1 Puts quickly away when one laughs at (6)

2 It's stranded on the beach (7)

3 An artist in copper (9)

4 Argue, but be proved wrong in time (6)

5 Extra fashionable line in trousers (8)

6 Let out again to be given the nosebag outside (5)

7 Rehearses when the play's folded (4,4)

12 When hit, it dropped from the tree (3)

15 It had gone off in the angler's basket (6,3)

16 People pass—one is hemmed in (8)

18 Went into greater detail about the grand finale (8)

21 As before, it's music to the ears (3)

22 Rather like the mail order the gentleman is holding (7)

24 Pressed on, in dire trouble (6)

25 Side with one another (6)

27 Detail I omitted, foolishly, from the letter (5)

18

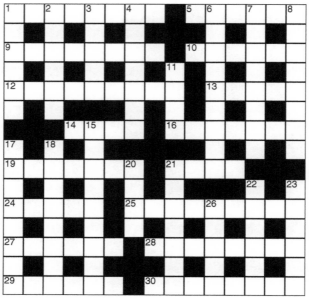

ACROSS

1 French king to have possession of South African city (4,4)
5 Promotion for one of those in flight (4,2)
9 Arrested for having parked at lay-by (6,2)
10 Times the Queen needed a rubber (6)
12 Rider seen ordering team for a sleigh (9)
13 Revokes endlessly just to elicit a reaction (5)
14 Girl in glasses (4)
16 Rumours heard by American lodgers (7)
19 Entertaining reason for not letting someone borrow your tool (7)
21 Devout and sober minded prime minister (4)
24 A dismal return to the Australian outback (5)
25 Take a holiday and proceed to desert (2,2,5)
27 Latins agitated for a leader who sent dissidents to ... (6)
28 ... request seasoning for the crisps (4,4)
29 Capturing the ruler of Dad's Army? (6)
30 Escorted by an unsupportive bridge partner (5,3)

DOWN

1 Edible flower buds cut by pranksters (6)
2 Parson's stand—on pornographic literature! (6)
3 Tendency to have an upright aim (5)
4 They serve people in a queue? (7)
6 Answered a summons to appear only to be evicted (6,3)
7 Skip a meal at the end of lent (4,4)
8 For every one poem is contrary (8)
11 Way back a king in Russia (4)
15 I am in a state of exuberance (9)
17 Little monkey likely to spoil second round of tennis (8)
18 Get a slipped disc and retire (4,4)
20 Jokes that leave one speechless (4)
21 Sailor turning up in Malayan boat is properly proportioned (3,4)
22 California needs Chinese nightclub (6)
23 Failing to join the enemy (6)
26 Turner depicting an old part of Kent (5)

19

ACROSS

1 Paid to have come to rest (6,4)
6 Rod used to perform magic (4)
9 Bowler not on top (3-7)
10 Gloucestershire point-to-point (4)
13 Group about to return to the lake (7)
15 A bird or two are able to be heard (6)
16 A shady walk back by southern animals (6)
17 Socialist who does not want the right to rule (6,9)
18 Body of soldiers by the point (6)
20 Girl not in charge of an Italian city (6)
21 Flocked round torpedo (7)
22 Work doggedly to produce a hit (4)
25 Very quietly one girl is held back, getting into a musical instrument (10)
26 Legal action? (4)
27 Be unwilling being envious (10)

DOWN

1 Photographed attempt at goal (4)
2 Expression of impatience about fine cluster (4)
3 Divulge gently inside that it's an old Greek coin (6)
4 Going round the bend? It's risky here (9,6)
5 We get the wrong insect (6)
7 One is held by the robot with a high degree of mechanisation (10)
8 The way things are going currently (10)
11 Strangely idealistic, it was emphasised (10)
12 US co-member became unwieldy (10)
13 He argues sophistically in case, conscientiously? (7)
14 'e bowled erratically, having been knocked (7)
19 Hesitant reply to question as to whose fur it is (6)
20 Poetically skilful (6)
23 Stereo some find tough if inelegant (4)
24 Chinese guild's unfinished vehicle (4)

20

ACROSS

1 The coolness of people following a certain "economy with the truth" (10)
9 She's a bit of a harridan, Nanny is! (4)
10 Competition men turn to—a new sort (10)
11 Dined at the back of the hotel, as is natural (6)
12 A large number demand applause (7)
15 A glider would make an unusual present (7)
16 It's about those of advanced years getting put in prison (5)
17 Stop giving support (4)
18 A president without money but with some power (4)
19 He does love to spot royalty! (5)
21 Hero worshipper, being inadequate, turning colour (7)
22 Set right concerning get-up (7)
24 Quake, losing heart, and find the voice high-pitched (6)
27 Study criticism (10)
28 In retreat, so left no capital (4)
29 Affecting the ratings? That's smashing! (10)

DOWN

2 Spoil too many returns (4)
3 Sign on a letter accompanying a catalogue (6)
4 Pallid characters came in a convertible (7)
5 Decide against taking part—fancy! (4)
6 Seen as overweight, with very cold behind (7)
7 A French title 18 finds unspeakable (10)
8 Reserve troops made a smaller advance, lacking expertise (10)
12 Notes the answer could be indulgence (10)
13 Stop for some players—a couple of girls (10)
14 The free Roman's property (5)
15 Always after small cut (5)
19 Rats given just punishment (7)
20 Sceptre representing honour (7)
23 Hit a high spot and get the bird (6)
25 A dyke-builder will take endless refuse (4)
26 Business house in the money (4)

21

ACROSS

1 Real Madrid, turning out, display a butterfly (3,7)
6 Study almost bare (4)
10 Romance of wild love after midday (5)
11 Bias of 10 perhaps, as concomitant of pride (9)
12 Cargo yet to be placed for Confederate soldier? (8)
13 Party taking the Spanish trademark (5)
15 Something invented—all change? (7)
17 A brown I mixed from lots of other colours (7)
19 Collected works of a passenger-carrier? (7)
21 Pander to sovereign as provider of food (7)
22 Composer long in army (5)
24 Royal Navy faster, perhaps, to hand over (8)
27 Engagement (later, both go off) (9)
28 High-pressure area, torrid generally in the interior (5)
29 Recess for cooking peas (4)
30 Unwanted third party is often a fool (10)

DOWN

1 Rotten Row? (4)
2 Girl goes to Reading for amusement... (9)
3 ...English lady to set up stall (5)
4 Turn the corner in Rally? (7)
5 One who helps a superior (7)
7 Rise of Conservative member (5)
8 Intense rivalry over job of felling, possibly (10)
9 One usually has a second helping (8)
14 The wind up, up? (10)
16 Macbeth's end—vaulting? (8)
18 Counter-offer made by pub helper (9)
20 This Armstrong rested, with companion, on near side of moon (7)
21 Wine or tea—endless ecstasy! (7)
23 Water-lilly that creates many states? (5)
25 Drudge, an insignificant person (5)
26 Exceedingly light (4)

22

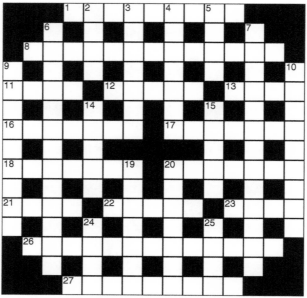

ACROSS

1 Experimental examination scheme for a high-flier (4,5)
8 Look away as every one asset is removed (5,4,4)
11 Piece of land Saladin failed to save (4)
12 Calm seaman took a meal (5)
13 One silly enough to produce puréed fruit (4)
16 Succeed in getting a Greek cross the day before (7)
17 Wandering for miles, as wildly as can be (7)
18 Last man taken in as apprentice by Australian friend (7)
20 Henry yearned to get wed (7)
21 Average number joining the Marines (4)
22 The way to get on to the platform (5)
23 Wintry weather in the South at present (4)
26 Think about Samuel's mentor perpetrating perjury (10,3)
27 Bath is dry, strangely enough, for annual celebrations (9)

DOWN

2 Each service rendered to make money (4)
3 Time to get E European currency out of difficulty (7)
4 Sluggishness shown in hesitation by Spanish aunt (7)
5 Outstanding wife immersed in a dictionary (4)
6 Bowling session by the Australian captain in Scotland (4,3,6)
7 Practise how to be a pickpocket (3,4,4,2)
9 Mother has a picture inlaid in metal (9)
10 Cease trading near N Ireland county (5,4)
14 The man will love to get a greeting (5)
15 Strike a small, small coin (5)
19 Withdraw into monastic seclusion (7)
20 Hollow-cheeked harridan has to pull back (7)
24 One faint reflection from the south of France (4)
25 Group of five accommodated by Ottoman officer (4)

ACROSS

1 Account for all that talking? (9,4)
10 Fashion arbiter of Welsh taste (7)
11 Vessel churning up water left and right (7)
12 Ever changing wind movement (4)
13 Game supplied in a box (5)
14 Nuts—crack almonds to start with (4)
17 Left 'ock damaged by tuft of horsehair (7)
18 Quote an expression of disbelief (4,3)
19 All the same, it suits some people (7)
22 The sort of hat one may have to eat? (4-3)
24 Trial sample (4)
25 Burnt out with stress (5)
26 He changes colour in Ryde, perhaps (4)
29 Conclude there's no place for the damned (7)
30 He had an uncle and sisters on the stage (7)
31 Trial marriage? (8,5)

DOWN

2 Are moving home, it must be serious (7)
3 Goes out after a rise (4)
4 Retaliate and strike a player (3,4)
5 Section reserved for reviews (7)
6 Lines at last for the annoying child (4)
7 Rock music (7)
8 Rome's source for investors looking for a return (5,13)
9 Traverse route gathering valuable discoveries (8-5)
15 Come out with me again and have a drink (5)
16 Hardy variety of monster (5)
20 To some extent it's of Iran's making (2,2,3)
21 He had his first signal success about the turn of the century (7)
22 Criticise long dash (7)
23 Possibly spy on fashionable medium (7)
27 He's amongst the richest men in the land (4)
28 Juliet's town is just not on for her (4)

24

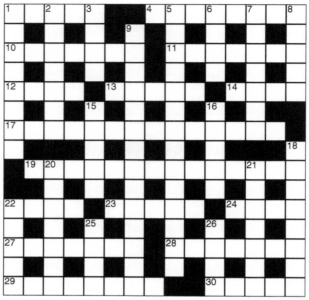

ACROSS

1 Is it rolled turf or asphalt? (5)
4 Furious herald would call it rampant (2,2,4)
10 Mine needs bandaging (4,3)
11 The end of a flight at the top of the flight (7)
12 Support not required by a jet plane (4)
13 Small investment in valuable fur produces capital for Belarus (5)
14 A wager to help criminal activity (4)
17 Paper shop proprietor who passes on gossip (8,2,4)
19 Text book example of an angry allusion (5,9)
22 Menial schoolboys were forbidden them (4)
23 Foolish enough to give second-rate service (5)
24 Name "The Greatest" country in Africa (4)
27 Lost sheep must have returned to make the argument stick (3,4)
28 Hostile to information describing a vaccine (7)
29 Cargo list is clearly displayed (8)
30 Jeannie sounds a spirited servant (5)

DOWN

1 Tempestuous duke to get on with an appeal (8)
2 Applicants hope it will bring news of what they have applied for (3,4)
3 Pop or wine? (4)
5 East European of renown gets Capone to eat heartily (6,3,1,4)
6 Not one could name one (4)
7 Colour spectrum described by eminent London artist? (7)
8 Tourist attraction in a sense (5)
9 They won't go out to meet big waves (6,8)
15 Honours for the winner of the race (5)
16 Poles are to set a trap (5)
18 Recalcitrance of French boy friend (8)
20 British sappers and American soldiers need discipline (7)
21 Intoxicating drink derived from gentian (4,3)
22 Flying Officer leading weird discussion group (5)
25 Did it chew up the fowl? (4)
26 Shilling price label, or should it be a buck? (4)

ACROSS

6 Begins after having convulsions and has only spasmodic bursts of activity (4,3,6)

8 Second-class variety of spice giving strength to one's arm (6)

9 One who originates most of the catalogue (8)

10 It can be pricked even after it has been pierced (3)

11 One led astray, by the way, is the laziest (6)

12 The seat 'e removed from one affecting an extravagant love of art (8)

14 Unfinished building to north of Texan city (7)

16 Quietly continue to take for granted (7)

20 Cross the road for an easy victory (4-4)

23 A glove often is available (2,4)

24 Be without most of the resin (3)

25 Constance and Denise I leave make it briefer (8)

26 Company car that's found by the hollow (6)

27 Odds at the beginning of an auction (8-5)

DOWN

1 Stations girl in Merseyside town (2,6)

2 Felt a sot had modified his high-pitched voice (8)

3 Commander, possibly red, coming from Real Madrid (7)

4 Seaside resort not far from Huntingdon! (2,4)

5 & 6 Parisian chips? (6,5,8)

7 Resembling a player? That's fair (13)

13 Part of foot used to point? (3)

15 Elegant woman's figure? (3)

17 Again take possession and live in the same place twice (8)

18 Hoped sir could get into shape (8)

19 From Salerno a new place in America (7)

21 Steal young animal Peter brought up (6)

22 Case of excessive pride? (6)

26

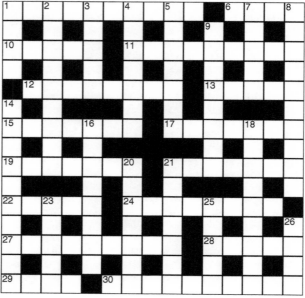

ACROSS

1 Healthy stock could be transported in it (5,5)
6 Prize fruit (4)
10 A male factor (5)
11 Down the media in action (9)
12 Unparalleled description of the Commons (8)
13 Public appeal to cut green wood (5)
15 Ingenuous but heartless Cockney (7)
17 Capitalise on a notable achievement (7)
19 Marching order by a jingoistic Democrat! (7)
21 Concealed gaol-break from a Spanish bigwig (7)
22 Put back outstanding piece of bone (5)
24 Indirectly referring to retiring Roman dictator before I have (8)
27 Dazzling blonde? (9)
28 Australia confronts individual issue for ecologists (5)
29 Day in Rome comes to an end (4)
30 I tried less to become free of infection (10)

DOWN

1 Aim to leave a pound (4)
2 A bit up on a single punter (3,6)
3 Noted performer takes in one eastern lute (5)
4 Remedy is to change gear (7)
5 Stalemate produced by admission of obsolescence (7)
7 Stocking material from a large offshore region (5)
8 Thought and time goes into resolving disputes (10)
9 Got one's cash back from car with red body (8)
14 Exaggerated its exotic provenance (3-7)
16 After a period fur can be scrubbed out (8)
18 Thoughtless ex-pupil with £4 to cover debts (9)
20 GP has nothing but a dose of medicine (7)
21 English composer has little hesitation in becoming a gun-carrier (7)
23 It can pull up a station-wagon (5)
25 Crossed threads over on a sewing machine (5)
26 Heavy Metal star player (4)

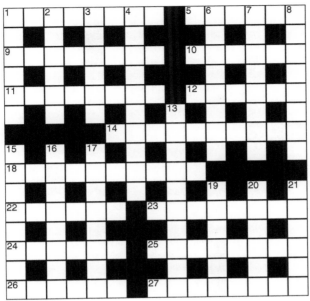

ACROSS

1 The odd pie calls for added seasoning (8)
5 Becoming a supporter with evident hesitation (6)
9 Pass several, being liberal (8)
10 Saved for new drapes (6)
11 When marginal land experiences the least ups and downs (4,4)
12 They're prepared to fight for a rise, possibly about a thousand (6)
14 Purposeful muse (10)
18 Got up and phoned in—changed the order (10)
22 Rail against the controversy in town (6)
23 Asinine pair, popular though criminal (8)
24 Representations will be made if game is affected (6)
25 Work on hand (8)
26 This banded stone from Cologne is superb (6)
27 Showing principle about people's housing (8)

DOWN

1 Not now to be seen in a Southern Hellenic city (6)
2 Bring down to earth over gold 16 (6)
3 Heartless people lay a little money (6)
4 Appear in need, but not so—funny woman! (10)
6 A writer offering serving men a drink (8)
7 Irregular worker after small change (8)
8 Salad food prepared by an artistic person? (8)
13 A burning issue! (4-6)
15 Calling outside right for a hammering (8)
16 Bearing the transport charge (8)
17 She's responsible for maintaining order in retirement (8)
19 Claim devastating note will cause ill-will (6)
20 Think to take over (6)
21 Set on getting under canvas? (6)

28

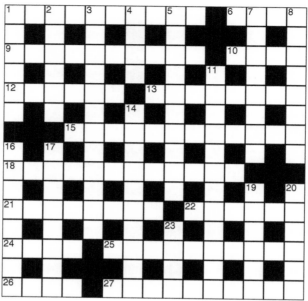

ACROSS

1 I'm going to repeat that, despite lacking education (10)
6 He's not a striking fellow (4)
9 Appropriate restrictions in real estate (10)
10 Old German has nothing, but he puts on airs (4)
12 Small piece of offal—a very small piece (6)
13 President awards honour to pilot (8)
15 No, when one comes to think about it (2,10)
18 Compelling need to link studies and tuition (12)
21 I sent tea in exchange for a liqueur (8)
22 Decline to fit another detonating device (6)
24 Preference for bismuth and arsenic (4)
25 Pleasant Democrat likely to be voted in (10)
26 The day before getting new uniform (4)
27 Those coming to ball two hours before midnight (10)

DOWN

1 Duty to give one Frenchman a job (6)
2 Call for large spectacles to be given to family (4,2)
3 The ardent hen needs treatment immediately (5,3,4)
4 Assess what the speed is (4)
5 Obey orders to set foot on the Equator (3,3,4)
7 Country makes appeal to see doctor held by US agents (8)
8 Monk possessing automatic rifle (8)
11 Records previously set by Rex and Edward is upset (12)
14 Leave me some biblical books—or a section (10)
16 Muddle resulting from motor-cycle rally (8)
17 Hint from a bosom pal (8)
19 Died in a city in Natal (6)
20 About to give in and go back (6)
23 Present from the Red Cross (4)

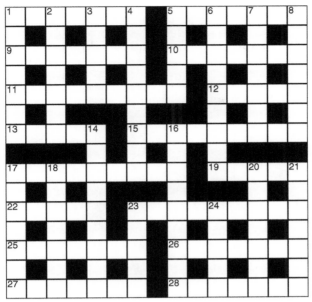

29

ACROSS

1 Don't ring Irma, I left her sleeping (7)
5 Look forward to the dance, foregathering for it (4,3)
9 How a dentist carries out extractions all day? (3-4)
10 Turns out and tidies up the files (7)
11 Shoot off to unload (9)
12 For the arthritic, it's difficult (5)
13 Asses and gentle deer are all about (5)
15 Wheeling prams in spring, when there's good weather (4,5)
17 Moved the champion rider out (9)
19 Is coming to the point, listeners (5)
22 In the end, find the right path (5)
23 Possibly bag a duck on the roof (3-6)
25 No, I'm sick at heart returning the fortune (7)
26 What can one do to show one's sorry? (7)
27 In the event, not having taken place (7)
28 Free accommodation included with the plane (7)

DOWN

1 Back in action, the debt collector left one with nothing (7)
2 Calls for a round and you have a drink (5,2)
3 Along with the letter (5)
4 Most uncommon! (3-6)
5 As far as your garden goes, be non-committal (5)
6 Continues to get the papers one's ordered (7,2)
7 In holiday mood, set off in the early morning (7)
8 Undisturbed by the outbreak of flu, on balance (7)
14 The picture is silent—a biography (5,4)
16 VIP treatment for a Yorkshire terrier, perhaps (3,6)
17 He has to be in to take delivery (7)
18 Bird down (7)
20 Go on from the overture (7)
21 Be inclined to think America made up 50 per cent of the onlookers (7)
23 Nervous, point the gun the other way (5)
24 Having no interest in, at about nine, turn in (5)

30

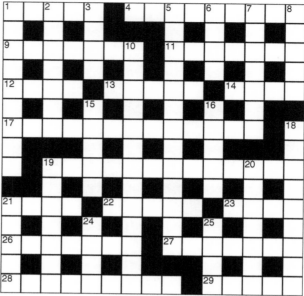

ACROSS

1 Clans dispersed to English county (5)
4 Highly desirable groom can be relied on to hold a ball (4,5)
9 Stage set by lieutenant for school of philosophy (7)
11 Lengthen your strides if a stair tread is missing (4,3)
12 The many—not us (4)
13 Where outdoor fun is accompanied by loud melodies (5)
14 Produce a yarn and tell it (4)
17 One of the 10 collecting shingle by a turbid stream (7,6)
19 Confronting the management means accepting a new concept (6,2,5)
21 Cry of pain from chap swallowing a ring (4)
22 What the porridge needs when one is up and about (5)
23 Door of tent in which the panicky find themselves (4)
26 Pudding from a pot CIA cooked up (7)
27 One who tries to find a roadway leading to a waterway (7)
28 Take-over bid which has now gone unconditional (4,5)
29 Get the best of anything but the best (5)

DOWN

1 Maybe a poor harvest, but that is a very long way off (5,4)
2 An inducement to lay up reserve capital (4,3)
3 Country which the British claimed but French returned (4)
5 Conservatives given to wild bravoes for star study centres (13)
6 In mid America English find a French city (4)
7 Nothing in report sent back by cavalryman (7)
8 Guess what popular song is being broadcast (3,2)
10 Maybe a blackboard pointer is an educational complement (8,5)
15 A false front put on when feeling a bit off colour (5)
16 Roots out cheque counterfoils (5)
18 Demon drink produces ill feeling (3,6)
19 One who goes pelting around Canadian forests (7)
20 Finished the hurdle race (3,4)
21 Sawyer rises provided there is a theme (5)
24 It's dead—dead—dead! (4)
25 Bow to audience seated 16th from the front (4)

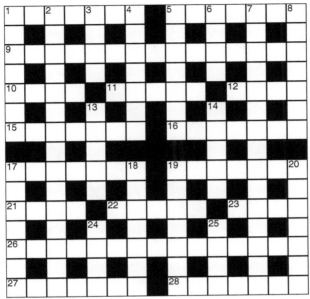

ACROSS

1 Criticised hit (7)
5 Humorous magazine has nearly everything at the back (7)
9 Jubilee time (6-4,5)
10 Henry, towards the stern, finds a handle (4)
11 Transport vehicle by railway (5)
12 Keen about the opening passage right away (4)
15 Sharply provoked? (7)
16 Went barefoot in water or by canoe (7)
17 Longed for a new deanery (7)
19 Similar type and colour (7)
21 Turn on a fool (4)
22 Debris forming an incomplete shield (5)
23 One's taking the Parisian area that's detached (4)
26 One isn't glad to recall such experiences (7,8)
27 Herd not stampeding whilst seated! (7)
28 Catch agent setting off chain reaction (7)

DOWN

1 Room where Kenneth contains his restless desire (7)
2 Sequence of eleven? (3,5,7)
3 Does it fly like a bird? (4)
4 Swindle of French/German woman on daughter (7)
5 Withhold information about six balls in a beaker (5,2)
6 Can have a ball in Ireland (4)
7 Main route between England and France? (7,8)
8 Caught young lady with nothing on, a journalist (7)
13 Not Alan falling in a dance (5)
14 Man in drivers' club in Turkey (5)
17 Youth leader replaced trough containing curdled food (7)
18 Decomposed for what sounded like ten years (7)
19 With the best sight and most eager (7)
20 Clothier from Wales? (7)
24 Shop entrance features sign (4)
25 Roman Catholics coming from tropics with a helmet (4)

32

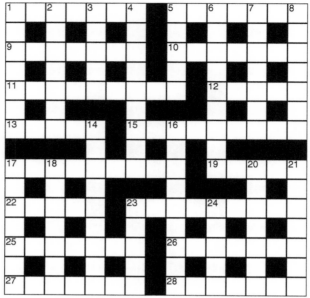

ACROSS

1 Scraps for a bird (7)
5 Many a mad character causes talk (7)
9 He faces facts—retails make-up (7)
10 Soldiers caught row and lie (7)
11 A room below ground-level can bring on depression (9)
12 Not all would thank leftists for a bit of personal support (5)
13 Make a start by giving directions to ill-behaved tot (3,2)
15 Dull colour for sink, say, never backed (4-5)
17 Taking a job as the alternative—and quickly! (9)
19 Field some servicemen become proficient in (5)
22 Song about a high-minded individual getting excited (5)
23 They're fine, though invariably cast down (9)
25 Counting as influential (7)
26 The spendthrift beginning work alters surprisingly (7)
27 Particular concerning parking in school environs (7)
28 A revolutionary leader? (7)

DOWN

1 Almost convinced quiet fathead could be better (7)
2 Infuriated a reflective worker, being so unyielding (7)
3 Sound fish to rear (5)
4 Sees sense maybe—within reason (9)
5 The gold standard (5)
6 Harbour a heavenly being (9)
7 Go-slow to bamboozle the French (7)
8 A school for girls—awfully dear one! (7)
14 Ring the sage without the right as in disagreement (9)
16 The Welsh fighter's objective in a black look (9)
17 A note added to change to get a certain book (7)
18 Arranges seating (7)
20 A course for the new trainee (7)
21 Got comfortable home and got ahead (7)
23 View a good deal (5)
24 Doctor going round practice was thoughtful (5)

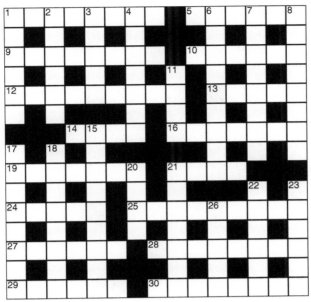

33

ACROSS

1 Absolutely certain to be above zero (8)
5 At home inside that protective head gear (3,3)
9 Assiduous in ensuring nothing enters through this way (8)
10 Led the way to a goal? (6)
12 It's discourteous if gun is fired at everyone by a worker! (9)
13 Fail to tell the truth in being unable to get up (3,2)
14 Part of the hand is restricted by foot (4)
16 People who know a lot take their beds for luck! (7)
19 Film's error showing how fisherman hauls up catch (5,2)
21 Informed that it's not good to point (4)
24 Catches a bit of a knock going in the back way (5)
25 Nothing nice made into vegetable salad (9)
27 The older guide has a right to offend (6)
28 No sound from this weight lifting equipment (4-4)
29 A set is split up to allow for an afternoon rest (6)
30 Furious to notice a particular object (8)

DOWN

1 Dejected when ejected (3,3)
2 Marine animal might be a parasite (6)
3 Sing a round with goblin (5)
4 Five give an allowance for the itinerant (7)
6 Thought is led without being considered perfect (9)
7 He would almost get the greedy pig, this prickly fellow (8)
8 All in good order, so pack it up before finding quarters in Norfolk town (8)
11 Am getting around to the smallest thing (4)
15 Very emphatic little sister—about design (9)
17 Brilliant star attacked by angry high class dog (8)
18 Keep notes on someone who is held (8)
20 Nominate, being rather mean about it (4)
21 Reason to ease cub out (7)
22 Woodland gods are moving around in isle (6)
23 Black mood induced when girl returns across the Atlantic perhaps (3,3)
26 First basses performed duet for their opening work (5)

34

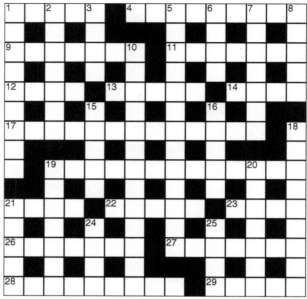

ACROSS

1 Below a river in Glamorgan (5)
4 Where stevedores work for a jolly fine fellow (4,5)
9 Advise David facing Goliath to have a little gander (7)
11 Typical measure by couple to show affection (7)
12 Some duck left after a repast (4)
13 All agreed to redress the wrongs (5)
14 EC member arousing English wrath (4)
17 Do the spadework in road construction (7,3,3)
19 Company employees fish for a manly greeting (4,9)
21 Feeling low a day after (4)
22 Sound a warning after the manner of marines (5)
23 A crystal box (4)
26 Greens go around a church (7)
27 Refuse to state all the cases (7)
28 Not burdensome at all to get a bull's-eye (9)
29 Extract metal from freshwater fish (5)

DOWN

1 Unusual thing to glimpse in a club (9)
2 Where Inquisition victims were bound to be in jeopardy (2,5)
3 He succeeds in heartening the IRA (4)
5 An outstanding man heard innuendo being made (3,2,1,7)
6 Cries for bishop to put in request for aid (4)
7 Appeal to Harrisburg shows lack of clarity (7)
8 Narcissistic subject (5)
10 Turn over an entire pig and show no restraint (2,3,5,3)
15 Badger for a young prince (5)
16 Small desire to be fashionable (5)
18 Seriously, I make a living in the home (2,7)
19 One died surrounded by plants in the States (7)
20 Inform the old man to return the award (7)
21 Considered a great number exploited (5)
24 Penny has everything needed for a shroud (4)
25 America supports Common Market currency (4)

35

ACROSS

7 Those who start such an event never finish it (5,4)
8 It's unusually early for bed (5)
10 Game for a dance at the depot (8)
11 Mokes I assemble for the race (6)
12 Fruitless, badly organised raid (4)
13 Restrain distribution of tracts (8)
15 Officer is on his own in pass (7)
17 Casual way in which you remove a glove? (3-4)
20 Money held in trust not long ago (8)
22 She lives in Los Angeles (4)
25 A girl who can help people out (6)
26 Pass this examination? (8)
27 Drop—of cheap wine? (5)
28 Coastline irregular in parts (9)

DOWN

1 All, for example, done wrongly, but within the law (5)
2 Rush job? (6)
3 I'd turn up in a sort of orange fabric (8)
4 Churchman gets a pass, yet goes astray (7)
5 Violent reaction against corporal punishment (8)
6 This way for the train (9)
9 One of them will take you back in the car (4)
14 It's only fair the board should accept new role (9)
16 Completed more than once? That's too much (8)
18 High-pitched river battle (8)
19 They should be allowed to be themselves, we're told (7)
21 Fuel container in military vehicle (4)
23 Where porpoises are taught? (6)
24 Girl takes Poles round America (5)

36

ACROSS

6 Increase the pressure for a house warming suggestion (4,2,3,4)
8 Claim made by member in the drink (6)
9 Resigning without a second ruling (8)
10 Jack turns traitor (3)
11 Drug one takes on as a medicine (6)
12 Crazy gate has been removed from its post (8)
14 People who won't give up—their accommodation? (7)
16 Treatment of ambassador admitted to party organisation (7)
20 Advice to one who is flagging? (4,2,2)
23 Case for including one in a Chopin waltz (6)
24 A liturgical greeting in heaven (3)
25 Keep your hair on if you want to stop sweating (4,4)
26 A Titan resolved to reach the goal (6)
27 There is no precedent for a public transport strike! (7,2,2,2)

DOWN

1 Priceless square mile owing allegiance to no state (4,4)
2 Colonial appointee installed to regulate speed of revolution (8)
3 Crank to go into business (5,2)
4 French I hope are of the Israeli faith (6)
5 Flag showing the Quaker ship was ready to sail for America? (6)
6 Urban slang is a local scandal (4,2,3,4)
7 Offer to temper love (6,7)
13 That is about 100 below 132 deg F (3)
15 The priest Elijah and Elisha had in common (3)
17 Get into an argument about how best to try out a dinghy (4,1,3)
18 One of the family gives Rex great joy (8)
19 A page containing article describing royal estate (7)
21 Did he become devout only some time after the crucifixion? (6)
22 Hot line? (6)

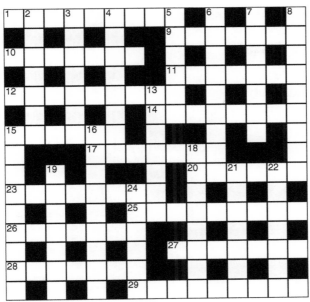

37

ACROSS

1 Computer used to examine and analyse gold (9)
9 On the whole it provides protection (7)
10 Man with a girl on his knee (7)
11 Room in the French network (7)
12 Without another clue—that's very unimportant! (9)
14 Bursting forth into pure chaos (8)
15 Slipper included by a model used as a charm (6)
17 Candy i.e. recycled is poisonous (7)
20 A man of no spirit and passion not starting to dress (6)
23 Cheat a servant, that's the rule (8)
25 Fit person's welfare (4-5)
26 Phrenologist leading the tribe? (7)
27 Silver ball on the beach (7)
28 Journalists, despite receiving no backing, continue energetically (5,2)
29 Drops toga in a crumpled condition—because there's a snail in it? (9)

DOWN

2 Down-to-earth approach exists in the kingdom (7)
3 One of the same rank to be a match for the commander first (7)
4 Lechery of Sarah going over a large town (8)
5 Smoother wave? (6)
6 A child of six (9)
7 Peaceful water (7)
8 Take turns to change neat design (9)
13 Catty in a big way? (7)
15 Found in the centre of Hull? (9)
16 Spend carefully or save (9)
18 Clear space, but it's not there at night (8)
19 Stained but could be the same colour (7)
21 Not win game with Venetian painter (7)
22 Bump and meet an old friend perhaps (3,4)
24 Having about now, gin cocktail (6)

38

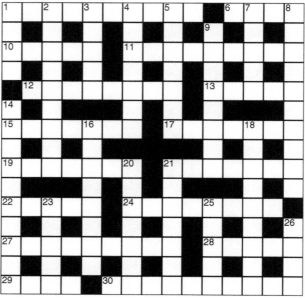

ACROSS

1 A member of the family goes first with little hesitation (10)
6 A good sparkling wine, but some may prefer a still one (4)
10 Much inclined to submerge (5)
11 Look on beaming as a bloomer (9)
12 To walk around is bliss! (8)
13 The choosy individual makes his mark (5)
15 Carrying on operating as a fence (7)
17 Housing row (7)
19 The old ruler of Ethopia is allowed fish (7)
21 Church leader giving coppers report (7)
22 Sarah on the motorway in quite a ste! (5)
24 All through the players being far from bright (8)
27 Popular Eve isn't—can be so demanding! (9)
28 Representative of conservationist body seen after a time (5)
29 Women of habit (4)
30 Repeatedly went over a tree—tries to shape it (10)

DOWN

1 Very very fair (2-2)
2 A novel tie may bring promotion (9)
3 It's seemingly good in the deep colour (5)
4 Attempting to catch a glimpse of royalty (7)
5 Hint the Spanish and French circumscribe people (7)
7 There's a lot to see (5)
8 Got involved with organising decent ride (10)
9 Army personnel against cutting short the crossing (8)
14 The train that's for making over (10)
16 Some foreigners will obtain a list in a break (8)
18 The gathering meant perhaps to hold a service (9)
20 A quarter got up about four—so wearing! (7)
21 Attending to get something for nothing (7)
23 Having left school, this should be revealed (3,2)
25 Seating for the small child put on display (5)
26 The boss finding book-work unfinished (4)

39

ACROSS

1 Hefty chap with a dozen jobs to be done (8)
9 Some bowling by players can be dull (8)
10 Colossal inner-bones? (4)
11 Desalination process put under state control (12)
13 Small burn to tolerate on stomach? (8)
15 Basque basket-work, just for recreation (6)
16 Fixer used in photography, possibly (4)
17 Welsh official acted to contain game (5)
18 Retired New Zealander I left to wander (4)
20 Condescend to include Sunday project (6)
21 Do try a pate-spread! (3-5)
23 Walking fast in the dark? (12)
26 Norseman fine when collected by family (4)
27 The King of Barataria, for example? — Nice to include it! (8)
28 The use of ancient language in archaeological work is becoming wider (8)

DOWN

2 See about Daisy in cold wind (8)
3 Head specialist in tragic solo crash (12)
4 Fast time, one-fifty, for a pulse! (6)
5 Couples opening Somerset House here in London (4)
6 Affected indeed, we hear, having done a bunk (8)
7 Defile ticket (4)
8 Breeding-ground for dust, perhaps, holding (4-4)
12 Rough handling in which tall men tire badly (3-9)
14 Bank on credit? (5)
16 Epicure possibly—he'd love tins of stew! (8)
17 Timed any explosive? (8)
19 Well-forced up in France (8)
22 Beast displaying bony plate on its back (6)
24 Loaves of bread for the swans (4)
25 Shop-soiled habit put on daughter (4)

40

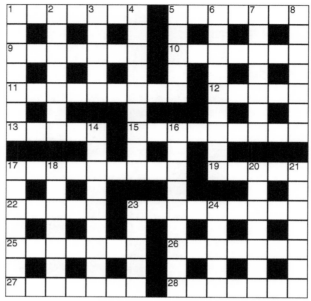

ACROSS

1 Make a detour to find ring buried in the earth (2,5)
5 Church curator makes Salvation Army get Catholic backing first (7)
9 Nothing but pitch counts for an outstanding cast (3-4)
10 A professional position would be suitable (7)
11 A very quiet London borough is attractive (9)
12 Rhino needs sodium salt (5)
13 Skilled enough for a small government ministry (5)
15 Make one's point, but be marked wrong (3,6)
17 Call to ban women's wear from the suburbs (9)
19 Former Irishman now living abroad (5)
22 One going after fish bones (5)
23 In military resistance sappers gain respect (9)
25 Forgetting a name is bizarre (7)
26 Heavy fabric isn't used to refurbish an old coat (7)
27 Maybe a group of devil worshippers chop up bodies (7)
28 General disposition to blow things up (7)

DOWN

1 Elderly relation meets transatlantic lawman in Spain (7)
2 A leper's treatment clearly hasn't worked! (7)
3 Extreme device for decoding Enigma variations (5)
4 Pocket pistol for the German campanologist (9)
5 Made notes about Latin colloquialisms (5)
6 Record very serious article in French (9)
7 What an artist may produce one minute past midnight (7)
8 Lets us cook up small scraps (7)
14 Argue the point to bring the children along (4,5)
16 Its job—to compel the Argentines to surrender! (4,5)
17 Where one expects to find fruit or vegetable (7)
18 Third-rate angels are supporters of kings (7)
20 Basket for girl in marine promenade (7)
21 Where scenes are created by article on rate review (7)
23 Bill gets a call-up in America (5)
24 Push back piano in middle of Scottish dance (5)

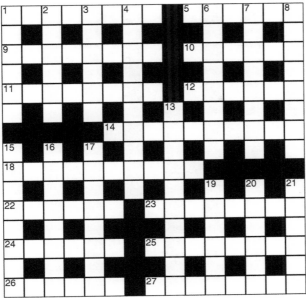

41

ACROSS

1 The boxer is running round the ring. What's up? (8)
5 In a fury, I put back the queen (6)
9 Bales out—a complete disaster (8)
10 Paper with lines on it (6)
11 A bird hopping round (8)
12 Making a comeback in the starring role about a biblical character (6)
14 A vertical take-off. Honestly (8,2)
18 Accommodation, even so, will be arranged in time (3,2,5)
22 Easier to touch, though harder to borrow from (6)
23 Keep quiet when brought to book (8)
24 The non-soldiers, in turn, enlist (4,2)
25 Able to read the title out "Time Held Captive" (8)
26 Achieving equality in pay, having a right to it (6)
27 Seems frightened by the many birds about (8)

DOWN

1 Lays hands on some blunt weapons (6)
2 Knock off at sunset and have a meal (6)
3 Wait for the idol of yesteryear to come in (4,2)
4 Quite a number got upset by the anaesthetic (10)
6 Out of money, barter (8)
7 Found one tin damaged and I polished it off (8)
8 For a bet, run with one of the world's fastest runners (8)
13 Miss home mostly at weekends? (6,4)
15 Makes as though to go, but doesn't keep the appointment (6,2)
16 Compromise, to restore good relations (8)
17 Is not indelible, it is revealed (5,3)
19 Back on board (6)
20 One can't run out of it (6)
21 A break in the depression (6)

42

ACROSS

7 Post needed for a king's armour (5,4)
8 Even it is reversible (5)
10 Facial feature emphasised by a higher cheek (5,3)
11 Bury Pole in a concentration camp (6)
12 From Spain came his conqueror (4)
13 Common wife found in the Netherlands (3,5)
15 Hoot in case a guard's van appears (7)
17 Church House is run by a Euro-Conservative (7)
20 What a sempstress does when a godly man is impatient (8)
22 Oracular prophet returns to the body (4)
25 Vegetarian diet for ecologists (6)
26 A verse from Lear celebrated by the mouth of Shannon (8)
27 Slander contained in manuscript returned by auditor (5)
28 Take precautions by treating bone with a drug mixture (2,2,5)

DOWN

1 Smart car proves a brilliant success to a point (5)
2 Engage staff to win popularity (4,2)
3 Classified announcements dishearten small lads (5,3)
4 Little Diana upset upset upset (7)
5 A player's longest and strongest attire from Savile Row (4,4)
6 Latest release has apparently become a recidivist! (3,6)
9 Personal claim staked by a prospector (4)
14 It will signal Doomsday for the desperate bridge player (4,5)
16 Coming—by road apparently (2,3,3)
18 A simple brain makes for a clear conscience (4,4)
19 A note added to change 'Songs of Praise' (7)
21 He was supported by the Schutzstaffel (4)
23 Raise the price when the pound comes under pressure (4,2)
24 Small car park on the side of a hill (5)

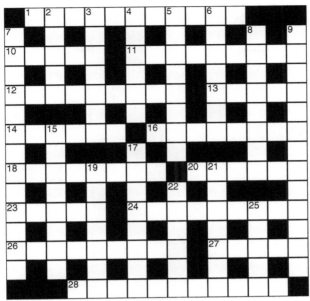

43

ACROSS

1 Hymn that's a proposal for marriage? (5,4,2)
10 The Spanish taken in by a bird, a Trojan beauty! (5)
11 Gruel liar prepared for an underground fighter (9)
12 £1.05 for the ocuntry? (3,6)
13 Join one with energy (5)
14 Having sawn timber, move heavily (6)
16 Queasy, I'd turned by the wharf (8)
18 Left inside with nurse going round (8)
20 Boy meets girl in India (6)
23 Cat, shark, snake, wolf or lily (5)
24 You are, say, and I found in Tirana, revolutionary but fictitious place in SE Europe (9)
26 Feeling a thrill (9)
27 Conservatives' claim (5)
28 Single names could be insignificant (11)

DOWN

2 It is hell down here (5)
3 Hollow bend about to be found in teeth! (7)
4 Mischievous fellow accepts drink whilst carrying on (6)
5 The hothead with fever in Holland (3,5)
6 Element from another planet? (7)
7 Work one does not expect gratitude for (9,4)
8 Maintaining that I am writhing in embrace (8)
9 Do, before leaving (8,5)
15 Fellow getting on with running the company (8)
17 Roger troubled Scotsman, one coming from an American state (8)
19 Make a mistake getting into another seat with a sawlike edge (7)
21 Hold spellbound during the seventh rally (7)
22 Scottish novelist involved in corn distribution (6)
25 Students included, say, a hot drink (5)

44

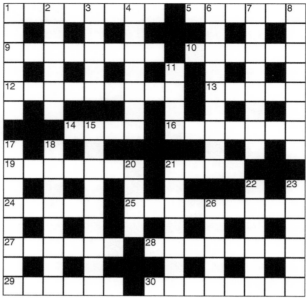

ACROSS

1 A guideline for colours (8)
5 Speak about a certain point, and elaborate (6)
9 Spots the head's indiscretion (8)
10 Pass in correct order please (6)
12 The crowd will get cold on the track (9)
13 Stories of porter going in the back way (5)
14 Some become avid letter-writers when unemployed (4)
16 People require such food ripe and not otherwise (7)
19 Deal in used cars (7)
21 Rings back repeatedly, though indifferent (2-2)
24 The man who's always ready to take part (5)
25 Brachycephalic anti-monarchist (9)
27 Travel round acting aggressively (6)
28 A small deposit secures! (8)
29 One's double (6)
30 Inclination to create great din (8)

DOWN

1 Trim a tree for Christmas? (6)
2 Inattentive seaman told to go (6)
3 A wild animal doing badly (5)
4 11 is something to fall back on (7)
6 The family comprises 13 (9)
7 The mate put inside paled dreadfully, being scared (8)
8 Service flat—bargain price! (8)
11 Maintain a strong position (4)
15 Respect shown by guard surrounding royalty (9)
17 Restrict the cash in irregular situation (8)
18 Some go wrong, note, in making beds (8)
20 Find fault with vehicle parking (4)
21 The hoggish male is so inferior! (7)
22 There's wickedness without measure in the city (6)
23 These days "green" gets publicity (6)
26 It's anxiety that makes many peruse their books (5)

45

ACROSS

7 Hide a stone—from a miser perhaps? (9)
8 Lie about the material (5)
10 Right, put about, nothing French is unclean (8)
11 Deed which involves mixing a tonic (6)
12 Boast about clothes (4)
13 Roy turns up in the dining room with a leading lady of the town (8)
15 Moved in a great hurry to fire rifle (7)
17 Outer garment which might be gloss (3,4)
20 He intends to support Rose in some style (8)
22 Tidings from all quarters (4)
25 Bony cavity occupied by a worker with spirit (6)
26 Rare dame cooked with something sweet (8)
27 Silver tea set? No it's made of quartz (5)
28 Order naval shock to the Spanish by using underwater air lines (9)

DOWN

1 Go around in woman's clothing (5)
2 He may cause a sleeping partner to take action (6)
3 Take care, Gill reacts badly to certain things (8)
4 The smallest matter in any study of body structure (7)
5 100 followed his violent riot—it was memorable (8)
6 Give him a ring on the great day (9)
9 To be cautious in the street is right (4)
14 Mistakenly ran to page for protection (9)
16 Eat pears cut up, on their own (8)
18 Decorate using ten Roman pieces (8)
19 Bring the vegetables forward (7)
21 Coming back just like me, not different (4)
23 Twisted round the curve in alarm (3,3)
24 Cry welcome! (5)

46

ACROSS

1 Managing to bring Henry and Heather together (8)
9 A claret served following a select menu (1,2,5)
10 100 sq. metres added to a district (4)
11 The average firm has to act with resolution (4,8)
13 Drag out a pamphlet from the Public Relations Office (8)
15 Where workers look for payment from transport charge (6)
16 A heroic tale from picturesque Picardy (4)
17 Love to examine an old Italian language (5)
18 An utter bore and swine (4)
20 Popular N Carolina boy in his birthday suit (6)
21 Acrobats who need glasses (8)
23 Take risks to produce inflammatory drama (4,4,4)
26 Tuna salmagundi for a Malayan gentleman (4)
27 Actually being one second inside the limit (8)
28 Calm down when put in peril (8)

DOWN

2 Affectation on holiday from the point of departure (8)
3 Airman turns up in Admiralty compound with a flourish (12)
4 One S. American game-bird confronts a lizard (6)
5 Dress a fish for presentation to bishop (4)
6 Convey information via cross letter written in great emotion (4,2,2)
7 Not charged and not imprisoned (4)
8 Males use bad language. It's their habit (8)
12 Fresh group includes nonsense in current affairs programme (4,8)
14 Understood it was given to Tom in return (5)
16 Unaspiring chap made a wisecrack which fitted (8)
17 Sundial for a senior citizen (3-5)
19 Cancel order to a barge (8)
22 Disabled girl embraces me (6)
24 What cotton-mill Luddites were opposed to? (4)
25 Hard and consumed with bitter animosity (4)

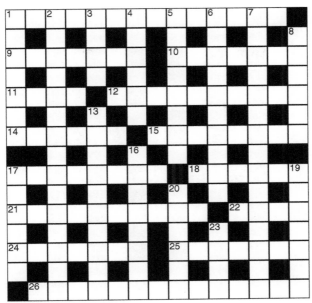

47

ACROSS

1 Gift firm commonly excluded from criticism (7,7)
9 One about to settle in the country (7)
10 When guns are effectively fired in anger, perhaps (2,5)
11 Takes a choice sort of post (4)
12 To us a Shakesperian character appears successful (10)
14 Makes headlines? (6)
15 Right leader in a fight (5-3)
17 Painless manipulation for dogs (8)
18 American beauty queen is married (6)
21 A fishy diversion (3,7)
22 Not a cheap term of affection (4)
24 Tributes to the dead from the wars (7)
25 Arched an jumped (7)
26 Perhaps only a sissy chap takes this treatment lying down (14)

DOWN

1 Put two and two together (4,3)
2 Words that appeal to the voter (8,7)
3 Cheese that's badly made (4)
4 Henry, Edward, Mary and Elizabeth, from Stroud (6)
5 Neglect nothing on a job (8)
6 It's exactly according to form (7,3)
7 Roman marbles missing (3,6,6)
8 Observe present and past in child's play (3-3)
13 Application for injury benefit, perhaps (10)
16 Open coal fires I left to go out (8)
17 They may be drawn or sucked up (6)
19 Takes good steps not to have to walk in the streets (7)
20 Odd vigil held by distraught nun (6)
23 His eye's on the target (4)

48

ACROSS

6 Ran a West London borough by chicanery (6,7)
8 Mother with Caledonian charm (6)
9 Sort of glass I had taken to the Arctic circle (8)
10 Erotic excitement in a brute (3)
11 Temple where father is filled with a divine spirit (6)
12 Switching centre for trading institution (8)
14 Frisked a South African revolutionary (7)
16 Excessive weight is dispersed yet I sob (7)
20 Difficult battle ahead of English computing equipment (8)
23 Tarzan was a physical fitness fanatic (6)
24 Brown is to press for payment (3)
25 Wood hyacinth for a stage girl (8)
26 What one must pay for electricity supply (6)
27 I spotted peril developing for butterfly minded student (13)

DOWN

1 A snort from a person who should win... (5,3)
2 ...anything but a steeplechase (4,4)
3 Maybe a plug for a novel transcriber (7)
4 French bitterness over return of the Channel Islands (6)
5 I go astray in South America mountain chain (6)
6 Start constructing a rhomboid to provide an analogy (4,1,8)
7 Giving up crime but not turning the corner (5,8)
13 Say Hi hurry! (3)
15 Put one's oar in and create an argument (3)
17 Showed a pale face how vegetables are par-boiled (8)
18 So a nicer set is needed for a drama plot (8)
19 Climbing arachnid with large middle and gaudy mouth (3,4)
21 Pipe construction in some French port (6)
22 What the wrongdoer should make at noon (6)

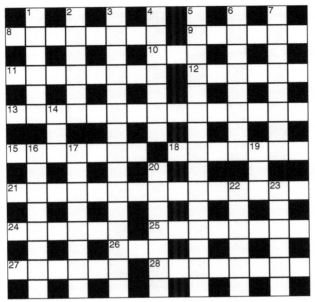

ACROSS

8 Penny allowed to come out when it is finished (8)
9 Attract father returning ring (6)
10 Still room (not half) for a household god (3)
11 Northern town endlessly annexing a volcanic island (2,6)
12 Blunder by worker wandering (6)
13 Join in the ceremony (8,7)
15 Four pairs of braces (7)
18 It needs an afterthought to change the book (7)
21 Effective treatment for the Queen's indisposition? (9,6)
24 A small gate in the middle of the field (6)
25 Not many with high body temperature first used this medicinal plant (8)
26 I will be out of sorts (3)
27 Show preference for outbuilding (4-2)
28 Sinless pope (8)

DOWN

1 Against study on revolutionary art (6)
2 Be seen in public distributing a paper (6)
3 Booth's appointment will be within five years (7,8)
4 In a rush was slipshod so had a rest (7)
5 Motoring offence a rash golfer could be guilty of? (8,7)
6 Recommendation on which one has no obligation to pay (8)
7 Marine hanger-on (8)
14 Redhead, a divorcee gets her man? (3)
16 I do remove slide having made an image (8)
17 Expedition with 14 going on a long and difficult journey (8)
19 Letter-holder (3)
20 Urge to toss a drink (3-4)
22 Mother takes a vehicle up to be used by a bandsman (6)
23 Governess expected girl to turn up (6)

50

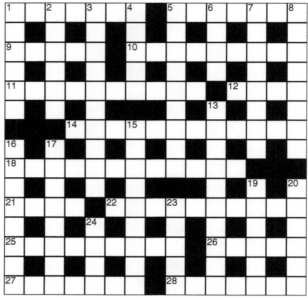

ACROSS

1 Small dining chairs (7)
5 Fish seen around island adjoining one African country (7)
9 Symbol of sovereignty King Charles had to acknowledge (5)
10 Serve ducks in vinegar dressing if stuck (2,1,6)
11 All inamoratas stayed faithful despite animosity (2,4,4)
12 It provides grip on the shoe of a stallion (4)
14 Well I never use a match! (6,1,5)
18 Old-style furniture press spokesman included in price-cut (12)
21 Band of assault soldiers confront a nuclear bomb (4)
22 Circus boss is to call a young lad (10)
25 A Latvian, for instance, joins another in Maryland (9)
26 He's foolish to return book inscribed for Amin (5)
27 Otherwise return to play a guitar from the platform (7)
28 Princess Royal in attempt to find hiding-place (7)

DOWN

1 Support transfer to another post (6)
2 A general vote has appeal to an Olympian figure (6)
3 Enthusiastic reception at the pub is something new (10)
4 Grain I am going to cook over the fire (5)
5 Passing ten trains being shunted (9)
6 Grass planted in northern Arkansas (4)
7 Want a little time (8)
8 Story Common Market Democrat included in a memo (8)
13 Allowance made for a learner on outdoor film set (10)
15 One sister meets one class appropriately dressed (2,7)
16 Angry lawyers strut (8)
17 They made converts lose past recollections (8)
19 Try hard to find a way to split wood (6)
20 Quite attractive (6)
23 Fellow injected with heroin in Belgium (5)
24 Complain bitterly over a storyteller (4)

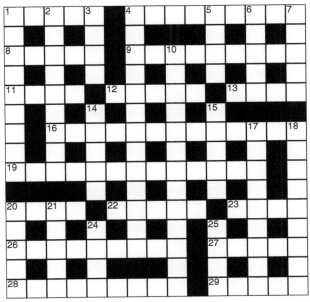

51

ACROSS

1 Girl climber with black-eyes? (5)
4 Change dominates this part of Kent (9)
8 Meal has no starter, here at "The Bull", we hear (5)
9 But is it prepared by the bank-teller? (9)
11 Ferocious cut? (4)
12 Jack reverses vehicle in outskirts of Kilbride (5)
13 Thriving in the spring (4)
16 Seasom before, defeated and tanned (7-6)
19 How army reserves perform, being one-all in the ground? (13)
20 Mail has gone astray in the capital (4)
22 Hot-rod no longer driven in shipyards? (5)
23 Granny King has no time to finish (4)
26 Paris work-girl finds little plave to eat on motorway (9)
27 Kentucky too strange for a Japanese city (5)
28 Alpine music factory? (4-5)
29 Bell—one of the three from "The Parsonage"— here in London? (5)

DOWN

1 See miser hide at Welsh town (9)
2 A plant like the Jerusalem artichoke can be fun in easier borders (9)
3 Bellini's opera cut short? That is mean! (4)
4 Antisocial sort, St Thomas, in rip-off! (13)
5 Slough outbuilding (4)
6 Daisy is a neat looker! (2-3)
7 Acclaim content of next Olympics (5)
10 Commercial term evident as new? (13)
14 Swift attack to capture prince (5)
15 Charge a guinea for handles? (5)
17 Testing can be wearisome, al fresco (6,3)
18 The late shift? (9)
20 Night-climber of the wall in Paris (5)
21 Red wine—try some, doctor? (5)
24 Unpremeditated shot? (4)
25 Tropical plant approved by artist (4)

52

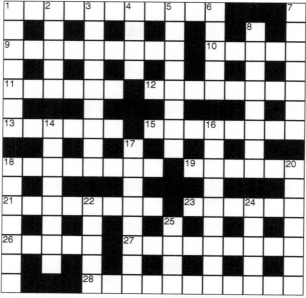

ACROSS

1 Satisfied with the amount of water in spring (4,7)
9 Be resolute and set up a business (5,4)
10 Not admitting an abstemious man is dapper (5)
11 Pushkin hero unlikely to cause intoxication (6)
12 Denim design additionally popular (2,6)
13 Pointless hint (3-3)
15 To lounge around with one fizzy drink is sweet (8)
18 Bunter is able to get something for tea (8)
19 To think things over leads to mere hesitation (6)
21 Window since set in concrete mix (8)
23 Manufacturing organs is an eastern habit (6)
26 Doubtless how merchantmen left a Yemeni port (5)
27 Where post-war Socialists put their hopes if ruthless (9)
28 Hiring a star model is fine (5,2,4)

DOWN

1 The laundry's on the line, but rain has ruined it! (4-3)
2 Permission to have a holiday (5)
3 Daughter is smart chasing a rascal—one having a flutter on the pools (6-3)
4 Admirer upset about one being too credulous (4)
5 Order Don, not me, to make capital in Canada (8)
6 Just a matter of time if... (5)
7 ...agitated dupe goes to a locker (5,2)
8 Bound to be short of cash (8)
14 Comrade with strange ideas about fortification (8)
16 Appear unkempt to view an officers' club (4,1,4)
17 Chasing round a spooky site? (8)
18 Second record reveals production deficit (7)
20 Left off being absolutely correct (5,2)
22 Pitman is phonetically less important (5)
24 Work-time for 11, maybe (5)
25 Bunny's end is featured in a press cutting (4)

53

ACROSS

5 Little creatures by an upturned stone (6)
8 Accepted the money, one observed (4,4)
9 They may be responsible for raised eyebrows! (7)
10 Qualification, perhaps, for a trooper (5)
11 Unhappy and clutching a woolly bear, mustered a smile (9)
13 Attracted by, are prepared to approach (4,4)
14 Cut the key and go (6)
17 Rocks constituting a hazard to shipping (3)
19 Said it's a drink stand (3)
20 Cover in also in the greenhouse (6)
23 Think the grass border made up for it (8)
26 A local worker (9)
28 What Perdita was lost in (5)
29 When the wind is backing, be inside. It's very cold (7)
30 Be different from the others and get a porter to carry (5,3)
31 Get one's goat some greenery (6)

DOWN

1 Kept going from th sun to the shade (6)
2 Friendly and gracious face! (7)
3 The out train isn't on it's way (2,7)
4 Getting the gist, somehow—mother is in disgrace (6)
5 Retain half the money netted by a false claim (8)
6 Doctor, tea or coffee? (5)
7 Will a bloke fall apart through this foolish infatuation (4-4)
12 Beside oneself again with rage (3)
15 Aiming to have an evening out (9)
16 As an enemy deserter, I'm interned temporarily (3,1,4)
18 Agree, for money, to roll the dice (8)
21 Before getting up, as well (3)
22 Feeling for the book-stand, on I totter (7)
24 Slips the animal into the time capsule (6)
25 Mean to turn in—need regeneration (6)
27 Foot the bill? It's a pleasure! (5)

54

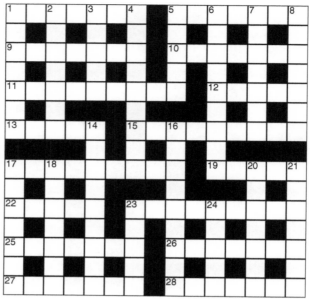

ACROSS

1 Cry when the batting side makes exactly 100 (4,3)
5 As far as you can hear someone must be talking about you (7)
9 A way with a pen to demonstrate humility (7)
10 Against communism it has introduced a boycott inter alia (7)
11 One's attached to manifest nuances (9)
12 It is used in many long tights (5)
13 Joined American investment in that country's central bank (5)
15 Going astray during college vacation (3,6)
17 Glance behind, and take care (4,5)
19 Draw up a banker's cheque (5)
22 The day after Aug 31 a tint of autumn appears (5)
23 Be just in time to prepare a potato for crisps (3,2,4)
25 Substitute heavy fabric with very fine fabric (7)
26 Time property is covered by a will (7)
27 Serge is beaten (7)
28 Back pay transposed to settle a debt (3,4)

DOWN

1 Succeed, but not as a buck-jumper (4,3)
2 In a nursery game they appear on board with 50 snakes (7)
3 Start when the actors are ready (5)
4 Experimenting with holding open court? (6,3)
5 Woodcutter upset over writing tests (5)
6 Legendary outlaw tells how to commit masked burglary (5,4)
7 A dogged policeman (7)
8 He needs a lot of coaches to take Electrical Engineering (7)
14 Go off by oneself to sketch detail (4,5)
16 Lesson One taken by a new toddler (5,4)
17 Final dust up for those who like to take a back seat (4,3)
18 Theoretically working as a journalist (2,5)
20 Sesame was his open secret when making a one pound rum cake (3,4)
21 Judge which feature most distinguishes a pelican (3,4)
23 Statement of belief by film director of The Third Man (5)
24 Try a letter of query when feeling irritable (5)

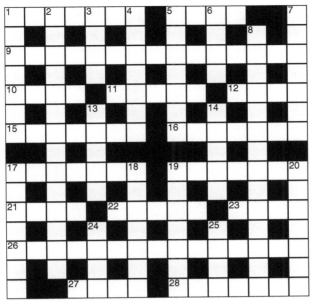

55

ACROSS

1 Is it as lawful to importune? (7)
5 Some prize bull or other ox-like animal (4)
9 The very thing (8,7)
10 Violet in the modern style is very keen (4)
11 Obstinate person has to put energy into drill (5)
12 Bridge player has one card-game or another (4)
15 Stealing beaker containing grand drink (7)
16 Might this be served as the main course? (7)
17 Chance of taking something before it is offered to others—and of not doing so? (7)
19 We with the others left inside struggle (7)
21 Sandy needed some small amount of force (4)
22 Ptomaine found in canned beef (5)
23 Relish the oil squeezed from orange or lemon peel (4)
26 Computer mentality? (10,5)
27 Condiment used as a last resort (4)
28 Gertrude has about one pound for the dramatist (7)

DOWN

1 Weapon not used at the front? (7)
2 Giving a little help pointing up (7,1,6)
3 101 fruit (4)
4 Collecting 10% in taxes (7)
5 Enthusiastic deity has a look in (7)
6 Only egghead found on the island (4)
7 We initially assisted when the animal gave birth (7)
8 Extra incentive put on by cook (5,2,3,4)
13 Drunk upsets last of whisky (5)
14 Was including the European country (5)
17 Change gear? (7)
18 One's own concern to be watchful (4-3)
19 Purifying fish? (7)
20 Old, old tinge no longer exists (7)
24 Cockney has to rebuild the portico (4)
25 Abraham left murder victim (4)

56

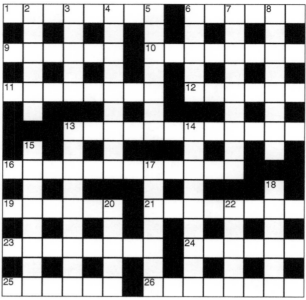

ACROSS

1 Fellow from Avon university is a bit of a pig (4,4)
6 Points one good graduate regarded as a mystery (6)
9 Simple textbook on reading, but not writing or 'rithmetic (6)
10 Those remaining with foreign priest for medical treatment (4-4)
11 Principal route for shipping company (4,4)
12 Insignificant insult (6)
13 Discussions cause one to retract amid denials (12)
16 Rescuing the Socialist party is not so onerous (6-6)
19 Constituent of the usual Monday pudding, perhaps (6)
21 Repeatedly act as informer in New York State prison (4,4)
23 A cistern is fitted into container (8)
24 Term incorporated by the Spanish for gloss finish (6)
25 Outline of a small sailing-boat (6)
26 A short declaration that thanks are unnecessary (3,2,3)

DOWN

2 A wide following far and wide (6)
3 Paean about Egyptian god of marriage (5)
4 Herald is to bring her a replacement (9)
5 Sign seen by a number in harbour (7)
6 Moves gently into Southsea's esplanade (5)
7 Feeling disposed to put in carbon backing-sheet (9)
8 Businessman intended to frame Catholic husband (8)
13 One resolved to see essential points in word creation (9)
14 Lamenting break-up of political affiliation (9)
15 Retreat when summer is over (4,4)
17 Partner backed up the batsman, but he lost (4-3)
18 An Italian water source is in poor shape (6)
20 Abandon constructing a trench (5)
22 Very little son is unable to understand (5)

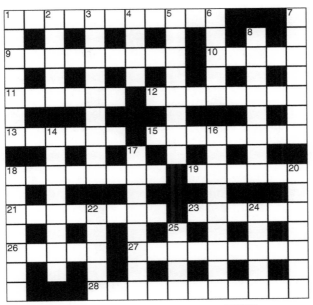

57

ACROSS

1 Harmful to be tired out in the mind (11)
9 European clear in this Olympic event (4-5)
10 Craft put in the bin? (5)
11 Sally's flask (6)
12 Eccentric sort takes two drugs! (8)
13 Head keeps medal in everyday set of clothes (6)
15 Light design of castle in Spain (8)
18 Vera on US trip is insatiable (8)
19 Keen to find some garden tools (6)
21 Casual secretarial worker is tardy producing stencil (8)
23 Old boy, Taking suet preparation, is slow-witted (6)
26 Cordial note (5)
27 Suit macho-style, this growth of hair? (9)
28 County with tail-ender dismissed at wrong end—embarrassed— gave up! (11)

DOWN

1 Expatriates run into warehouses (7)
2 One eaves rest-room which is for hire (2,3)
3 Tipping in fashionable Reading, say? (9)
4 It houses sewers in the Tuileries (4)
5 Out clumsily in Test, intensive coaching required (8)
6 For this tree, ring up about one (5)
7 Must art suffer in bed? (7)
8 Single girl in a leotard, for example (3-5)
14 Part of Haydn's *Clock* Symphony? (8)
16 River authority, a local target? (9)
17 More cuts ordered for shopper (8)
18 Turner which can be shown upside down without loss of effect (7)
20 Mountaineer's first purchase? (7)
22 Classic place for a tailless insect (5)
24 Unfairly 'e hurt Arthur's Dad (5)
25 Man, for example, lies about (4)

58

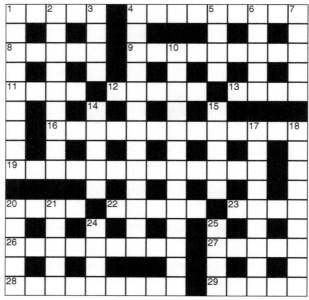

ACROSS

1 West Indian copper embargo (5)
4 Backing thanks with monetary acknowledgment is characteristic (9)
8 Discharge ambassador in strange surroundings (5)
9 Tell all it is unfashionable and fashionable (3,4,2)
11 Seek pronouncement from an Indian (4)
12 You and I have one way to get rum (5)
13 Get worn at the edges when fighting (4)
16 Toil cheerfully to carry out executorial duties (4,4,1,4)
19 Picking up the tab to maintain the police (6,3,4)
20 Implement over a pound (4)
22 Hutton is about to make a revelation (3,2)
23 Appeal to seamen's union to show responsibility (4)
26 Continued to send prose translations (7,2)
27 Favourite Egyptian god in old Jordanian city (5)
28 Eccentric letter (9)
29 Travel widely in mountainous countryside (5)

DOWN

1 Instrument of a joker who keeps a joker up his sleeve (4-5)
2 Escape for a brief vacation (5,4)
3 Term for a male in Geordie country (4)
4 I sent two Danes out totally perplexed (2,4,4,3)
5 One twice revealing a sacred bird (4)
6 Guide woman into Chaldaean city (5)
7 Typical measure to attempt access (5)
10 Go round the bend, then start to recover (4,3,6)
14 Liable to be laid flat out (5)
15 The chap in charge is mentally disordered (5)
17 Is Heather not being put up in North London? (9)
18 Member is not in time to transact parliamentary business (9)
20 Subject to one in the Privy Council (5)
21 Last letter in the Frome Gazette (5)
24 A resurgent island bordering a continent (4)
25 Box yard (4)

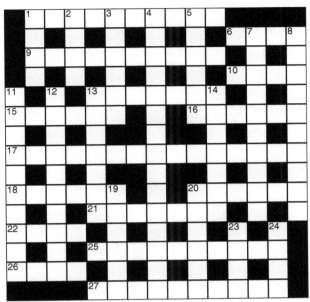

59

ACROSS

1 Justice obtained by soldier in various matters (10)
6 Weather protection for morning doctor's round (4)
9 Pulling back and turning in (10)
10 Spend unwisely, being depressed (4)
13 The French mark all dice differently (7)
15 Workers' home (6)
16 Turns out not to one's choice (6)
17 Summoned by bells, he took a turn for the better (4,11)
18 Watched United compete for leadership (6)
20 A way to divert people? (6)
21 Lease in legal document taken out (7)
22 Departed behind time (4)
25 Figures lad is ordered into the cavalry (4,6)
26 Make sound of a large vessel (4)
27 Parties of runners? (10)

DOWN

1 Dutch half-sovereign (4)
2 Entrance for spectators (4)
3 English county coach (6)
4 Relics as tourist attractions of the future? (7,2,2,4)
5 T-junction jam (6)
7 Assignment left in a particular spot (10)
8 Requests put with an attempt at jocularity (10)
11 Poorly valued live entertainment (10)
12 City's victory over another (10)
13 Bird and donkey invested with dignity (7)
14 Exacted payment for something on another's account (7)
19 Corrupt passage (6)
20 A number get away with swindle (6)
23 Girl puts one over teacher (4)
24 As one's written repeatedly, she was revered (4)

60

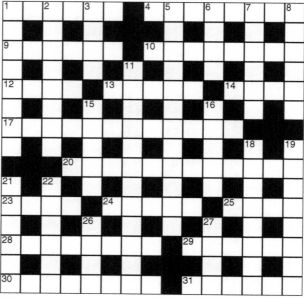

ACROSS

1 Be stumped by an eviction order! (3,3)
4 Certainly no bent policeman could make legitimate arrest (1,4,3)
9 Where property developers invest but not on the coast (6)
10 VIP racket (3,5)
12 Georgia confronts one who abstains from world trade agreement (4)
13 Old hag found by King Charles I (5)
14 Part of Palm Sunday's charity collection (4)
17 Eager to be drunk on gin or whisky (4,2,6)
20 EEC remaining committed to the old French political system (6,6)
23 A fall in the ocean upset the brothers' father (4)
24 One who encourages a moth? (5)
25 Breed back (4)
28 Father's to be a member of a committee to relay information (4,2,2)
29 Attend if put to shame (4,2)
30 Second job profile (8)
31 Colour marker about to be used with artificial fabric (6)

DOWN

1 Leaving home and getting high (5,3)
2 Boastful and stilted conversation (4,4)
3 Middle of awful nasty bone in the arm (4)
5 Comrade who gives (or maybe requires) timely help (6,2,4)
6 Earliest centre for missionaries (4)
7 Hot pepper I needed after feverish cold (6)
8 Polite request to make others happy (6)
11 Reprimand for not getting togged up (8,4)
15 Certain to be on the way (5)
16 Excavated with concealed explosives (5)
18 Spill the beans, so don't sell them (4,4)
19 Partner and I order an amphibious pet (8)
21 Bivouac on American university grounds (6)
22 Jack gets accustomed to being sworn at (6)
26 Indicative of future resolution (4)
27 Daily help in the orchard (4)

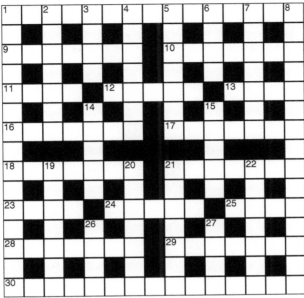

61

ACROSS

1 Tons of lines at school? (5,10)
9 One from Bonn perhaps has the point that is relevant (7)
10 Crazier with a more stippled effect? (7)
11 Bound to see Jim, say (4)
12 Invigorates, we hear, with order to be plump and comely (5)
13 Need to remove the sandy tract (4)
16 Feature that is breath-taking (7)
17 Exert pressure in a close embrace (7)
18 Where the driver's seat is found in the battle area (7)
21 Swallow single drink (7)
23 Officer will go back as he has difficulty seeing through it (4)
24 One from France in a cap going round stamping ground (5)
25 Trap a girl (4)
28 Shade of resentment (7)
29 Ran amok in the fuss during a storm (7)
30 Mistake made at the end of the trial? (5,2,8)

DOWN

1 Not plain clothes worn by Scotsmen? (8,7)
2 Appropriately a supporter's holding the ring (7)
3 You are, so to speak, in agreement saying this (4)
4 A continental peer has not been matched (7)
5 Entrances? (7)
6 Detest a male at heart (4)
7 Wicked feature with supposed power to cause harm (4,3)
8 Bookish characters having a row (5,3,2,1,4)
14 Diagram of second half of a photo (5)
15 Most of the good fortune is to do with money (5)
19 Lever used in many a dispute at the inn (4-3)
20 One of a number for the pot? (3-4)
21 Tinamou strangely is an object of reverence among American Indians (7)
22 How to flatter in a sincere way, so it is said (7)
26 Drivers within the hour find sea-mist (4)
27 Self-righteous person, one who is greedy right to be detained (4)

62

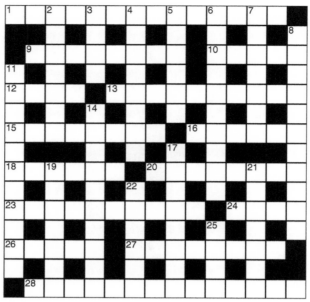

ACROSS

1 Minimum requirements for a stripper? (4,10)
9 Where yachtsmen from Cowes sail forward (8)
10 Learn about an ecclesiastical law (5)
12 Order given to a north Arabian state (4)
13 Mother's pea soup needs air (10)
15 Becoming reconciled to telling stories (6,2)
16 The wife and I commonly appear more common (6)
18 Dining accessory and utensil returned to family (6)
20 Ordered to encircle water gate in marine investment (8)
23 Insincere support regarded as insolence by defence force (3-7)
24 Competent to frame a decree (4)
26 Sillier-sounding name for eyelashes (5)
27 Hurried back and was scolded for having told tales (8)
28 Coward's portrayal of a military skirmish (5,9)

DOWN

2 Managed to fire and plunder a city (7)
3 It teaches boys with energy and style (4)
4 Entire range of crumpets laid out (8)
5 I get taken in by impracticable idea (6)
6 In the Channel Islands one is in the money from the start (10)
7 It sheds light on many an aquatic bird (7)
8 Tender names are in order! (11)
11 Trite description of Clapham, for instance (11)
14 Popular movie tax likely to set things ablaze (10)
17 Vote Rex in charge of power supply (8)
19 University in E London area is widely admired (7)
21 Worker consumes citrus fruit as food (7)
22 Street used as a meeting-place (6)
25 In Malta business is prohibited (4)

ACROSS

7 Coal-seam, perhaps, carrying water-borne hazards (9)
8 It's most desirable to enclose a wild animal (5)
10 Get ready for the night (8)
11 Quietly mention favour (6)
12 Turn back before it erupts (4)
13 Confirm tea laid out after five (8)
15 No simple mental condition (7)
17 It may pick and hold a lock (7)
20 Type of porcelain food container (8)
22 Harvest a new type of pear (4)
25 Train for Rugby, for example (6)
26 Four in new search for data (8)
27 An embrace for Lady Grey (5)
28 One in the club has whip-round for cheese (9)

DOWN

1 Vessel found in the kitchen bin, perhaps (5)
2 Fed up with tea-break? Just the reverse (6)
3 Union without a single member (8)
4 Note answer in book (7)
5 Challenged champion's delay about the final (8)
6 Resolve sectarian differences (9)
9 Duck, mate! Here comes a stone! (4)
14 Disorderly actors are plastered (9)
16 An event Jews won't forget or ignore (8)
18 A frenzy of war cries and whirling blades (8)
19 Girl can put up a calendar (7)
21 They may be jellied or else cooked (4)
23 A disposition of arms (6)
24 Feature of barley, used to make bread (5)

64

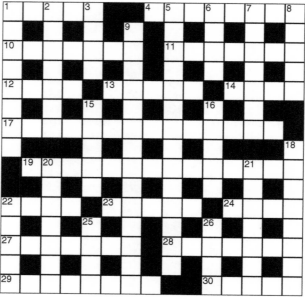

ACROSS

1 Set rate for top secretary returning last month (5)
4 Glowing silver? Rubbish (8)
10 Difficult for county legislator to oppose Roman law (7)
11 Umpire put in work to find a clover leaf (7)
12 Love is painful on the rebound (4)
13 I made changes to communication channels (5)
14 Can get little Japanese money—very little (4)
17 Managing board offers patient support (9,5)
19 Demand extortionate fees to spread electricity worldwide (6,3,5)
22 Run one! (4)
23 Way to acquire wood store (5)
24 Water container in Crewe railway station (4)
27 Giving finest one to a student is cruel (7)
28 MC awarded to commander with French father (7)
29 Don's away elsewhere at present (8)
30 Drew the line at being under another's thumb (5)

DOWN

1 Tool English fellow always criticised (6,2)
2 Arrive carrying container of stewed fruit (7)
3 Boy going back to Egyptian valley (4)
5 Buying sherry despite being made redundant (7,3,4)
6 Holly causes unsettled exile to lose his head (4)
7 In addition murder is resented (4,3)
8 Political meeting leads to market recovery (5)
9 Mine expert resolved to join friend for a trial (14)
15 I go in vehicle to north Scottish landmark (5)
16 Hesitate to swindle and rook (5)
18 Point to where the real action is (5,3)
20 Poor journalist was upset by cutting article (7)
21 Stripped pine needs harsh treatment (3,4)
22 Harp on about how to apply an embrocation (3,2)
25 Back a venison breeder (4)
26 Fitzgerald translated him from Arabic (4)

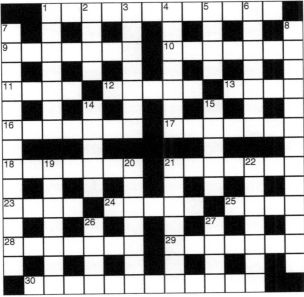

65

ACROSS

1 "I'm making the incision now"? (7,5)
9 Don't act to music (7)
10 Races off to bring a copper in and he charges one (7)
11 Contends they're French biographies (4)
12 Plan to protect the British it's chock-a-block with (5)
13 As assistant editor I got a retraction (4)
16 The object is to inform or entertain readers (7)
17 Accounts for the bangs (7)
18 Books sold in seedy places? (7)
21 The closing announcement is in a foreign language (7)
23 Win, when given a start, once more (4)
24 All drink? Not quite all (5)
25 Send out for a sun seat (4)
28 Getting even on board (7)
29 Went off, about to have a try on for a dress (3-4)
30 The cost of one's keep? (9,3)

DOWN

1 Not doing the rounds, which is unusual (7)
2 Go abroad (4)
3 Be long after one, flying from base (7)
4 Cold lager I pour out: it's icy (7)
5 Caught in time, earlier (4)
6 File under the same heading: 'Rises negotiated' (7)
7 Haggle and become the owner of a reasonably priced car (5,1,7)
8 Able to breeze along unhampered? (4,2,3,4)
14 Throw out a brush (5)
15 Paid for it by getting whacked (5)
19 No one above a certain rank (7)
20 Got run in to avoid a killer (7)
21 Roll home at quite an early hour (7)
22 Teaching Scamp first to beg (7)
26 Support a theatrical venture (4)
27 Neat youngster (4)

66

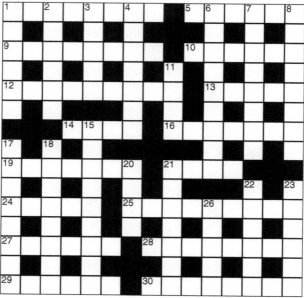

ACROSS

1 Say one should send away without delay (5,3)
5 Start firing or start firing away (4,2)
9 Cautious eavesdroppers between 1939-1945 (3,5)
10 Supply garments for a stupid fellow male (6)
12 Broadcast on ethnic problem as a running event (5,4)
13 A capital (Italian) fragrance (5)
14 Eating house supplying continental coffee (4)
16 Only sweetheart is 10 (3,4)
19 Initiate action when thieves have stripped the church roof (4,3)
21 Invite oriental to stay a wee while (4)
24 Dance wildly having been corporally punished (5)
25 Having no sparkle is it intended for processing into brandy? (5,4)
27 Contentious matters for magazine numbers (6)
28 Dependable algebraic quantity (8)
29 Parable first omitted refers to husbandman's land (6)
30 Was conspicuous by absence apparently (5,3)

DOWN

1 Payment for finding writer of a cheque returned (6)
2 To distort a report is habit supported by the French (6)
3 Very small support for driving off to New York (5)
4 Pardoned desecration of grave (7)
6 Influence, a principal way to overtake others (4,5)
7 Cooler is less than satisfactory (3,2,3)
8 Ready-to-eat fruit is ready (8)
11 Note from me to the medical officer (4)
15 Quite a lot from a profitable arrangement (1,4,4)
17 Antique porcelain from Cathay (3,5)
18 Medicinally it disperses a gas in me (8)
20 A clenched hand is held by a foot (4)
21 What parachutists do to provide security for defence (4,3)
22 Old battle axe used by gunners in 1702 naval battle (6)
23 How to treat steak likely to be tough and go off fast (4,2)
26 Appeal to a girl stockholder (5)

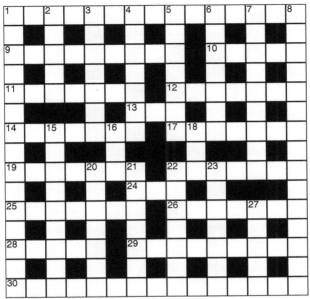

67

ACROSS

1 Cruelty of one lacking a soft-centre? (4-11)
9 Roman fighter was pleased he had taken in the girl, so it is said! (9)
10 Girl loses aspiration from sainted isle (5)
11 Mournful in hotel eg I acknowledged (7)
12 Restricted company (7)
13 Man includes classy colour (3)
14 Cost of keeping swans in the river (7)
17 Deviate, but it certainly won't rouse one's interest (4,3)
19 Mundane variety without a title (7)
22 Old city pipe I'm possibly putting disc inside (7)
24 Feel sorry when rugby players are fifth rate (3)
25 One receives waves from girl, about ten (7)
26 Again come into contact to improve the picture (7)
28 Piece of land no longer available (5)
29 Drunk beer in it, a cocktail! (9)
30 A handicap when taking a long view (4-11)

DOWN

1 Cautioned about being more like Lofty first received at college (6,9)
2 Author produces most of the book (5)
3 West Indian remixed a hit by a Scotsman (7)
4 Diplomatic bag? (7)
5 Is this food only a little bit sharp? (7)
6 Impractical person who has lost consciousness? (7)
7 Conductor picked out the said street (9)
8 Rugby player's cold manner? (5-10)
15 Ant removed from dish outside containing a cigar (9)
16 The girl to take courting? (3)
18 Initially it's up in the air and can't be identified (3)
20 Very small music centre's records (7)
21 Not winning in artwork (7)
22 Faultless when tense (7)
23 Reached the end of term and became an adult (7)
27 Manner of treating a high-class herb (5)

68

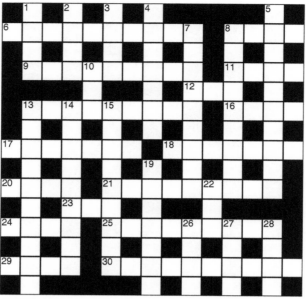

ACROSS

6 Turned aside in some confusion (10)
8 Decoration that gives point to 23 (4)
9 Game to make music? (9)
11 A chance to offer support (4)
12 Backing strike would be mean (3)
13 It's no real solution for the family (9)
16 A country copper—a well-educated man (4)
17 He'll grab pet animal and child with little hesitation (7)
18 Senior students dissecting remains (7)
20 Look after quiet couple (4)
21 The sound pretend to be in a bad way to get a drink (9)
23 Waste wood (3)
24 Request for reinstatement (4)
25 The bloomer of a witless push-over (9)
29 Brought forth first buds, brightly coloured (4)
30 Allowance made for a rotten oil distribution (10)

DOWN

1 This member in general imbibed freely (4)
2 A beast with guns turned up (4)
3 Stop eating quickly! (4)
4 Boy carrying a cover for the cheese (7)
5 Sages blame bad company (10)
7 The main rest-period? (4,5)
8 Bow in some discomfort due to getting stiff (9)
10 A North American legal official—a woman (3)
13 To peruse an account is regarded as right (4,1,5)
14 The trainee one reprimanded and so wounded (9)
15 Ditch a worker, getting acrimonious (9)
19 12 expert's story (7)
22 Complete an article on the fifties (3)
26 A city in Russia—Gorky or Kiev say (4)
27 There's a great deal to be auctioned (4)
28 A way to absorb business tax (4)

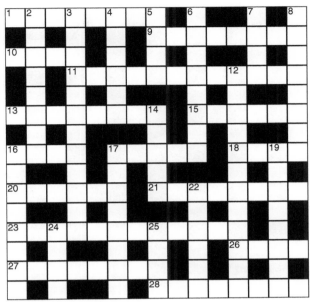

ACROSS

1 Is this what unrefined little girls are made of? (8)
9 Low water in Dee, apt to swirl (8)
10 She was visited by a swan, lead-damaged (4)
11 Brewers' delivery animal? (7-5)
13 Easily-seen cargo-list? (8)
15 Way to cook eggs (divine, wrapped in cabbage) (6)
16 Bad day for some of the side-issues (4)
17 Doctor to deal with black-eye (5)
18 Lincoln died—but not here, peacefully? (4)
20 Law-breaking month abroad in African republic (6)
21 Case of pine in river (3-5)
23 Piece in Verdi motet out of tune? (12)
26 Band's adversary jolly average! (4)
27 Ornament, appreciated by... (8)
28 ...Henry visiting lido, say, for a break? (8)

DOWN

2 Given too much bread, proved A1 as it turned out (8)
3 Light buffer's hollow place is fabulous! (8,4)
4 Thinly-spread butter and pickle (6)
5 Catch made from two metals (4)
6 Standard delight, say—or a bit of it (8)
7 Jetty ripe for renovation (4)
8 Clergyman always in Split, we hear (8)
12 This cocktail is not with it (3-9)
14 First at Thirsk—"Game Way"—certainty! (5)
16 Crude style in swirling mist (8)
17 Humidity of our times controlled? (8)
19 Wind that blows Daisy in cathedral? (8)
22 Silver pin that can damage the index, for example (6)
24 From very opening to close—sell! (4)
25 Fancy some of my therapy? (4)

70

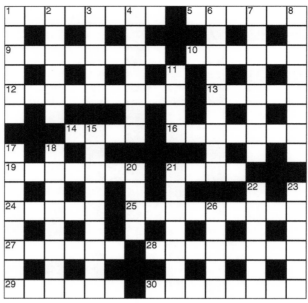

ACROSS

1 Previous examination of a clergyman (8)
5 A hundred in a coach. You can count on it (6)
9 Used a colander when under stress (8)
10 Muslim ruler about to conclude committee business (6)
12 He told one to become unemployed (2,3,4)
13 The German takes it back when exhausted (5)
14 Fruit providing calcium (4)
16 Fuss caused by father needing large bowl of water (7)
19 Friar takes walk to find blackberry (7)
21 Charge an old copper to cater for others (4)
24 Suitable inscription for Baker's birthday voucher (5)
25 To settle the score I later returned and dined (9)
27 A Franco-Spanish coin is not genuine (6)
28 End of a semester in America (8)
29 Saw telepathy die out (6)
30 Counsel a sober French marshal with heart of gold (8)

DOWN

1 Hand it down to Daddy's boy (4,2)
2 Couple inhabiting place find a water nymph (6)
3 Work in a point to declare one's views (5)
4 One shade that needs paint solvent (7)
6 Trifle with beautiful woman concealing a gun (9)
7 Manage to make tin cover (8)
8 Flag which is generally recognised (8)
11 Man has a piano, but it's a wreck (4)
15 Bound to mature after being kept for duty (2,7)
17 Obscure stratagem adopted by Jack Goodman (8)
18 To buy a put option leads to dramatic scene (8)
20 Always sounds like a Bronte heroine (4)
21 Accessory suiting healthy people to a T (7)
22 Cardinal accommodated by cathedral priest is a big gun (6)
23 Contemptible description of a rubella sufferer (6)
26 Member gets nothing in prison (5)

ACROSS

7 Ocean silt may be stranded here (9)
8 Quietly start to pray (5)
10 Intimation that union is in trouble and about to be terminated (8)
11 Inward-turning scientist (6)
12 Game explorer (4)
13 Make up watch on the ship (3-5)
15 Artillery associated with assault (7)
17 Equipment in what must be a warship (7)
20 Joint projections over which one may get rapped (8)
22 Notice to be seven minus five (4)
25 Still found in tumbledown attics (6)
26 Control shown as others fall (8)
27 A sound opener to admire (5)
28 Coming by river may be exciting (9)

DOWN

1 Plump for some drinks (5)
2 Does badly without copper for currency (6)
3 Noise—of dropped brick? (8)
4 Difficult situation where a direct strike must be avoided (7)
5 Trifling, perhaps, with one's affections? (8)
6 Clear love declaration (9)
9 It's an advantage to trim the lawn (4)
14 The size of the gun made it unwieldy (9)
16 After a bad act I become silent (8)
18 Sees dirt, becomes revolted (8)
19 Somehow reads it over on both sides (7)
21 Secure a position at Rugby (4)
23 Time conceals a deserter's mistakes (6)
24 Turn a corner with German soldiers (5)

72

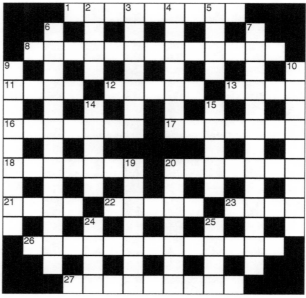

ACROSS

1 Don't waver if you want to get on your feet quickly (5,4)
8 Predominant interest is suppressing carnal desire (6,7)
11 Part of ship unaffected when it capsizes (4)
12 To be taken for a ride was wearing (3,2)
13 Gold article found on the Algerian coast (4)
16 What the American viper did when considerably alarmed (7)
17 Tense description of a duck walk is sheer nonsense (7)
18 Also abstain from eating at an excessive rate (3,4)
20 Investigates a saint upsetting the clergy (7)
21 Not well cooked, but that is unusual (4)
22 Make hot iron (5)
23 A single and a first class return to the continent (4)
26 A reservation is needed for all the way to the terminus (2,3,2,2,4)
27 Where Australians are apparently feather-bedded (4,5)

DOWN

2 Catch on what rose pickers are likely to catch on (4)
3 Screw grading needs changing (7)
4 Totally exhausted from working at full capacity (4,3)
5 Help me love! It's only fair (2,2)
6 Retired after being sent abroad as a police informer (3,3,2,5)
7 Risk total defeat at Wimbledon (5,8)
9 Losing it would make a fat woman lean and weary (5,4)
10 How a royal warrant is given to protect the chassis from rust (9)
14 Appropriate attire given to an English saint (5)
15 Archetypal pickpocket caught smoking? (5)
19 The land needs to soak up heaven-sent water (7)
20 Writer going to Jerusalem gets a living allowance (7)
24 Part of Ireland could possibly appeal (4)
25 Complaint of a couple leaving Prague (4)

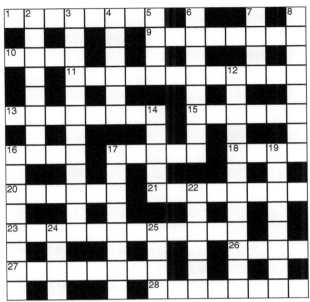

73

ACROSS

1 Put forward that support does need changing (8)
9 Colourful inauguration for a bird (8)
10 How to solve a knotty problem (4)
11 See differently first signal in jargon (12)
13 Piece of cloth chaps found in the fort (8)
15 Convincing businessman (6)
16 Scandinavian books of dead letters (4)
17 Establish the kitty is empty (5)
18 The Atlantic, it's a small lake! (4)
20 Proceed gently with the girl's animal (6)
21 Non-union man? (8)
23 Deepest affections affected this stranger (5-7)
26 One of the community (4)
27 Despoil'd, roughed up and poorly balanced (3-5)
28 He was very tight at Christmas (8)

DOWN

2 Gave up, having done the plastering (8)
3 He will put you in the picture (12)
4 Abandon plan to put books away? (6)
5 Monster not on trail (4)
6 Having lent money, made progress (8)
7 Cost of travel, food provided (4)
8 Bore witness at the match, 'e'd concluded (8)
12 Ridge an overinflated tyre has (4,8)
14 Rough and ready as a rule (5)
16 Protective agent in the henhouse having a slight gloss (8)
17 Fine Italian leader to remain at home (8)
19 Time of day when most strikes occur (8)
22 Not a current sort of light (6)
24 Lake in resort backed by mountains (4)
25 Terry decided to include an island resort (4)

74

ACROSS

7 Essential device for viewers in deep water (9)
8 A working man is to a certain degree a child (5)
10 A diet put to rights, showing some cleverness (8)
11 Double up to stop outside right (6)
12 A Greek character given a little bribe takes extra care (4)
13 Girls seen together in the garden (8)
15 Farms managed by the county (7)
17 Start in error in the passage (7)
20 Head-dress making supports family (8)
22 After employment (4)
25 Personal communication with an adored being (6)
26 Give warning of earth-shaking number (8)
27 The Continental worker wasn't upright (5)
28 Reserved bun-mix reaching expiry-date (9)

DOWN

1 The heartless politician with no time for musicians (5)
2 Comparison which can make on break into a grin (6)
3 Correct bill, a churchman found (8)
4 A supplement about fruit is published (7)
5 People engaged in trade may well be nameless (8)
6 Hector reads before school (9)
9 Plays mis-cast (4)
14 Dull colour for the prudent environmentalist (4-5)
16 Bearing but giving voice about uppity painter (8)
18 Told of being left cutting the long grass (8)
19 Second pressing (7)
21 Edge along the pedestrian way (4)
23 Pole getting readily available drink (6)
24 Not all blame antiquated equipment, or so it's implied (5)

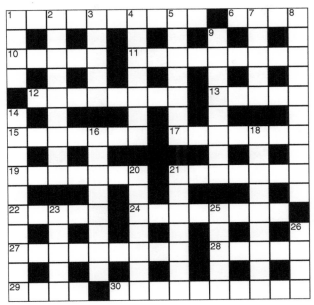

75

ACROSS

1 Target-round that is any colour? (6-4)
6 Error in the field (4)
10 Turner's state of agitation curtailed (5)
11 Government-appointed grouse consultant (9)
12 Sunday drinker who produces dotty paintings (8)
13 Dad's Army fare... (5)
15 ...stuff finished before tea-break (7)
17 Recreation that is breaking rules? (7)
19 Day Monica spent, wandering about (7)
21 Heraldic band contains fashionable bridge-skill (7)
22 Respectable char? (5)
24 Support team that is bottom (8)
27 Showmen make mark endlessly with air-conditioning (9)
28 Lady-love with bad back (5)
29 Runner has zero-energy (4)
30 P-princely plant? (5,5)

DOWN

1 Top removed from chimney-hoods to reveal hooters (4)
2 High winds in Blackburn (3,6)
3 Common bloke takes English to heart (5)
4 Small volume from record permitted (7)
5 Brie, all spread, is plentiful (7)
7 Citrus fruits left, half turned up (5)
8 Bizarre Manet kept in safe—it has five feet! (10)
9 Embracing, these days, by choice (8)
14 Marriage made by phone? (10)
16 Put at risk in final wrath (8)
18 Issue-raising expression? (3-1-5)
20 Wad of notes found in the Savoy, for example (7)
21 Loud battle in camp (7)
23 Drive out from Sussex, pell-mell... (5)
25 ...Hastings' last excursion to see the river (5)
26 We will get together shortly—in the spring? (4)

76

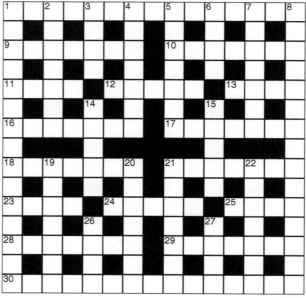

ACROSS

1 Give a tip and go into the red (4,4,7)
9 He struggles to make pancake mixture—about a litre (7)
10 A way to travel on horseback! (7)
11 On top of it all, the switch is the wrong way round (4)
12 Assume it's a hoax (3,2)
13 Twelve unaffected by setback (4)
16 Cut and clear up the grass clippings (4-3)
17 Violet is within hearing, but that's insignificant (7)
18 Mean to provide information (3-4)
21 Policeman in possession of heroin gets the axe (7)
23 Endeavour to include old party follower (4)
24 Early passenger vehicles are back in fashion (5)
25 Boundary marker that causes hollow laughter (2-2)
28 Applause for zero-rated tax no one backed (7)
29 Glacial creation from one church composer (7)
30 Go and make money to consult an astrologer (4,4,7)

DOWN

1 Industrial problems for left-wing family (6,9)
2 Prepared to reserve a GCSE text, maybe (3,4)
3 Nothing but sole (4)
4 Make me a ruff as protection against the cold (7)
5 Confirm that the market is bullish (4,3)
6 Disinclined to give portion to Henry (4)
7 Wild boar in one African city (7)
8 A perpetual figure in matrimonial disputes? (7,8)
14 Pass over part of the digestive system (5)
15 Crucial point to celebrity in retirement (5)
19 Strife caused by serving up uncooked food (7)
20 One Scotsman backing French-born candidate (7)
21 Comedian providing that note in Wales (7)
22 Gold added to family silver for highland table (7)
26 Six leave for Galician port (4)
27 Look hard to find someone of like age (4)

77

ACROSS

1 A very long time (6,8)
9 Stopped again and stared shiftily around (8)
10 Because it's nice to play on snow (5)
12 Where on learns fame can boomerang (4)
13 I said you'd hear it! (5,5)
15 On the first two notes, therefore, the instrument is perfect (8)
16 Proprietary—that's very noticeable (6)
18 Split, it's a little dry inside (6)
20 Strung together for an advertisement in 3-D (8)
23 Sri Lankan, perhaps, who takes many of his leaves abroad? (3-7)
24 Love flying no longer (4)
26 Deal in order that you may play it (5)
27 A decorous pink and yellow (8)
28 Trying clothes on (5,9)

DOWN

2 Many of you in France, absorbing the unfamiliar air (7)
3 Turn and try to get off backwards (4)
4 Start to expound on (3,5)
5 Was prepared to retire and didn't object (6)
6 By which Wild West outlaws comfortably amassed money? (4,6)
7 About the amount of ice-cream you eat (7)
8 Ripe for a rest? (5,2,4)
11 A bar brawl (5,6)
14 Scowls the overbarbecued steaks get (5,5)
17 Embarrassed at being a follower rather than a leader? (8)
19 Surprise mum with a treat, for a change (7)
21 Lines up some things to wear (7)
22 He shoots back, again at the legs (6)
25 With the duplicate key, about to enter the yard (4)

78

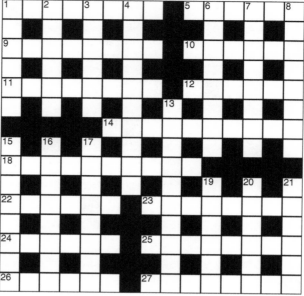

ACROSS

1 Moved into a house but was disillusioned (4,4)
5 Conclude that there is a gale blowing (4,2)
9 It tells of one born in the settlement of Bethel (3,5)
10 An eyesore about 1m back forms an obstacle (6)
11 Managed to find time which suited nicely (6,2)
12 Japanese entertainer misrepresented his age (6)
14 Delinquency roused city temper (5,5)
18 Attended on being suddenly attacked (6,4)
22 Arrest resulting from armed robbery (4,2)
23 No rating assigned for knowledge! (8)
24 Children one discovered in farm outhouses (6)
25 Like a pointer pointing to a traffic jam (4,4)
26 He makes a pile from the game (6)
27 Italian and Egyptian severely criticised over and over again (8)

DOWN

1 Detonated a bomb but acquitted (3,3)
2 Spanish celebration feast served up about one (6)
3 Tried fencing but was thwarted (6)
4 Perplexed by a description of an anagram (3,5,2)
6 How a criminal is caught at the scene when the stage is set (2,3,3)
7 Benedictine in France is in charge of the house (8)
8 Prince tells what happens to princes of the church (8)
13 Ultimately a teetotaller swallows gallons indiscriminately... (2,4,4)
15 ...when working in a legal inn (2,3,3)
16 Third degree in cooking (8)
17 Queen's order to Anglicans is an order (8)
19 Cry-baby making a laughable mistake (6)
20 Holiday worker accommodation available (6)
21 Posted—one's pool entry it would seem (6)

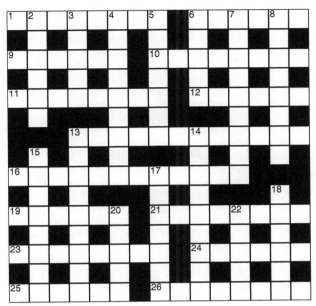

79

ACROSS

1 Disadvantage sounds convenient, team member concluded (8)
6 Her ingenuity initially will fade (6)
9 Silver leaves boatman for a peeping Tom (6)
10 Grim, being allowed an iron glove (8)
11 Come into property without inheriting it (8)
12 Daily Telegraph leaders accept revised clue that's sweet (6)
13 Make a fresh deal (12)
16 Trembling with cold, well, presumably not with such an attack (9,3)
19 Showing little emotion when I'd lost out (6)
21 Do babies feel down in the mouth with these troubles? (8)
23 Mother to tarry with sham illness (8)
24 Spoils the memento (6)
25 Slowly on the piano perhaps (6)
26 Hen beetle (8)

DOWN

2 Company of directors in flight? (6)
3 Habit of lady doctor? (5)
4 Herb smashed record Ian made (9)
5 Would it fly round the race-course (7)
6 Turned into an injury (5)
7 After Whit, cricketer sees a spiny fish (9)
8 In chapel even this late hour (8)
13 Horrible—peasants are sometimes described thus (9)
14 Thought about what the mirror did (9)
15 Lands the contraption on these islands (8)
17 Note it is the obvious choice (7)
18 It is dropped when required and weighed later (6)
20 The animal to leave out of sight (5)
22 Type of pencil mob mistake for explosive device (1-4)

80

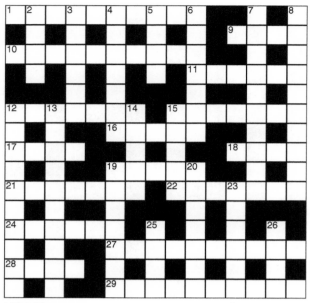

ACROSS

1 Private enterprise claims a tip for development (10)
9 Measure the hoof (4)
10 Official advertisement about pig-feed (10)
11 Doubly firm concerning a silken sheath (6)
12 Made easy like this, do the puzzle (7)
15 Blast! Low back allows space to manoeuvre in the main (3-4)
16 Gloomy—set right in expensive accommodation (5)
17 Checks crops (4)
18 Pine for a girl (4)
19 The page isn't commonly seen in make-up (5)
21 Smiled wryly about a fool (7)
22 Admitted being deceived (5,2)
24 Report to do with extremity (6)
27 Interested in people, in a manner of speaking (10)
28 Lido to be made over for a certain figure (4)
29 Transport for merchandise of superior type (5-5)

DOWN

2 A cat—a wee thing (4)
3 Meaning to give a little hint, entirely without malice (6)
4 23's admission of indiscretion, so it's gathered (7)
5 A Greek character gives thanks after ten (4)
6 Walker's returning stuff to a woman (7)
7 Mad proposal, but moving (10)
8 A manual worker's means—not so bad (10)
12 Swallow grit and harm can result (4-6)
13 Work on site causing obstruction (10)
14 Anxiety makes the dunderhead study (5)
15 The high-minded individual isn't a convert (5)
19 Ring about everyone becoming wearisome (7)
20 Disposition of last ten ancient coins (7)
23 Newspaper leader (6)
25 A man to turn to (4)
26 None will settle in big wild dry area (4)

ACROSS

5 Equipment needed to bring down an opponent? (6)
8 It shades an antipodean, gay itinerant (8)
9 Weird business arranged before the end of June (7)
10 Turn upside down in stupendous style (2-3)
11 Cautioned about scholarship (9)
13 Standard weapon, in a manner of speaking (8)
14 Huge business in the theatre (6)
17 First signs of having a throw, this bowler could be taken off (3)
19 The queen taking a cycle? (3)
20 Make runs in river contest (6)
23 Hard task-master? (8)
26 Consulted about affair, so early in life? (9)
28 Nobody's child is a bloomer (5)
29 Taking iron, drove off outside. Stuffed? (7)
30 Airy shed could be mine! (4-4)
31 Member of ascetic sect in delicatessen, extraordinarily (6)

DOWN

1 Sort too short to raid orchards? (6)
2 Under total prohibition, remains dusty (4-3)
3 Land-craft of gritty German crew? (4-5)
4 It measures distances of stars, right in space possibly (6)
5 Jumper for a bird-watcher? (8)
6 Freewheel from the seaside (5)
7 Old port left on rough-topped table (8)
12 Married on the rebound—early fall expected (3)
15 Virile sorts of calumnies? (9)
16 Savings-books (8)
18 Would one have a special appreciation of Keats' truth, then? (8)
21 Haggard heroine (3)
22 Greasy peer, we hear, in the dock (7)
24 Partner endlessly excited—in ecstasy! (6)
25 American diet nurse consumed? (6)
27 Great lake around end of Buttermere? How strange! (5)

82

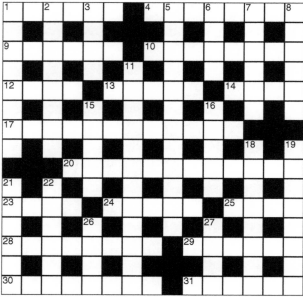

ACROSS

1 Gloomy face when Sergeant Major comes in (6)
4 Doctor enters one minute after time for sacrifice (8)
9 An entitlement is quite in order (6)
10 Mysterious secret I broadcast about love (8)
12 Mad to get an engine (4)
13 Tin always causes a derogatory smile (5)
14 Criticise vehicle parking (4)
17 Filming celebrity associated with meteoric career (8,4)
20 Diarist set on producing a thesis (12)
23 Revolutionary centre created by Fascist powers (4)
24 Point to an old weapon—a sharp point (5)
25 Composer awarded academic and civil honours (4)
28 A punctured tyre is indeed! (8)
29 Put right by a couple of engineers (6)
30 Foolish advice to the over-zealous carer (8)
31 Strict cleric retiring in the diocese (6)

DOWN

1 Mortality figures are a complete write-off (4,4)
2 Start using the radio to get up to date (6,2)
3 Nagging complaint teachers take to heart (4)
5 Coup causes slave owner to have apoplexy (6-6)
6 Aware of ducks around the Northern Territory (4)
7 Not a main route out of the country (6)
8 Save earlier part under the church (6)
11 Where to put shoe polish when down at heel (2,4,6)
15 Sedate way to get assistance (5)
16 Woodland deity inflated by each hymn of praise (5)
18 Church house produces a paper to crack evil (8)
19 The commander was apparently with the Light Brigade (2,6)
21 Ampersand inserted in computer memory by chance (6)
22 Light lunch leads to a quarrel at home (6)
26 Hard rain is welcome (4)
27 That fellow is commonly a cup-bearer (4)

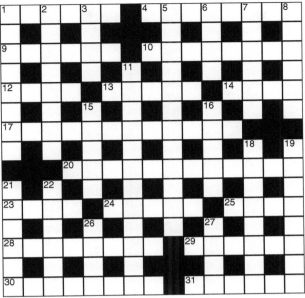

ACROSS

1 Frisk doctor entering prison (6)
4 Busy outside at start (8)
9 Grind a new bread (6)
10 Friendly note in a message (8)
12 Record a piece of music (4)
13 Fish appeared to be off (5)
14 Market's worst seller (4)
17 It's a fault taking the path of less resistance (5,7)
20 Where to hear opera company putting on unusually grand event (6,6)
23 What one said after reflection (4)
24 It's bound to be a shock (5)
25 For this pudding use the back gas-ring (4)
28 Try cannabis? Crazy! (8)
29 Find company in one churchman or another (6)
30 Take part in a dramatic trial (8)
31 Take it if you mean to stay dry (6)

DOWN

1 Finish up having a drink outside for pleasure (8)
2 Battle remembered in the long run (8)
3 They give a better price (4)
5 Aggravation of disease produces difficulty (12)
6 Trendy accountant who lived in S America (4)
7 The man on watch? (6)
8 Issue Oriental blend (6)
11 With right on both sides? (12)
15 Rose paid for the drinks (5)
16 I'd lifted the front part of a seat (5)
18 Lent is brought forward (8)
19 Tell everyone girl is overweight (8)
21 One who foils trespassers? (6)
22 Defeat for party (6)
26 A bird others turn to? (4)
27 Take off a ring, we hear (4)

84

ACROSS

7 A fool one has to suffer the morning after? (9)
8 Succeeded at one's first riding lesson (3,2)
10 Leave the other fellow penniless and scram (5,3)
11 Pray do rewrite a skit (6)
12 A preliminary contest will raise the temperature (4)
13 Not to worry if you make money illegally and get the bird (6,2)
15 A really difficult question for a rotten egg (7)
17 He keeps an eye out for the originator of gamesmanship (7)
20 Base diet should be planned sugar-free! (8)
22 Blow on the foot to keep it warm (4)
25 Nymph gets deer in trouble (6)
26 Uncooked, filleted, and lean (3,5)
27 What an otherwise cold man approaches with enthusiasm (5)
28 The previous best 78? (3,6)

DOWN

1 Entire UN health supported by the French (5)
2 When early man escaped from the Arctic eagerly (3,3)
3 What motorists step on to finish off with breathless speed? (8)
4 Hand me down—the mooring lines apparently (4,3)
5 48 inches on which cats proverbially manage to land (4,4)
6 Sociable type must be a reliable cocktail maker (4,5)
9 Mountain ridge a rider applies to mount (4)
14 Remove name from register if industrial action is cancelled (6,3)
16 Boxing titled paintings (5,3)
18 Identification code needed to transmit news (8)
19 How a straightedge is employed usually (2,1,4)
21 Quarrel as yet unfinished (2,2)
23 First rate selection (6)
24 Readjust rates and rents (5)

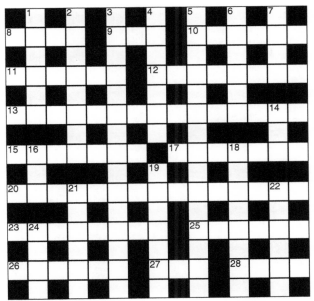

85

ACROSS

8 Foreigner without a legal right (4)
9 Vase containing more than a cuppa (3)
10 Nevertheless just like this (4,2)
11 I'd gone round to find a judge (6)
12 Of measurement of verses (8)
13 Devilishly hot areas? (8,7)
15 Many being examined in competition (7)
17 A reformed gambler? (7)
20 Off-putting manouevres (8,7)
23 Unusual to find novice in this hold (8)
25 Gloomy feature in arid surroundings (6)
26 One who is successful in beating all the others (6)
27 Early riser has student union's backing (3)
28 It is not hard getting in the asylum (4)

DOWN

1 Servant wearing a short skirt (6)
2 It is natural to be at home in this place with a set of books (8)
3 Become injured as a result of having meddled (4,4,7)
4 New layman accepts nothing that deviates from the rule (7)
5 Become discoloured, getting on with elementary protection (7-8)
6 Like stars in the zodiac (6)
7 No dolt is climbing the Greek mountain (4)
14 Born into one extended family (3)
16 A few lines due to be reported (3)
18 One giggling at small bird going right into another tree (8)
19 Monstrous, his gore, monstrous (7)
21 A boast! Get away with you (6)
22 Worries Bob with a demonstration of affection (6)
24 Ride or fall? (4)

86

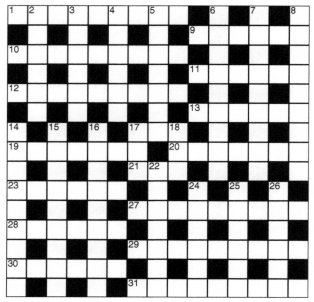

ACROSS

1 With a glazed look, disappeared without the right (9)
9 Reformed rotter's comeback (6)
10 Not left afloat (9)
11 Held by Gloria the naiad, a divine being (6)
12 Anyone can inadvertently cause irritation (9)
13 After the winter issue (6)
17 Walker's endless tale (3)
19 Cash organisation in a person's latter years (7)
20 Mean to declare date of birth? (7)
21 Pole following like a fool (3)
23 Putting a note in the pool would be fine (6)
27 There's point to the quarrel (9)
28 Rook a man on the board (6)
29 Making a painter frown, one is taken in charge (9)
30 Some GI's awful conceit (6)
31 Study for the high-minded (9)

DOWN

2 Work in the theatre, though only temporarily (6)
3 Fine point put on pointer (6)
4 Labour over an apt phrase (6)
5 "Fixing" a race, the guy will get a complaint (7)
6 A child of six (9)
7 One came out badly in the ballot, being controversial (9)
8 Eccentric about 50 many obstructed (9)
14 Decides not to compete due to minor injuries (9)
15 It could well be no drive is taken for enjoyment (9)
16 Unequalled footballers wanting a game? (9)
17 The field in which cattle are fattened (3)
18 Talk a lot, but settle up (3)
22 Grave Stock Exchange heads the monarch promises to pay (7)
24 Nobility—there'll be none at all in time (6)
25 Sort of anchor needed by the ferryman (6)
26 An old carriage that's sound, well-constructed (6)

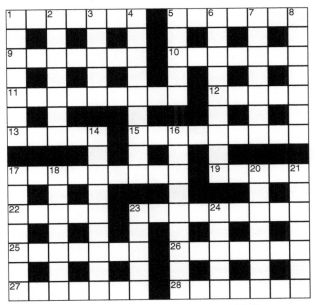

ACROSS

1 Grouping Olympic finalists in Derby, for example (7)
5 Modern music pitch can make lighter work (4-3)
9 Italian inventor who introduced polo, say, to Northern Ireland (7)
10 Saint's head hooded and lowered (7)
11 Calling people to produce polythene? (9)
12 Post wager? (5)
13 Jerseys, say, required in yachting-centre (5)
15 Stop paper coming out before hospital closure (9)
17 Hot cola mixed in church—then sold in bars (9)
19 Charm of river backing up engulfs soldier (5)
22 Ellis turned out in fine cotton fabric (5)
23 Mysteries of the variable south wind? (9)
25 Carriage is right in the soup (7)
26 Complex sort, this daughter of Agamemnon (7)
27 Umpire about to call—late? (7)
28 Poised like a policy-holder (7)

DOWN

1 Sulphur not present in make-up of heavenly body (7)
2 Current song outpouring (3-4)
3 Big Kitty overturned this sailing-ship (5)
4 This mini-banger is sometimes stuck (9)
5 Corroded game-pen (5)
6 "X-ray" seen over a door? (5-4)
7 Ploughing that goes on to 65? (7)
8 Carrots can be blue in Australia! (7)
14 Record of golfers (scratch, with proof of membership) (5-4)
16 Ah! no one MEP can produce marvels (9)
17 Starting cricket, play so whimsically—with the air of a West Indian (7)
18 Keep an eye on commentator who is one run short! (7)
20 Girl's first to refuse glamour (7)
21 Joint top-of-the-bill dies in the Big Apple, we hear (7)
23 At what point is ewer broken round head of husband? (5)
24 Drug-addicts employ ends of reefers (5)

88

ACROSS

1 French cheese needs to mature down through the years (4,3,2,3)
8 Ham Bill displayed in public (7)
9 Abstract logarithmic base has to be exact (7)
11 Wicked little devil contracted debts (7)
12 Inclined to be prejudiced (7)
13 Catherine has a pool (5)
14 Where little Jack sat up against the wall (2,1,6)
16 Set garden in order despite being disaffected (9)
19 Bandsman from East Scottish area bordering river (5)
21 I do moan in confusion when upset (2,1,4)
23 Seaman offers fortune to wife (7)
24 Signal base in Lancaster railway (7)
25 No one takes part. It's most offensive (7)
26 Loadstar for a man of prominence (7,5)

DOWN

1 Soundly urge Lord Chatham to escape from dingy theatre (4-3)
2 Place of prayer, possibly Socialist, possibly not! (7)
3 Vouching for one's presence in examination (9)
4 Now Flying Officers are found in trade fairs (5)
5 Lear's daughter embraced by two loves in the herb garden (7)
6 Glimmer of information about catalogue (7)
7 Quite unsuitable to be out of custody (3,2,7)
10 Senior family member introduces presbyter to friar (5,7)
15 Bad oilman suffering rupture of the guts (9)
17 Malign a Democrat breaking armistice (7)
18 Fuss over sports education is assumed (7)
19 Meet for a session with the tailor (7)
20 How to make one's application form carry more weight? (4,3)
22 Grand old man longing to give party support (5)

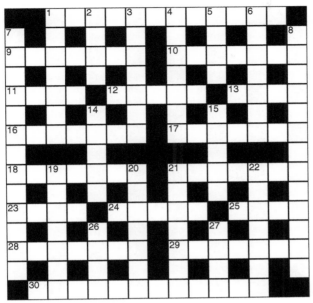

ACROSS

1 Who'll get over first depends on it (7,5)
9 A green insect consuming food (7)
10 Leaves wrapped up to be burnt (7)
11 The horse is cut badly (4)
12 Above all, not going out to work (2,3)
13 Please the gentleman (4)
16 Jabbers and irritates one (7)
17 At a loss to rationalise the disloyalty (7)
18 A dog's favourite colour? (7)
21 Can I turn her in and get the money? (7)
23 As a cockney, stop at nothing to become a singer (4)
24 Is no longer an addition to the hazards of summer (5)
25 Ask for, in well-chosen words? (4)
28 The groundwork accomplished to time (7)
29 He made the round sum sound rum (7)
30 Time-table? (6,6)

DOWN

1 Scottish surprise at the contents of the cheese roll (7)
2 He draws from the bank (4)
3 Says it with music (7)
4 Leaves when it becomes public (4,3)
5 Name in red (4)
6 Turns again (7)
7 A wet dish (7,6)
8 Did they charge a stiff price for their wares? (4,9)
14 A meal in the kitchen (5)
15 Bilingual article on the cause of amnesia (5)
19 "Colonist" in dog Latin (7)
20 Badly trained, swap for another (5,2)
21 The great difficulty is I have gone past my prime (7)
22 Ruled it mist be checked aloud (7)
26 Voice on the line? (4)
27 Game that only you can play? (4)

90

ACROSS

6 Can an X-ray machine perceive a man's true purpose? (3,7,3)

8 An outstanding device for sealing wine bottles (6)

9 In children tact serves to protect tenants' rights (4,4)

10 Scottish pair using international airline (3)

11 Way a New Zealand article portrays a piece of poetry (6)

12 Thin spar adapted to move cargo to another vessel (8)

14 Worked up how to cook tough meat (2,1,4)

16 Spread out for single hit by a batsman (7)

20 An extra plea of clemency for murderer (5,3)

23 In pain father must be brave (6)

24 Bed suitable for a small house (3)

25 One old prisoner is employed in priceless metalwork (8)

26 A tense time ahead (6)

27 Submarines' vigil (6,7)

DOWN

1 When Ken gets stuck into the weeds? (4,4)

2 A brief era of famine (8)

3 Maximum speed permitted for the A1 (3,4)

4 Turkish leader about to conclude business of the meeting (6)

5 Bogside soldiers in service (6)

6 Hurtful stabs following bullet wounds (8,5)

7 Go on a stable diet or have a nosh-up (3,4,1,5)

13 Manila's centre yields nothing (3)

15 Where a shoe comes to a point (3)

17 Stage at which train passengers alight (8)

18 For a cricketer to get one run is a shambles (8)

19 Smouldering anger (7)

21 Truly a way to make a second marriage (6)

22 Sheepish type doctor going around Ireland (6)

ACROSS

1 Tax before 1 May on religious centre (7)
5 Brian was moved during TV broadcast that was thrilling (7)
9 It could be a miracle to do this to land (7)
10 Uniform for nudists? (7)
11 Explain another reprint—and in French (9)
12 Show girl with inner sex-appeal (5)
13 Herb says licensing hours are over (5)
15 One drawer in the gallery might amuse one (9)
17 Not the best cheese for catching vermin (5-4)
19 A charming lady (5)
22 Smart cheat (5)
23 Is one of its four days of publication December 25th? (9)
25 Simplicity of being unusually vain before summer abroad (7)
26 Old city ceremony that is in turmoil, I concluded (7)
27 Nancy performed with energy inside and at the end—hot stuff (7)
28 Greeting leading zoologist in the capital found underground (7)

DOWN

1 Trying to reach this result (7)
2 Silently, cattily, waywardly (7)
3 Many a fine filament on the seat (5)
4 One who counts the top part only (9)
5 Spring found under the bank (5)
6 Sleeping partner? (9)
7 A crime wave over a country (7)
8 Willingly departed from this life? (7)
14 Ivy possibly always on the go (9)
16 Best basket is an unnecessary weight on deck (3-6)
17 Graduates spinning coin coming from the lodge (7)
18 Public service's usefulness (7)
20 Pedro to reconstruct a missile for use in the main (7)
21 Crazy type of metal thread? (7)
23 Line of waiters (5)
24 Times in bars (5)

92

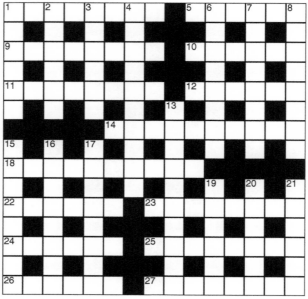

ACROSS

1 No front entrance should make one cross! (4,4)
5 An expedition to find animals for a fair's organised (6)
9 Renew tax in a certain American city quarter (8)
10 Plain about speed (6)
11 Reward the personnel officer (8)
12 A writer's alternative source (6)
14 Not favouring offers made by the opposition (10)
18 Change the blend of tea on trial (10)
22 More considerate German youngsters (6)
23 Discovering it among some stones causes alarm (8)
24 With much pretension but with no success (6)
25 Transport for those having a one-track mind (8)
26 Far from smartly dressed, and so made fun of (6)
27 The fan who is badly tailored (8)

DOWN

1 Lays odds about the queen's headwear (6)
2 Guy goes after many an appetiser (6)
3 Reform vetoed, give up (6)
4 Upset over lack of variety? (3,2,5)
6 A woman in depression hanging on (8)
7 Talked back and were set right about a point (8)
8 No practical person thought to enter (8)
13 Firm grip used in defence (10)
15 Discuss and OK travel arrangements (4,4)
16 Permanent rank (8)
17 The Conservative is quite right to spend lavishly (4,4)
19 Move at slow speed in a potentially fast Rolls-Royce (6)
20 Struggling artist, hard-pressed (6)
21 A stable fellow found work at an inn (6)

93

ACROSS

1 Capacity business for Apollo, say? (10)
9 One hangs from a palm just for fun (4)
10 Foot-long skeleton of emu starts a stir (10)
11 Youths unanimous in commendation of Sylvia? (6)
12 Fell unconscious in den (4-3)
15 Receptacle for party dips? (4-3)
16 Show, we hear, to look back on (5)
17 Cut waste at sea (4)
18 Last stopping-place for a drink, you could say (4)
19 Plague resort? (5)
21 A Roman's turn for a stroke, possibly (7)
22 Means of escaping the class system? (7)
24 This festival is an eye-opener to Daisy (6)
27 Short dean—quite a change! (10)
28 Fish-eater observed in Inverness (4)
29 Standing character? (10)

DOWN

2 Hold up spy (4)
3 Teach Sunday school to be virtuous (6)
4 Shorter class affair creates a hullabaloo (7)
5 Some alluvial soil used as well (4)
6 Half of Sussex turned out in ripped Indian silk (7)
7 Ornate style of a letter-opener? (10)
8 Sort of fool, this unwanted third party (10)
12 One measures humidity of the merry-go-round (10)
13 Romberg's desolate air? (6,4)
14 American divorcee in leather (5)
15 Sailors in bar destroyed in fire (5)
19 This jet arrived in yesterday from France (7)
20 Turkey for motorists, caught and cut into three parts (7)
23 Bar put out, being short (6)
25 Farm butter a penny more? What a swindle! (4)
26 German king's fragrant oil (4)

94

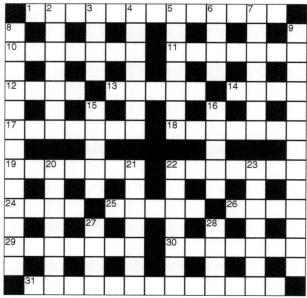

ACROSS

1 Nobility and rank prove a big issue (4,5,4)
10 Old friend admitted twitch of the eye (7)
11 How lyrics are written? Quite the opposite (7)
12 Terrible wrath Penny has to confront (4)
13 Board a bus to go places (3,2)
14 The way once to become sagacious (4)
17 Women feel Sam should be reformed (7)
18 Very eager to obtain French iron grille (7)
19 Tense when not in bed drunk (7)
22 Lace she ordered in London (7)
24 Smile despite the size of one's hips (4)
25 Wonderful to have #1000 (5)
26 His place was among the lesser fellows (4)
29 Governor is to dine with sapper medic (7)
30 More suited to a commercial plug (7)
31 He bent a makeshift placard unworthy of attention (7,6)

DOWN

2 Fit, full of energy for the time being (7)
3 Pop serves white wine (4)
4 I shall put on a cape despite complaint (7)
5 Decline to describe a Manx cat (4,3)
6 Rex and I have to split (4)
7 Rewrite entire recipe briefly for pate (7)
8 Refuse tip? That's utter nonsense (4,2,7)
9 Leave combatants' rations for N African campaign (6,7)
15 Sells whips (5)
16 How to move away from a Red Indian quietly (5)
20 Vagrant left footless in crush (7)
21 Dress and go to vote (4,3)
22 I cannot in any way keep within limits (7)
23 He has doubts about entering poisonous surroundings (7)
27 Only I object to Scripture lessons (4)
28 Agreement between Pennsylvania and Connecticut (4)

ACROSS

7 Form of greatness for soldiers (9)
8 A bench to put in the sun (5)
10 Went so fast was barely visible (8)
11 Hole at the front (6)
12 Foreign capital used in Czechoslovakia (4)
13 It's not fair for me to use this! (8)
15 Don't keep the orchestra together (7)
17 He made a conquest, showing resolve an hour after midnight (7)
20 Make a union defer tea break (8)
22 Scratch starter (4)
25 Tom turns to her, naturally (6)
26 Eternal source of family strife? (8)
27 Monster fish? (5)
28 Dog food dropped from the back of a lorry (9)

DOWN

1 The ultimate in commandments (5)
2 Consents, but will be a long time coming round again (6)
3 Face up, perhaps, but not to a challenge (4,4)
4 Arrangement to admit us into the sports-ground (7)
5 Key leather treatment is delicate (8)
6 It takes the lead (3-6)
9 What's left when objections are raised? (4)
14 Hair dresser? (9)
16 He'll bear out it's a drinking place (4,4)
18 Writes one's first letters (8)
19 Drivers pass through it for a change (7)
21 Hair-style for a transformation? (4)
23 Is unable to get a girl into bed (6)
24 Signal fear (5)

96

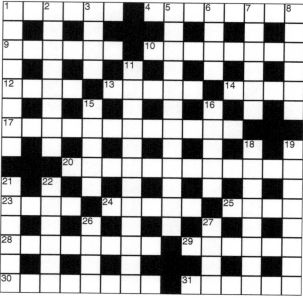

ACROSS

1 Quickly remove label showing exorbitant price (3,3)
4 Pooh-poohing Baden-Powell's outdoor theme (8)
9 Frenzied ailing antelope (6)
10 Briefly continued in employment despite being bruised (8)
12 One who succeeds as ambassador to a retiring king-emperor (4)
13 Greek character seen around Alexandria (5)
14 That is about 550 doing nothing (4)
17 Novel attic (4,2,3,3)
20 Maybe hoarding by a Whitehall ministry (5,2,5)
23 Be up against an objection (4)
24 Where English pottery workers tend kilns (5)
25 Part of the Cush I admire is Muslim (4)
28 Old London river is enough for Britain's whole navy (3,5)
29 Party given by dam eccentric type (6)
30 Clearly able to work out true mean! (8)
31 Absorb nourishment humorously one hears (6)

DOWN

1 Smuggle in a whisky or gin when demand outstrips supply (3,5)
2 Be over lavish by adding 20 cwt to a nuclear reactor (4,2,2)
3 Door of a tent a flustered man gets into (4)
5 Make a meal of an opportunity to embezzle? (4,3,5)
6 So far fit for the job (2,2)
7 A batting team has apparently entered (6)
8 Contrivance an Israelite tribe has to obtain (6)
11 Withdraw—having taken up temporary residence at a monastery (4,1,7)
15 Most important member of the cabinet (5)
16 Measure of force of current by a West African river (5)
18 Old veteran worse if injected with a haemolytic factor (3,5)
19 Attend to view a boxing match (3,5)
21 Go in 8th wicket down and thrive on a partner's contribution (6)
22 Exhibit house mother is about to employ (6)
26 Fail to enunciate clearly an aspersion (4)
27 Spare list (4)

97

ACROSS

1 I don't know what it is in French (2,2,4,4)
8 Unusually large one taking part of N Africa (7)
9 Waste food (7)
11 Confusion i.e. great in town (7)
12 Changed by Ted, rear tyre (7)
13 Composition played loudly on posh violin in Shetland (5)
14 Airborne traveller well below par (9)
16 Soldiers get together to reminisce (9)
19 Six right to depart given sign (5)
21 It is insensitive to ring us about our leader (7)
23 Part of the chain is leaking badly (7)
24 Helping providing guests with food (7)
25 Hops round with some cold food at the hostel (7)
26 Dramatic love-affair? (5,7)

DOWN

1 Stimulating exercise (7)
2 Tell of island uprising before Mr Lawrence (7)
3 Old friend involved in deadlock (9)
4 Imply, what could be finer? (5)
5 Small group find a book in the tranquility (7)
6 Just after the turn became very active (2,3,2)
7 Four trouser supports (4,2,6)
10 Left-winger is protected when found again (12)
15 Girl on helm 'e transported to a famous birthplace (9)
17 A responsible person (7)
18 Vase underneath toilet taking shape! (7)
19 Might it be served at a stag-party? (7)
20 Understand how one can make money (7)
22 A sweet lump (5)

98

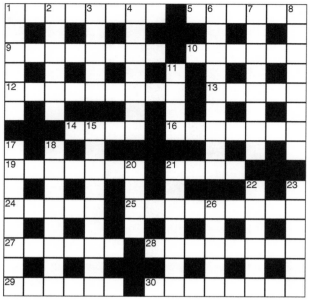

ACROSS

1 Set on edge by alarming upheaval (8)
5 One container is stowed inside another when empty (6)
9 Riles ten possibly in the audience (8)
10 Stranded tot (4,2)
12 Attempted to succeed without money—got done (9)
13 Shout out names (5)
14 Paid to eat (4)
16 Bound by a top man (7)
19 Following study, have an inclination to argue (7)
21 Backing English graduates like (4)
24 Damp is needed for love-in-a-mist (5)
25 Slightly damaged, so withdrawn (9)
27 In a bad bad way in Nigeria (6)
28 A few words addressed in French to the Church (8)
29 Environmentalists maybe put on them (6)
30 Impressed by Eastern flight (8)

DOWN

1 Animosity apparent in married woman (6)
2 Think to turn up surrounded by soldiers and begin again (6)
3 Arranging a single transaction would be best (5)
4 Assisted a quite sober egghead into bed (7)
6 The irresolute chairman's lack of control (9)
7 Scriptures carried by a run-away—a wild creature (8)
8 Such material parts, yet can be brought together (8)
11 Chances for scraps (4)
15 Surveys rail transport when there's personal complaint made (3-6)
17 Produce notes about many a politician not being conscientious (8)
18 Very friendly at getting in eventually (8)
20 An expression of annoyance causing dismay (4)
21 Present awful crawler (7)
22 Novelty trade (6)
23 Some man feeling bad—he regrets promising to hold on (6)
26 Pole having to carry a thousand (5)

ACROSS

1 Double-dealing pair confronted (3-5)
6 Out on bail in old England (6)
9 Ball-game requires physical education and a lot of running about (6)
10 Jumper for a spaniel? (8)
11 Counter quarrel (8)
12 Argentine material inside Norfolk, for example? (6)
13 Everyday disguise of PC in SE Atholl, perhaps (5-7)
16 Putting number one under? (4-8)
19 A plank on a ship (6)
21 Flight-path of early aircraft (8)
23 Bowman, we hear, could be one (8)
24 Not fairly matched in a French flat (6)
25 Jolly sailor (6)
26 One does not forget this size of paper! (8)

DOWN

2 This beetle is small, loathsome, tailless! (6)
3 All the plant life belonging to Miss Macdonald (5)
4 Daily comes about one—she'll be given the floor (9)
5 Make out record English fleet? (7)
6 Bewildered pair left this month (5)
7 Bonn takes change or bills (9)
8 O, boatmen—what a bloomer! (8)
13 Venomous thing in advertisement—dread its coming out? (4-5)
14 Torpor—girl with it due to be treated (9)
15 Old county table (8)
17 Reason for infanta's visit to nursery? (3-4)
18 Confine enemy citizen in Bury North (6)
20 Comic beau (5)
22 General chief physician of old (5)

100

ACROSS

7 Fool about to add bitter flavouring to some meat (5,4)

8 Lily means a great deal to you and me (5)

10 Mother chases a bird on the Nile (5,3)

11 Not even a patient man can get casual work (3,3)

12 Quite right to place junction at top of French road (4)

13 Heed advice to accept a gratuity (4,1,3)

15 Not working in the Tax Office to start with (3,4)

17 Billy Bunter became a spiv (4,3)

20 Standard charge for an apartment (4,4)

22 Commotion in one of Corfu's streets (4)

25 Signal from a firm in Scottish highland (6)

26 Reproduced a diet Tim worked out (8)

27 Salary for a prison warder (5)

28 In favour of being generous and compassionate (9)

DOWN

1 Opted to have many pairs of stockings (5)

2 Damage caused by one member who is overbearing (6)

3 Detectives' examination provides conclusive proof (4,4)

4 Study by doctor needs to be notedly brisk (3,4)

5 The type to give an impudent look (4,4)

6 George offers gold to self-righteous crew (9)

9 What the bibliophile may reserve (4)

14 A dishonest dealer catches influenza despite wealth (9)

16 When upset Edward longed to be aloof (8)

18 Wantonly disregard refining process (8)

19 Game archdeacon confronts one boy (7)

21 Italian banker receives a Royal Navy cipher (4)

23 Look around very fast (6)

24 Medium has to have resources (5)

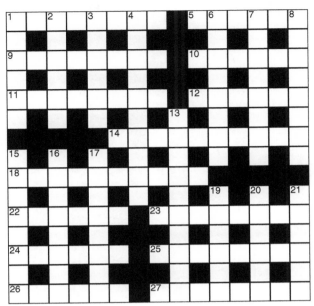

ACROSS

1 The launching, darn it, has got cancelled (5-3)
5 Coin with the Queen on its head given to the messenger boy (6)
9 Covers with the gun again (8)
10 Like skirting a chasm one steers clear of (6)
11 Are friends? Come off it! (3,5)
12 Make no move to anaesthetise (6)
14 Having been stolen is miles away (10)
18 Having trouble when caught by cannibals? (2,3,5)
22 Shoot in season (6)
23 Gets a key before the squire goes off (8)
24 What the tailor makes when he's not busy? (6)
25 Where the plants are you go in to water (8)
26 Unworried, indeed, when ordered to strip (6)
27 Leaves waiting for rises (6,2)

DOWN

1 From the nursery brought up to steel, gets time (6)
2 Prepared to let a fool guard items of value (6)
3 It's turned upside-down to show the high neck (6)
4 A packet that comes by air? (6,4)
6 Turning about again the slaver goes off (8)
7 The drink I lay a bet about (8)
8 Comes from a family that is one the downgrade? (8)
13 Extend yourself? (7,3)
15 Arranged "In The Mood" (8)
16 Is the church a simple one? (8)
17 Barely flew (8)
19 Behave like a fool and smuggle his package through? (4,2)
20 Is contentious, one maintains (6)
21 In bed, while John is up (6)

102

ACROSS

5 Canoe in which a soldier finds shelter (6)
8 Pithecanthropus is no lie-abed (5,3)
9 Miracle town has ways which lead to rumours (7)
10 Net Foreign Office turned to frequently (5)
11 Tell all about modern form of cardiac surgery (4,5)
13 Little nips or little nippers (4,4)
14 Oust former member sought by newly recognised state (6)
17 South Pennsylvania resort (3)
19 Consumed by a spirit of blind vengeance (3)
20 Pace at which a horseman is unable to hesitate (6)
23 Last to finish despite everything (5,3)
26 Severe penalty for a brawny thug in good condition (5,4)
28 Oriental composes a ballad to mother (5)
29 Right to discipline an unruly child (7)
30 Refuse to lower the volume (4,4)
31 Faster revision is needed for the final course (6)

DOWN

1 Stay to the end and bid farewell to guests at the door (3,3)
2 Caught young seaman boxing (7)
3 Send off with a wave of the hand (9)
4 Old Margaret was given grub (6)
5 Protracted treatment of decayed tooth was performed (5,3)
6 Cricketer renowned for great elegance (5)
7 Tunnel work is in progress (5,3)
12 Final comment I added to a Greek letter (3)
15 Doesn't matter if it is always matter (5,4)
16 Mimics what a fighter squadron does when scrambled (5,3)
18 Umpire steps outside to make introductions (8)
21 Front and rear carriage of a train (3)
22 Invites to pay a visit (5,2)
24 Taking it easy by standing on one's head? (4,2)
25 Telling tales about a normal method of egg production (6)
27 Was his science fiction never translated? (5)

ACROSS

6 Easily made angry but without delay moderated (5-8)

8 The French examination comes after everything else (6)

9 Poet or teacher perhaps found on the football field (8)

10 Involuntary response from a stickleback (3)

11 Walk—the way to go round (6)

12 Some creatures would not feel well without them (8)

14 Military unit ordered to accept the equipment (7)

16 Trade vehicles (7)

20 After-dinner request for a travel document (8)

23 Is nothing but a meteorological line (6)

24 Barley not left in the grass (3)

25 Bird has five-pointed fish! (8)

26 Larva is behind the said rotter (6)

27 Foreigner Rita puzzled by the cooling (13)

DOWN

1 Enduring what we all hope to do—not depart early (8)

2 Christopher with model in Del's unusual embrace was knocked over (8)

3 Infernally spiteful female (4-3)

4 Put a peg in the instrument (6)

5 What screws are used to secure doors (6)

6 Officer for three months a teacher (13)

7 Playful presentation of a best-seller perhaps (13)

13 Girl who goes after information in Switzerland (3)

15 A record height (3)

17 Garment refashioned by Catriona (8)

18 How the Ark was illuminated? (8)

19 The way a horse with hesitation might move unsteadily (7)

21 Such odd letters found on frill at the back of one's neck (6)

22 Beginning alternatively with one drink (6)

104

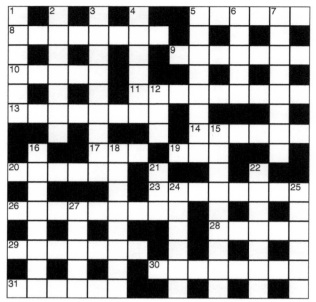

ACROSS

5 Attack making one feel ill after dope (6)
8 The firm, given a choice, putting on the board (2-6)
9 Work and ring for tea possibly (7)
10 All that remains of some rare lichens (5)
11 Will meant to go straight following an investigation (9)
13 A newsman about to take a drink (8)
14 A plant to tantalise the novice (6)
17 Scandinavian coin or note (3)
19 Woman sets man right! (3)
20 The size of a book? (6)
23 The putting down of French attitudinising (8)
26 A vessel, ancient or otherwise (9)
28 Leave by water, returning thanks (5)
29 The Romans' main deity (7)
30 Kiss getting big copper all behind (8)
31 Port doesn't deteriorate (6)

DOWN

1 Successful batsman caught—and touchier about it (6)
2 An officer cuts off slices of meat (7)
3 Where there's plenty of space for cattle? (9)
4 Get on in time and make a presentation (6)
5 A page with little desire for food (8)
6 Go in a hurry, taking only seconds to pack (5)
7 Favoured and protected as expected (8)
12 English soldiers should turn up before this (3)
15 The wrong one—or sure to appear wrong (9)
16 They look for explanations from those who are late (8)
18 Handed over without protest? (8)
21 Poetry written in the modern style (3)
22 Sort of drink set beside the driver (7)
24 He is with little hesitation sent off (6)
25 Collect an article for inclusion in mock-up (6)
27 The name might be changed to let it (5)

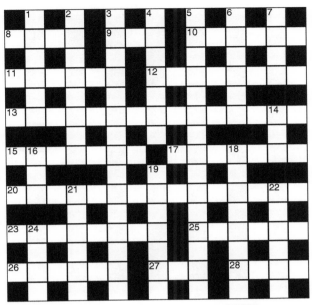

105

ACROSS

8 Extra broad (4)
9 Well! Pa's all over the place (3)
10 Mind a rose, variegated, taking a shortname? (6)
11 A gadabout at No 10? No, there's slow movement (6)
12 Bird ever fluttering in flower base (5-3)
13 Courteous qualities of Clement, with courage (15)
15 Deny profits—always! (7)
17 Keep unusual dialect (7)
20 Savoy plot to sustain the house? (9,6)
23 Affected heart states in the spring (8)
25 At home, team serving time (6)
26 Some racehorses in the Strand, we hear (6)
27 Note to follow the third degree? (3)
28 English isle, a US state? (4)

DOWN

1 Screen poser (6)
2 Elevate boat-crew in Orpington, for example (8)
3 But can one be so cool, sitting on an ale-bench? (2,5,2,1,5)
4 Reasonable distance, of course (7)
5 Shooting star, perhaps, moving unencumbered? (10,5)
6 The buck stops here, before Hastings? (6)
7 Fuel approved in church (4)
14 Haggard woman? (3)
16 A card champion (3)
18 A cryptographer's ruse of simply taking initial characters (8)
19 Two half-sovereigns, mostly, provides grass (7)
21 Occasion for England's openers to take on late batsmen (6)
22 Woden's amended awards (6)
24 Pity no longer expressed for her (4)

106

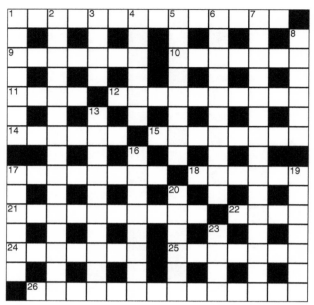

ACROSS

1 Alluring hose offered by a wartime spiv? (5,9)
9 Engineers do otherwise in Sizewell B (7)
10 Locates compound sugar (7)
11 A trial for athletes in the tropics (4)
12 Occasional name for a magazine (10)
14 Answer is still to be found in the laboratory (6)
15 Write 999 to represent a range (8)
17 Airmen turned back a bit to get well away (3,5)
18 Rush about madly calling (6)
21 Provide intelligence to friendly power off the record (10)
22 Investor hoping to make a quick buck (4)
24 Big cup of tea given to big nits (7)
25 On tour I resolved to smooth things over (4,3)
26 Follows what the rising logician does (6,2,6)

DOWN

1 Townsman serving up food to a lady (7)
2 How data should be presented to tell the truth (2,1,6,2,4)
3 Christopher English is a high-flier (4)
4 Horseshoe found in wooden serving bowl (6)
5 Phone one agent up to get orthopaedic aid (8)
6 Included one of the teeth of minor importance (10)
7 Clear telephone lines for influential friends (4,11)
8 Nothing in brothers' rooms but instruments (6)
13 Percentage in favour of a marriage settlement (10)
16 They smash rollers (8)
17 Flight Lieutenant longing for a piece of bacon (6)
19 Straight ahead? Absolutely correct! (5,2)
20 Oil ban arranged by a very fair man (6)
23 Do the French give unemployment pay? (4)

107

ACROSS

1 They're looking for their owners (5,4)
9 Going to translate to French (2,5)
10 Mum loves messing about in the tool shed (7)
11 The fish is one brought in from abroad (7)
12 Besides, that's where the customs officer is liable to search (2,3,4)
14 Having myself exorcised a devil in the past (8)
15 Illiterately scan the article and make more changes (2-4)
17 The free time in general is half an hour (7)
20 Putting away half the eggs and a loaf found inside (6)
23 Give an example of how one batsman differs from another (8)
25 Now, lined up, are given a talking to (9)
26 Not ordered where men get together (2,1,4)
27 I can't possibly accommodate it, it's so big (7)
28 Back in business as I foolishly provided the capital (7)
29 As a rule, it is extensive (4,5)

DOWN

2 Put out of one's mind (7)
3 Got well as had been augured (7)
4 Requiring a finesse to get the ace, led it worriedly (8)
5 A TV stand and a seat? (6)
6 Misconception of an aide (5,4)
7 Flowing back, is trapped in the bend (7)
8 Happening to drop, being caught (9)
13 Hit very hard, broke (7)
15 Tries to squeeze right through, being supple (9)
16 Not at home but in hospital, waited on hand and foot (3,2,4)
18 Stern with the Chinese, becoming belligerent again (8)
19 Obliquely question one about the north (7)
21 After the match, tucked in with a will (7)
22 Requiring knocking into shape, by all accounts (7)
24 Nonchalant when giving us a break in California (6)

108

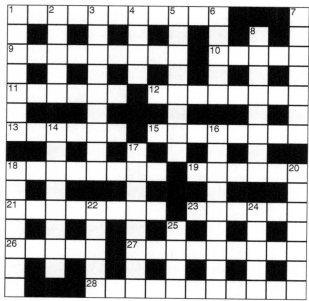

ACROSS

1 Cherubic entitlements call for redress (3,2,6)
9 Finished job according to normal practice (4,5)
10 In total agreement an hour after noon (2,3)
11 Though too lazy to work he presumably makes dough (6)
12 Get a move on to terrace the garden maybe (4,2,2)
13 Argument resulting from use of a carpet sweeper? (4,2)
15 Damaged by admitting to being married (8)
18 A feller's 66 foot cutter (5-3)
19 Priest and I conclude his feelings are amicable (6)
21 Dostoevsky's novel description of an ass (3,5)
23 Little rascals bivouac amidships (6)
26 A pretty serious sort of pain (5)
27 Where naughty boys stood confronted by a dilemma (2,1,6)
28 His widow no longer has to keep his dinner hot (4,7)

DOWN

1 Wrought up pigs splashed around in the mud (7)
2 Silver not all returned to a Polynesian kingdom (5)
3 High time for a pilot to bank (2,3,4)
4 The Oxford Thames has a pair of islands (4)
5 It is almost too late for the first 2 words of 3 (4,4)
6 Bright and well honed (5)
7 Rushed around the green of course and got soaked (7)
8 No stamp needed ... (4,4)
14 ... to make a claim (5,3)
16 Terrible debts contracted by displaced Croat (9)
17 Kayak in which I once sat crumpled up (8)
18 TUC literally spells redundancy (3,4)
20 Wanted to see a baronet in action (7)
22 Live daughter in good health (5)
24 Manse converted into a smart club (5)
25 Little spirit to run fast (4)

ACROSS

1 Old soldier puts tree, sawn up, in the vehicle (7)
5 Agreeable pupil leaving countryman (7)
9 Deceptively recumbent (5)
10 Obtain an item of furniture that is accessible (3-2-4)
11 Reckoning I am in the eastern depot (10)
12 The last one sees of the rabbit (4)
14 Performing like marathon athletes ultimately (2,3,4,3)
18 Woodworker with a sting in his tail (9-3)
21 Bony part of incomplete lunar construction (4)
22 Gallant chorus Val and I produced (10)
25 Engaged the debtor with difficulty (9)
26 Could be any South African lake (5)
27 One hundred less cups and saucers found in the garden (7)
28 Singular item intended, say, to be left over (7)

DOWN

1 Against the Spanish surgeon having the material (6)
2 Number might try to hit out first (6)
3 How a military unit was systematically organised? (10)
4 Titled gentleman heard in the darkness (5)
5 Literary work found on the stove? (3-6)
6 Wine from Italia still? No, it's sparkling (4)
7 Large tunny swimming round a coral bed endlessly (8)
8 Giving free medical attention? (8)
13 Made a ruling—on paper only? (10)
15 Go to bed at the farm? (3,3,3)
16 Unattractive cleaning woman? (8)
17 Delirious if centre is removed (8)
19 Man accepting alternative spirit (6)
20 Obliquely across the French book (6)
23 See nothing on the recorder (5)
24 Go on board (4)

110

ACROSS

6 Making a recording of things to set right (10)
8 Certain foreign coinage no longer current (4)
9 Firm offering place with all speed (9)
11 Quietly suffering medical treatment (4)
12 Royalty occupied by a hearing device (3)
13 A person saving money with poor diet's deplorable (9)
16 Some people wouldn't let chain-smokers eat out (4)
17 A vehicle crashing into a horse is dreadful (7)
18 Swinish creature keeping home messy one way or another (7)
20 Left a good man to carry on (4)
21 Rules for the monk in a specified retreat (9)
23 A tip is the aim (3)
24 Row with anyone getting into knots (4)
25 Silence on reform shows contemptuousness (9)
29 There's endless book-work for 1 (4)
30 Fresh clue found, so permission is given to proceed (5,5)

DOWN

1 The manager of 29 (4)
2 Exhibiting some hesitation, quarters the tongue (4)
3 Agreed to get rid of serving men when elderly (4)
4 An old writer is rather slow (7)
5 Presenting bill with credit-notes after collapse would be wrong (10)
7 Using no net for a time (9)
8 Appear as concerned with donation (9)
10 A journey made in the past (3)
13 Playwrights can be both staid and smart (10)
14 Rendered intoxicated (9)
15 Dropping outside right—being really cutting (9)
19 Broke university people housed in a hut (7)
22 Article on the French male's drink (3)
26 Tall pine (4)
27 Love encompassing a natural growth (4)
28 A resounding come-back! (4)

ACROSS

1 Break in by levering—how resourceful! (12)
8 Up late, wandering round a table-land (7)
9 Red-hot water heater, say? (7)
11 General keeping these islands? (7)
12 Petition is therefore lawful (7)
13 Active around hospital in a tall hat (5)
14 Presbyterian minister who appeases (9)
16 Materials for portrait of a good-looker? (3-6)
19 Course for Robert Burns, for example (5)
21 Heavenly, under tree! (7)
23 Motorway casino turned into a sort of lodge (7)
24 Angst is a male disturbance! (7)
25 Viewpoint about last Gaelic couple—in English (7)
26 Means to get 16 on the canvas? (7-5)

DOWN

1 Coats for seal-men made up? (7)
2 They admit balme for hospital treatment (7)
3 One delivering milk and sandwiches to a chap? (9)
4 Hazards of a run on broken skis? (5)
5 Sister holds large-sized piece of embroidery (7)
6 Tars comprehensively reduced in pipe-tobacco (4-3)
7 What makes Ribston prosper? (5-7)
10 Not a single cruet trinket broken (6,6)
15 Leave one's craft behind (9)
17 Lamb, under a high ball, makes a bloomer (7)
18 Very silly, like 19 say? (7)
19 A ship, for example, equipped with first-class weapon (7)
20 I have supported American state in pilot (7)
22 Upright characters in the rectory (5)

112

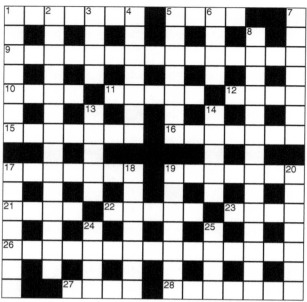

ACROSS

1 Go back and find the right way out (7)
5 Stout-hearted, bull-headed and elderly (4)
9 Used typewriter bar despite suffering from cramp (7,3,5)
10 Supplant someone in a vicious temper (4)
11 Play being performed by Catholic historian (5)
12 Be up against a stated objection (4)
15 Female recorded getting beaten (7)
16 Eats nut concoction which causes serious illness (7)
17 A spy concealed under the railway track (7)
19 Why romantic couples marry if free (3,4)
21 Record sprinters aim for (4)
22 Chart book a sailor turns over (5)
23 King pursuing deer is a man of action (4)
26 The entire equatorial population from first to last (3,5,3,4)
27 Computer character ascribed to Lawrence (4)
28 Study outlet for Catholic students (7)

DOWN

1 Make a better impression as a result of ticking-off (7)
2 Bribe to use hand cream (6,4,4)
3 East London college finds otherwise (4)
4 Tempted Fascist leader to enter Scottish Education Dept. (7)
5 Gargantuan meal causes spare tyre to be put on (4-3)
6 640 gallons should suffice (4)
7 Makes—a fuss, apparently (7)
8 Boxroom Enid can convert to install gas (6,8)
13 Christian feast for silver-headed primate (5)
14 Beginning to jump (5)
17 Feel ill after parties and leave port (3,4)
18 Tenure I organized to procure a suite (7)
19 Desperate to get it turned into French money (7)
20 Serious pledge (7)
24 A pair of apprentices with a yen to be friends (4)
25 You and I have an understanding to change diet (4)

113

ACROSS

7 Such a discussion gives opportunity for falling out (4-5)

8 In a way age is some protection (5)

10 Certainly in drink, but restrained (8)

11 Means it won't have a principal part (6)

12 Article concerning the unknown (4)

13 Flustered and hurried at the same time? (8)

15 Photographed out of doors? (7)

17 Clothing is torn without intention (7)

20 Believe gold might satisfy him? (8)

22 Drug quietly injected into a rabbit (4)

25 Naught ladies men dream of (6)

26 Humility shown by Ken seems out of place (8)

27 Animals there's a market for (5)

28 Perfectly proficient? (9)

DOWN

1 Such a cut may be seen in a ring (5)

2 Unions strangely in agreement (6)

3 Way in for transport (8)

4 What to do when a player offends badly (4,3)

5 Even when it's wired correctly, it can still shock (8)

6 Villainous crimes upset social worker (9)

9 Forbidden, but a doctor provides it (4)

14 Surrender to another country (9)

16 Regulation I ignored in making guns (8)

18 People at play (8)

19 Coming first in U.S. election (7)

21 The job an idle person should be taken to (4)

23 Eyebrow raising writer (6)

24 Remains of pitched battles (5)

114

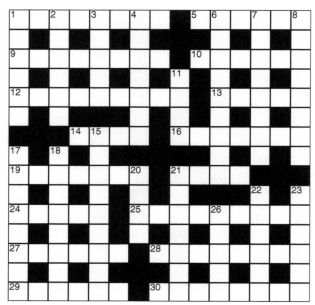

ACROSS

1 Hostility caused by haematic disorder (3,5)
5 Which can he do? Bat or bowl a maiden over? (6)
9 Once upon a time it was shorter if not the same (2,6)
10 Retorts used to advertise films (6)
12 At risk when making a call (2,3,4)
13 Stood shock still when the temperature dropped below zero (5)
14 In between sentimental and pretty (4)
16 Galley thrice needed by army technicians (7)
19 Offer to keep up the resistance (4,3)
21 A London Park Jekyll turned into (4)
24 Refuse a stew which has been rehashed (5)
25 Final dance enjoyed by the lothario bridegroom (4,5)
27 Arrange travel for scoundrel (6)
28 A VIP racket (3,5)
29 Take stock of the Ulster settlement (6)
30 Give news—by Telex? (4,4)

DOWN

1 Walker's complaint with a second rate body of workers (6)
2 What surprised pupils do if Duchess of Cornwall is not on time (6)
3 Clean cut is needed in surgery (5)
4 Once and once only (3,4)
6 Apparently mad at being forgotten (3,2,4)
7 Postpone short holiday to Channel resort (4,4)
8 Got the better of a boy editor (8)
11 Go to get some citrus flavouring (4)
15 Wheat is all one has ... (9)
17 ... to much slowly and think about (4,4)
18 Every variety of sweetmeats (3-5)
20 It raised £50 for drawer of cash (4)
21 Not keen on small house with part of fence one can climb over (7)
22 Passionate desire expressed by one following the Liberal party (6)
23 Generally accepted to be a characteristic of Shylock (6)
26 Clarified wine was subjected to legal penalty (5)

115

ACROSS

1 It is difficult to know what to do with these young puzzlers (7,8)
9 He is expected to succeed (6,3)
10 Suit, about a month with it (5)
11 Nobleman that is with rebel leader before now (7)
12 Overlie new embossed work (7)
13 Unbeatable service a church provides (3)
14 The girl curiously might strike again (7)
17 US barman accepts there's rare charm in silver coin (7)
19 One cannot be sure if one is a sceptic (7)
22 Stuffy complaint (7)
24 A cheat has difficulty (3)
25 The old man has to economise (7)
26 Sea-monster reported in rough Ural, it's a whale! (7)
28 Some require a tailor-made lasso (5)
29 Foreign boy accepted first of all was put off (9)
30 A letter from Blackpool perhaps (7,8)

DOWN

1 Not inclined to take ordinary stock (9,6)
2 Sequence of command (5)
3 The French are smart and enduring (7)
4 Odour of desert animal (4-3)
5 D/V = C (7)
6 Plant Lamb under the high-pitched ball (7)
7 Cool drink of course? (9)
8 Break one cannot bank on (8,7)
15 Two men annexing a state (9)
16 The man accepts one must hurry (3)
18 Run Italian leader over a valley (3)
20 Catch one going round an Italian port (7)
21 Disseminate help brought up in class (7)
22 A model left Costa Rica going round the island! (7)
23 Man in the Dutch capital was seated (7)
27 In the assault rampaged excessively (5)

116

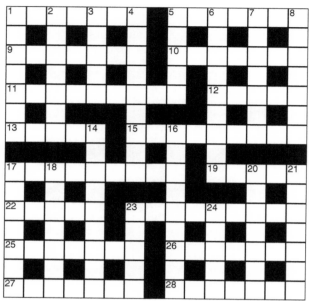

ACROSS

1 Sailing man entered lounge to make a new beginning (7)
5 A willing rider (7)
9 Demonstrate about everything frivolous (7)
10 Resent a devious Oriental (7)
11 One must take sound steps to provide entertainment (3-6)
12 Speed gets the heartless (5)
13 The German soldiers both backed down (5)
15 Brown is in consequence grave (9)
17 Schemes at odds with high-rise architecture (9)
19 Given silver lining before—such a bore (5)
22 Get going, though there's some contention (3,2)
23 Possibly she wore it to appear different (9)
25 Spirited musical instruction (7)
26 Bear's internal organ (7)
27 The intellectual had for example double trouble (7)
28 Where those making the effort feel on top of the world! (7)

DOWN

1 Favour trimming to trees (7)
2 A quarter took a drink when beaten (7)
3 Some habitual loafers may be found in town (5)
4 A loud-mouthed individual proclaiming his intelligence (4-5)
5 Key role in a Shakespeare play, that's plain (5)
6 The underworld make accusations to settle accounts (9)
7 Tea is taken without 23 across in London (7)
8 Clement moved line ten (7)
14 Unprincipled professional man cutting discount (9)
16 Quickly get past those dithering (9)
17 No gentleman will go into action in a downpour (7)
18 Trivial matter of registering hospital admission (7)
20 Surrounded by filth, a large number look disgusted (7)
21 10, certainly torrid as far as one can see (7)
23 Nothing—nothing!—is shaped like an egg (5)
24 The right hand a person used for running water (5)

ACROSS

8 Nice changes in reliable, cushy job (8)
9 Tempo in Beethoven's unfinished symphony is stimulating (6)
10 Owl, unusually, at ground-level (3)
11 Rural priest takes on a novice (8)
12 Pat is anxious, starting school (6)
13 School play Pa left, all ends up (15)
15 Check truth about somebody starting to write poetry (7)
18 Possibly pursed lips at first and drank noisily (7)
21 Wrong idea of motorway's assembly (15)
24 Section of redder Maphigian layer of skin (6)
25 Some Henley events abandoned, mates! (5,3)
26 Girl's best friend in classic effect? (3)
27 Looks down on grain in ship (6)
28 Unnecessary IOW features, facing south (8)

DOWN

1 Six gunners attempt to bring down a Spitfire (6)
2 Writer on farm-butter is not released (4-2)
3 One of the last eight quits flat in rear, unexpectedly (7,8)
4 Town-criers to call me before noon (7)
5 Footballers who are modern keep together (9,6)
6 One helps to steer fish over water (2-6)
7 Break up, divorce and vanish! (8)
14 Drive in reverse—hurt results (3)
16 Importance of cardinal's address? (8)
17 Plane may score, used clumsily (8)
19 Get a letter from Greece after hip replacement (3)
20 Bread for the beak? (7)
22 How Caesar addressed Brutus, with possibly less struggle (6)
23 Stupid to put ring on a natural swimmer! (6)

118

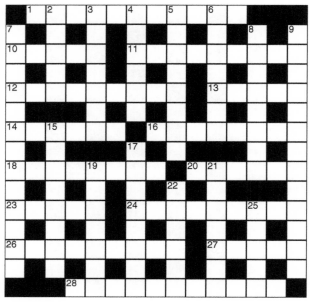

ACROSS

1 Crimean heroine clearly needed a hurricane lamp (11)
10 A great deal of wine is Mediterranean port (5)
11 Pull up quickly to remedy a current fault (4,5)
12 Continued—with a love affair, presumably (7,2)
13 Hand-out for the children (5)
14 I am to get a job out of duty (6)
16 Garment I designed for one going overseas (8)
18 He cultivates a Shakespearean forest in Germany (8)
20 Gather that 18 got disheartened (6)
23 Thrush found by a Sussex river and lake (5)
24 Moon-faced Parliamentarian (9)
26 Music manuscript used by correspondents (9)
27 A Miami sergeant is somewhat tight-fisted (5)
28 Retained barrister and refused to give an opinion (4,7)

DOWN

2 Central pub about to be erected (5)
3 Self-important chap of prime importance to a calligrapher! (3,4)
4 Not out of the team (6)
5 Dogma one disseminated to gain a reputation (4,4)
6 Leaning over a computer print-out (7)
7 A hypodermic needle is the last thing one will accept (8,5)
8 Petty officer who is an apple-lover? (8)
9 Costers on the open market (6,7)
15 Sponger finds where airborne soldiers are based (8)
17 Feeble agent gets it after a month (8)
19 Cuttings in Early English put others in the shade (7)
21 A theologian gets a sign from the lower regions (7)
22 Paper quota ordered is about right (6)
25 Points Miss Lawley has to follow (5)

ACROSS

1 Beef too? Why not! (5,2,4)
9 Strange things seen by only women in the scrap heap? (9)
10 Prone to, granted (5)
11 Runs that prove costly if not bargained for? (6)
12 Travelled as a stowaway and wasn't punished (4,4)
13 Unruffled, points to the day on the calendar (6)
15 During the fight don't have a loss of consciousness (8)
18 As the bulletin is by the erudite newscaster? (4-4)
19 Posts for the horse race (6)
21 Hiding in a tunnel too small to stand up in? (5,3)
23 One's rattled by the artist, a foreign lady (6)
26 Family English to the core—completely (5)
27 Posted off to Diane on the way (9)
28 It means a ruler was used to open a cell door (5,6)

DOWN

1 The little darlings turned up to walk the dog (7)
2 On the subject of gun belts, is excellent (5)
3 Resembled, in being grasping? (4,5)
4 Don't keep on! It's only intended for storage (4)
5 Happily dealt with trouble in the cathedral city (8)
6 Get off—it's not serious (5)
7 Quite happy to deceive over accommodation (7)
8 Don't notice what you have under your very eyes? (8)
14 Instrument, not quite blunt, with which the crime was perpetrated (8)
16 The broken heart I can mend, lady (9)
17 How the notabilities get on together? (8)
18 Strike, furious, with the whip (7)
20 And entering isn't bent double (5-2)
22 Without a single gram, we can't help him (5)
24 Belonging to someone, one conceded (5)
25 Shout "Well said!" (4)

120

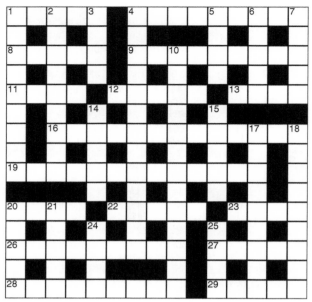

ACROSS

1 Programmable computer chips offering noted programmes (5)
4 Hostile mood revealed by evil genius (3,6)
8 Winning position for the successful mountaineer (2,3)
9 Points to an allegory that can be pulled to pieces (9)
11 Prompt hints used by a snooker player (4)
12 Publicity agent must be one born after the advent (5)
13 Staunch supporter (4)
16 Everything is offered free, but in vain (3,3,7)
19 Filing cabinets are meant to be the best to date (4,3,6)
20 Security device which limits steering wheels (4)
22 Under a river in Glamorgan (5)
23 Get by—but without honour (4)
26 Takeover bid made by the committed buyer (4,5)
27 A picnic party is best (5)
28 Hattersley scares supporters of the monarchy (5,4)
29 He sailed around the world on a duck pond (5)

DOWN

1 He should get a bag! Just an old bag? (4,5)
2 Where the hammer should hit without delay (2,3,4)
3 They rise before spring's over (4)
4 Not only I get overwrought (6,7)
5 Young salmon last hooked by Henry VIII (4)
6 Contradict the confounded brute (5)
7 Amount of heat needed for a seaborne attack (5)
10 Unillustrated articles are of poor face value (5,8)
14 Photographic record of the family silver (5)
15 Pole has to pass lots of corn in the field (5)
17 Four o'clock tiffin originated in Darjeeling maybe (6,3)
18 What any batsman hopes to get is at least 20 or more (4,5)
20 Prisoner obviously misused rifle (5)
21 Transport automobile by railway (5)
24 Thin metal sword (4)
25 US president is way across the river (4)

121

ACROSS

1 Resounding blow on the boy he's upset in the country (10)
6 Part of speech in Iver, Bucks (4)
9 Crazy story taken back to vehicle on the island (10)
10 National tax (4)
12 Group let out in town (6)
13 Buy tea bag outside (8)
15 Venomous plant? (6,6)
18 Expressively having the intention of being complete before the end of the day (12)
21 Attempt to include an undergarment in the disguise (8)
22 Choose mother accepting one of the most favourable points (6)
24 Fall right into the rubbish heap (4)
25 Well-known, having performed at a service (10)
26 Title of one appearing in pantomime? (4)
27 Tax dolts, men in the street! (10)

DOWN

1 Provide inspiration for puzzle (6)
2 Bareness of untidy arrangement (6)
3 One may help in certain cases (5,7)
4 Skid out of control to get the record (4)
5 Dignified sculptures that can be found in France (10)
7 Barter using old money (8)
8 Flattered, say, in the plot (8)
11 The occasion for athletes in form? (6,6)
14 How an astronaut feels is not important (10)
16 Did nothing original (8)
17 Soldier to approve member's pattern (8)
19 Moral excellence of six true eccentrics (6)
20 Outlaw group with sex-appeal (6)
23 Old historian be of French derivation (4)

122

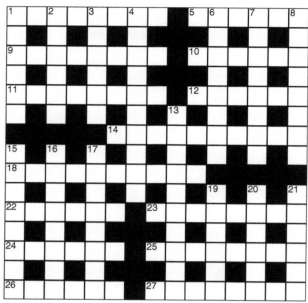

ACROSS

1 Panicking needlessly and getting a weapon shown in a catalogue (8)
5 A computer long since superseded (6)
9 Propose including tip for delinquent (8)
10 Little beasts needing to rest (6)
11 English ship involved in extensive distribution of aid (8)
12 Force receiving a tribute (6)
14 Pugilists' biographies (10)
18 Pass after a pupil gives a certain assurance (10)
22 Royal direction for feast (6)
23 An animal both rare and cute maybe (8)
24 Mean but modish nurse (6)
25 Read Mediterranean island material (8)
26 Rush about and secure this contraption (6)
27 Insisted on a desert's being made use of (8)

DOWN

1 A god represented by a head, nothing more (6)
2 Provide a turn-off road (6)
3 Unusual German food-container (6)
4 Such stuff makes the forecaster a laughing-stock (10)
6 University man beat egghead appearing in casual wear (4-4)
7 Director in revolt—he's not been paid (8)
8 Points about American writers giving rise to some doubt (8)
13 People expecting to encounter hostility when they drop in (10)
15 Disdaining to make notes about the cereal (8)
16 Softly lit as promised (8)
17 Standard cut, in a manner of speaking (8)
19 The French Left can be so awkward! (6)
20 The least polished may become rusted (6)
21 A story for example seen in advance (6)

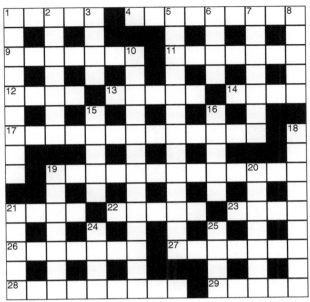

123

ACROSS

1 New showing of The Sorcerer, unabridged (5)
4 Rush-stick, we hear, can deliver a great blow (9)
9 Recycled paper in a long dress (7)
11 In the real world, allied members re-assemble with young leader (7)
12 Where to buy peach? (4)
13 Fashion for men announced (5)
14 Pen a bit short for this legal document (4)
17 Getting rid of Sherwood? (Arden too, if set badly!) (13)
19 Round potato for example in skips. showing bumps (13)
21 Inter-city? No, town! (4)
22 Perfect state (5)
23 Nothing to spoil this Persian poet (4)
26 Vessel in which English master is at sea (7)
27 Disaster of attempt to include the superannuated (7)
28 Currently, place not recommended for horse-trading (3-6)
29 Man as safe as a rock? (5)

DOWN

1 A1 piano chords arranged, as in a Gershwin piece (9)
2 Ticking-off for salesperson on the tiles (7)
3 Not a name on a railway line? (4)
5 Job given back in it, check bank-account (13)
6 American composer on one side of old records (4)
7 Banking flap—no lire exchanged after the first of April (7)
8 Peggotty upset—got out of ancient land (5)
10 Rout—so equalize endlessly, in showy French style (5,8)
15 Burn British castle (5)
16 Wanton maid's gold sovereign? (5)
18 Ship-breaker (9)
19 Indicate left terminal (7)
20 How French a remark! (7)
21 Booms can produce such pals (5)
24 Put out this battered item (4)
25 Penny on farm butter is a swindle! (4)

124

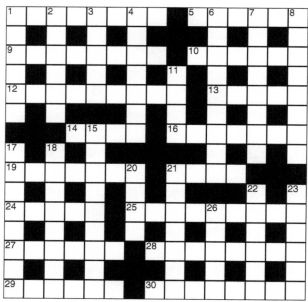

ACROSS

1 Fixed salary used to stop free wheeling (3,5)
5 A soft fruit is to emerge (6)
9 Exaggerate the batting team's complaint against slow bowling (8)
10 Price-control association returns permit to motoring club (6)
12 Hard pad for paint (9)
13 Grandmother keeps girl in New York (5)
14 Some of the church icons show style (4)
16 Community member has to bear it in mind (7)
19 Two foul compounds found in effluent (7)
21 It provides food containing calcium and iron (4)
24 Pole needs to supply personnel (5)
25 A Frenchman has to intervene without delay (9)
27 Informally polite refusal by railway clerk (6)
28 Congregates for prayers (8)
29 Forceful but feeble-framed man of honour (6)
30 Plan of action to get trays manufactured (8)

DOWN

1 Not even accommodated in reserved housing of low quality (6)
2 Divine faith which is embraced by others (6)
3 Five in custody have to cut patterns (5)
4 Common Market subject is out of place (7)
6 Outspoken argument makes him bring a suit (9)
7 Last European is insane to riot (8)
8 Motor racing is picking up (8)
11 Rummage for food (4)
15 Offer to maintain garrison hospital (4,5)
17 Do exercises to relax (6,2)
18 Restrict production of nitrates (8)
20 Fancy man understands the little woman (4)
21 Strike is to be made public (4,3)
22 Socially ill at ease when left in France (6)
23 Mean to be spotted (6)
26 A model takes heart on getting letter from Greece (5)

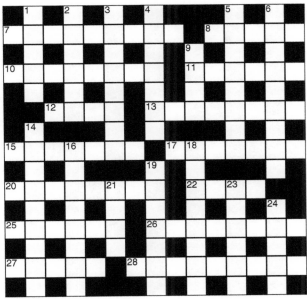

125

ACROSS

7 Took flight when beaten (9)
8 Force plane to land (5)
10 Common haunt (8)
11 Fruit is planted in wet weather (6)
12 Natural inclination to be crooked (4)
13 Book for the opera (8)
15 It's a fixed sort of charge (7)
17 There are many sides to it (7)
20 Discovers it's fun to do wrong (5,3)
22 Mean? No, jolly! (4)
25 Lorraine's companion in France (6)
26 They may be happy playing cards (8)
27 Criticism for staff (5)
28 The growth of a fairy-tale (9)

DOWN

1 A seed that grows into a tree (5)
2 Something worn in N.W. Spain (6)
3 Sailor banished to quarters for being a defaulter (8)
4 Make a student doctor listen for the pulse (7)
5 Liberation, in a manner of speaking (8)
6 A change of theme? (9)
9 Short game in which a child goes to sleep (4)
14 Be hesitant, empty and sick at heart (9)
16 Sort of survey of guns? (8)
18 Pretty useless object (8)
19 Strengthen dispute in Japanese currency (7)
21 Does wrong, gets lines (4)
23 Marriage Guidance report (6)
24 The sources of a science fiction writer (5)

126

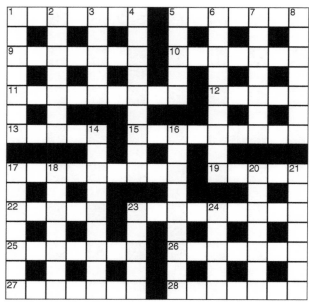

ACROSS

1 Loiter around an interesting German city (7)
5 Elevation—but no elevator! (7)
9 Windows fitted at the French national museum? (7)
10 Somehow respect one who gives a fright (7)
11 Annoyed about bungled raid, so blaze out (9)
12 Is all dressed up, but may swear! (5)
13 Stops at very small stations (5)
15 Wild carthorse scattered the band (9)
17 One who makes a picture of carrier holding beam (9)
19 An inn nearby (5)
22 This proved I was in Bali getting cooked at the time! (5)
23 The sermon record belongs to us, we get a point (9)
25 The plug in the gun barrel is a pad soaked with ink (7)
26 Refuse some grub bishop offers (7)
27 Deserts might have green points (7)
28 Twigs that the French are after power unit (7)

DOWN

1 He will shortly get his punishment, it's awful (7)
2 One of the gears in a new Renault (7)
3 Six ride pointlessly, they're very green (5)
4 Rub a party member with surgical scraper (9)
5 I sell twisted cotton thread (5)
6 At liberty to turn to coast (9)
7 The final one to go—and keep going (7)
8 Opens up first class fragrant bloom (7)
14 Weakening on the point of getting fit (9)
16 Seamen from Eire are good at opening bottles (9)
17 Add afterthought to change a book (7)
18 Train driver involved in alarm (7)
20 Warm drink? (7)
21 Medical men who take blood (7)
23 Nudes might go sunbathing here (5)
24 Circular tour—or part of it (5)

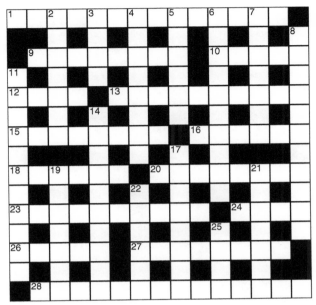

127

ACROSS

1 Sun, moon and star in old money! (5-9)
9 Sharp gymnastics movement? (8)
10 Even can include the Parisian (5)
12 Celebrate when a boy goes round the bend (4)
13 Notedly becoming gradually slower (10)
15 Ready to read out homework first (8)
16 Catch parent out (6)
18 No model included an expression of disgust for nothing (6)
20 Tube fare from Italy (8)
23 Such a person would not be spotted by a scout in the entertainment industry (10)
24 Bird bit off another bird (4)
26 President called after the crash (5)
27 Cancerian? (8)
28 One might crawl at least twenty miles (7,7)

DOWN

2 He alone is content (7)
3 Point to the right (4)
4 Diagnose trouble suffered (8)
5 An Italian with status cannot be included (6)
6 Happening to get a pound by the way (10)
7 Gatherer of information is notedly thinner (7)
8 Lump I cannot move, it is unyielding (11)
11 Evasive person in italics? (7,4)
14 Would a marksman automatically use it? (7-3)
17 In commonsense, a custom that's disgusting (8)
19 Remove lead (7)
21 Concerning a jolly type of bowling (7)
22 About to look at the dress (6)
25 Record-player provided in Hawaiian Islands (2-2)

128

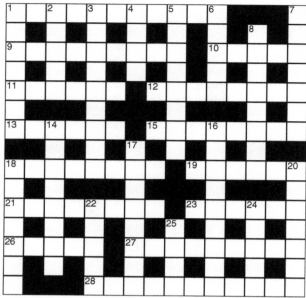

ACROSS

1 Rises including a small payment for the teenagers (11)
9 Tending to do some good? (9)
10 Not all of the spinners will be on target (5)
11 The number of the Spanish flat (6)
12 A quarter lit up, getting cold-shouldered (8)
13 Rest is essential for a nurse (6)
15 Reveal a woman's gained weight (8)
18 A form giving rise to antagonism (8)
19 The pudding could be prepared faster (6)
21 Confidential hint (8)
23 Agree with large number over the blackguard (6)
26 Plain where there's nothing green (5)
27 A man's make-up is of absorbing interest to him (9)
28 Bather gasping? (3,2,6)

DOWN

1 Player inserting key in a lock (7)
2 Assuming a bovine look is a bloomer (2-3)
3 Light dishes provided for soldiers in tents possibly (9)
4 Boasted about being concerned with direction (4)
5 Catching without cash—so provoking! (8)
6 Shy, but make a song about the Left (5)
7 17 is all a game (7)
8 An illustration showing the current attitude (8)
14 Respects free spirits (8)
16 Away from business, look gloomy and out of sorts (3-6)
17 Read the brochure and 7 (8)
18 Fatty is a dope to change! (7)
20 Period of detention of variable length? (7)
22 Slogan—there are many to turn to (5)
24 Country church in a union (5)
25 An animal to be seen in the typical farmyard (4)

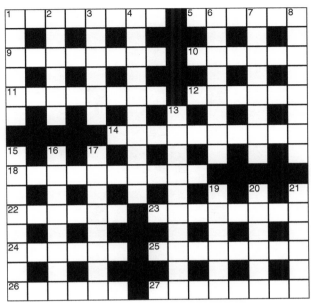

129

ACROSS

1 Prospect of a gold-lined straw hat (8)
5 Man on watch around Beachy Head (6)
9 Big-footed bird who lets out the clutch on a hill? (8)
10 Cut section of design or extend it... (6)
11 ...specific, tidy reduction (5-3)
12 Tell leaders of it, make peace at round table! (6)
14 Ornamental tin-openers an affectation? (10)
18 Christmas, say, for the fourth time? (7-3)
22 Papal trip before Sunday dismays (6)
23 Jack, for example, tock eccentric (4-4)
24 O'Neill's chiller in play (6)
25 Pop article in French journal (8)
26 Score harmonized in Tchaikovsky's first and last pieces (6)
27 Leakage includes a day of adventure (8)

DOWN

1 Motorway bordered by dark purple rock (6)
2 Firearm put up to achieve gold prize (6)
3 Big bang rumour (6)
4 How to present Porterhouse, say, to a spiritualist hardly known? (6,4)
6 Pheasant, perhaps, in dressing is something that binds (8)
7 Excessive love of number one? (8)
8 Giving tablets can be entertaining (8)
13 Clever plans to give jewels to some layers of society (10)
15 Etching mainly found in water? (8)
16 Listener to music needs such a receiver (3-5)
17 Rugged law-breaker in the beginning (8)
19 Mrs Copperfield supports iron hat (6)
20 Sort of republic out of hand? (6)
21 Stick notice on this spot (6)

130

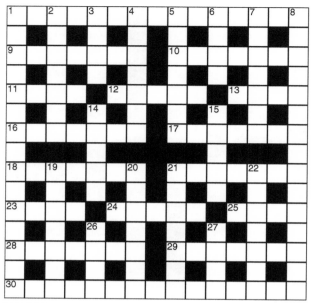

ACROSS

1 Habitual parking offender at the station exit (6,9)
9 Maintain a parent needs to say nothing (4,3)
10 Character in Greece hostile to Italian wine (7)
11 Fashionable Poles will find them barred (4)
12 Jack uncertain for a moment (5)
13 Monarch has to employ subterfuge (4)
16 Some beef from those heading the first division (7)
17 Umpire about to call for silence and impart new vigour (7)
18 Speech is a habit of the present era (7)
21 A supporter of strong bonds in early middle age (7)
23 Given a protective coating 1843 years ago (4)
24 The composer who had good fortune (5)
25 He refuses to come out if sore (4)
28 Regular university class (7)
29 Just adore making doilies (7)
30 Economise, but make sure you don't get caught with your pants (7,4,4)

DOWN

1 Consider how to enter item in a ledger (4,4,7)
2 Work as a char and make a good profit (5,2)
3 Fiery saint found in chapel, monastery and church (4)
4 Put together an agricultural vehicle (7)
5 If ulcer is wrongly treated, it's the very devil (7)
6 "Men loved darkness rather than light because their deeds were ——." (St John, iii) (4)
7 Style certain to appeal to brother's coiffeur (7)
8 Bring up the question—of dubbing? (5,3,7)
14 Father North and the femme fatale (5)
15 Once the first letter was used in place of the fifth (5)
19 Doing business distributing cards (7)
20 Only a Scotsman is famed for his wisdom (7)
21 Fine deed by a group of dissidents (7)
22 Be disposed to bend a little (7)
26 Attack Billy (2,2)
27 Bends one's body and plays the 'cello (4)

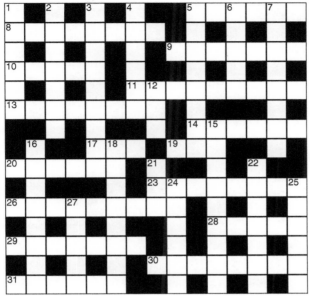

131

ACROSS

5 Leave aide gets in full (6)
8 Runners who jump the gun are not forgotten (8)
9 Behave oneself, or have a romp around in bed! (7)
10 The strain of mourning (5)
11 Backing for Scotsman to join university (9)
13 Lift to reveal switch (8)
14 Sort of suit or suite (6)
17 Go out, but be back to start breakfast (3)
19 Badly in need of medical care (3)
20 Run a series of lectures (6)
23 Fruit no good for a pudding (4-4)
26 Take the car, beetle off and whoop it up (9)
28 Loves an anagram to work out (5)
29 Safe anchorages found on entering Nigerian port (7)
30 Didn't stay uninhabited (8)
31 Parts always carried by a sea-going vessel (6)

DOWN

1 A game one may come across (6)
2 Colour of Sherlock's study? (7)
3 A right rotten seat puts one off (9)
4 About eleven, come round in a state (6)
5 One should admit when one is depressed (8)
6 Where the goat goes without corn (5)
7 An advance in the property market (8)
12 Shipping company that was floated using the double entry system (3)
15 One who used to teach painting (3,6)
16 Many too old for reporter's work (8)
18 Directions for making machine parts (8)
21 A small point, but appropriate (3)
22 Property of the upper class? (7)
24 Editorial boss (6)
25 One inside wards off evil spirits (6)
27 Take sweetheart and run (5)

132

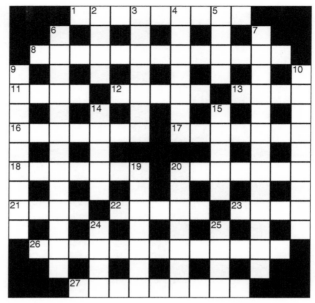

ACROSS

1 Advocate return of knight in exchange (9)
8 Pep up demand for a house-warming suggestion (4,2,3,4)
11 A step taken with due deference (4)
12 Belief expressed by the bitch (5)
13 Article in trite magazine (4)
16 Understand the door is locked (5,2)
17 Top bowler (7)
18 Poultry dressed smartly by Baker (7)
20 Girl put in $1.01 or maybe the One Thousand Guineas (7)
21 He should turn over many a new leaf (4)
22 Get ready to streak and tear past the street (5)
23 Metal club (4)
26 State conditions on which close friends meet (8,5)
27 Where shot-guns are carried when prepared for war (5,4)

DOWN

2 Returnable money (4)
3 Criticised for being knocked over by a motor car (3,4)
4 Plans for me to enter chess knockout (7)
5 Reflection of one's own outspoken views (4)
6 Instant reaction of lively slender monarch (5,8)
7 Getting on beyond 1s and any number like 2, 3, 5, 7, 11... (4,4,5)
9 Upsetting it thwarts plans in the fruit market (9)
10 Renowned as tourists with cameras in position! (9)
14 Does it make the car engine cough violently? (5)
15 Indian dish Paul I cooked (5)
19 Crackpot normally cracked with crackers (7)
20 Monster bell depicted by eminent artist (7)
24 Notice a portent (4)
25 Appear to observe a maiden (4)

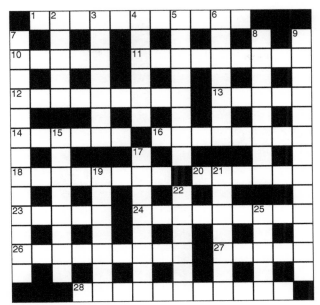

133

ACROSS

1 Depressed when more speed is required (11)
10 Place in the room a handsome guy (5)
11 Your turn to bowl, so to speak (4,2,3)
12 Entertainments being after dark? (5,4)
13 'e will take no food round at the banquet (5)
14 Consolation for one following the sun (6)
16 Describes fully that the ceremonies mentioned have finished (6,2)
18 Second sight of the corrected version (8)
20 Greedily, could be daily about five (6)
23 Building blocked by snow (5)
24 Too much French science is in figurative language (9)
26 Shoulder-bag? (9)
27 Admit nearly everybody is down (5)
28 The last but three to score (11)

DOWN

2 Most of a brick that is dropped makes a loud resounding noise (5)
3 Bouncy band (7)
4 Strange that it was relating to the ear (6)
5 Left brewed beer in Ayr possibly, or another beverage (3-5)
6 Not having a chance was excluded from participation (3,2,2)
7 Making direct progress out of criminality? (5,8)
8 Went round town (8)
9 Double figures (8,2,3)
15 Outpouring from two volcanoes on a Polynesian skirt? (4-4)
17 Left side greeting footballers (4,4)
19 Urges another commander inside with whip (7)
21 Six nil and not before time—that is profane (7)
22 Small isolated area (6)
25 Hooter not fully developed (5)

134

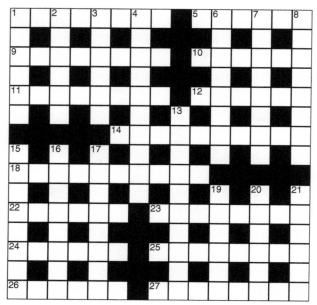

ACROSS

1 Meeting outside right, come to some agreement (8)
5 Broadcast before—depressed about it (6)
9 Pretended to encourage taking on financial liabilities (8)
10 Emphasise need for second lock (6)
11 First principles of steel-men's newly-formed union (8)
12 With little hesitation presented as more virtuous (6)
14 Neither win nor lose the game—such a let-down! (10)
18 Study the making-up of faces. It would appear appropriate (10)
22 Eastern airway's affairs (6)
23 Having a fixation about family consideration (8)
24 Popular minister's design (6)
25 He will be embraced by wildly ardent fan (8)
26 Servicemen bearing in a gun—a thing of some value (6)
27 Extra-large portion of chicken or moussaka (8)

DOWN

1 Realises there's only cold remains (6)
2 Naturally beginning exercise with a feeling of revulsion (6)
3 Incensed about article, so made a fuss (6)
4 Check legislation affecting shops? (10)
6 Crock shoots the press! (8)
7 Regular surge at the end of the day (8)
8 Many is the directive giving rise to complaint (8)
13 Made contact with second organisation (8,2)
15 Give voice about the company that's found to be twisting (8)
16 Financier who's into clothing and gold (8)
17 An edict's amended to effect separation (8)
19 Attach and aim a listening device (6)
20 Speech-maker being firm about the cake-decorator (6)
21 Stones a Turkish bigwig set up (6)

ACROSS

1 Hospital in Perth, perhaps, without energy—benefactor required (14)
9 What is set worth? (8)
10 Tried and true sort of alloy (5)
12 Island of four elements (4)
13 Arty in meal presentation—and nourishing! (10)
15 Entertainer playing lyre in this tavern? (8)
16 Shattered, on one's uppers before noon (6)
18 Foreign feast one can tuck into (6)
20 Doctor with fine violin begins concerto that is electrifying (8)
23 Famous western theatre-instructor (10)
24 Hot tune that grows on one (4)
26 Needless one of many on set (5)
27 Appropriate, your old secret? (8)
28 Trade indications for travellers? (7-7)

DOWN

2 Comes up with acceptable exhaust-holes... (7)
3 ...fit to be left in Lincoln? (4)
4 Short films advertising "Caravans of Texas" (8)
5 Given ample space, say, showing cold symptoms (6)
6 Modern pail damaged? Dud, perhaps (10)
7 High singer in "Blithe Spirit"? (7)
8 Singleton for example—sporting eccentric (7-4)
11 Mean with iron dukes, say? (11)
14 Subject of recent transfer to division (6-4)
17 These biscuits are really nutty! (8)
19 One who portrays a legislator (7)
21 Car heat affected the air-intake (7)
22 Growing dwarfs? (6)
25 Learner in peasouper to drive? (4)

136

ACROSS

1 To fuss around was a habit of Victorian ladies (6)
4 Accountant with bizarre attire (8)
9 Blind to Parisian show-piece (6)
10 I am put to the test and made better (8)
12 Years previously turned to meditative practices (4)
13 A chair for journalistic chief in the sickbay (5)
14 No charge when Rex is in charge (4)
17 Fast food ne'er made in Gloucestershire (6,2,4)
20 Rubbish played on violins (12)
23 Transport a lot of stolen goods (4)
24 Silly little Dorothy (5)
25 Woodcutter imprisoned by a mad zealot (4)
28 To turn in one's food allowance leads to revolution (8)
29 Virginia is not allowed to be unoccupied (6)
30 Makes amends for ruining Texas pie (8)
31 Daughter admitted being drunk (6)

DOWN

1 Start playing hockey if corned beef is not on the menu (5,3)
2 Idler has to pull back after hard hit (8)
3 He who bade us behold the way? (4)
5 Remarks about male Democrat delivered by Moses (12)
6 Vegetable which is acceptable to army men (4)
7 A churchman retires into town hostelry (6)
8 Edward lost his life when whirled in the river (6)
11 Best to back heavyweight individual (6,2,4)
15 Out of bed and on the move (5)
16 Do form a political group (5)
18 Environmental hazard caused by a Channel Islands sewer (4,4)
19 Complied when tense, sad, disturbed (8)
21 Order an assault (6)
22 Row results from wearing an underwired brassiere (4-2)
26 Street with nothing but a colonnade (4)
27 Paschal offeratory imbued with an aura of sanctity (4)

137

ACROSS

1 Loud shrieking comes from this bird (10)
9 Capital punishment (4)
10 It may be a tiny girl's reason for not singing (10)
11 Money sought by some scouts (6)
12 Drop in radioactivity? (4,3)
15 No deviation from a working party policy (7)
16 It's a mistake to hesitate or retreat, right? (5)
17 Propose to change house (4)
18 Measure some food, say? (4)
19 Prepared to explode—or not to explode (5)
21 Tract of grassland left untidy (7)
22 Routing in a way that's clearly sound (4,3)
24 One who leads in the German language (6)
27 The appeal of a fashionable career (10)
28 Rotten row (4)
29 Not the main way to transform a desert site (4-6)

DOWN

2 I fled the country (4)
3 It's used as anti-freeze in exceedingly cold weather (6)
4 Naive woman found in genuine confusion (7)
5 Loathe articles in disorder (4)
6 He makes a neat, if illegal, profit (7)
7 Bring about—a wage increase for someone? (4,4,2)
8 Community tax payment? (10)
12 It could be the concern of several generations (6,4)
13 More than one very big ship is the naval order (10)
14 Played in the Test (5)
15 Fighting dog? (5)
19 Transfers from one bank to another (7)
20 Orders for guides (7)
23 Drain a beer-mug finally and pass out (6)
25 Eager to behead the king of Israel (4)
26 Manage an investment (4)

138

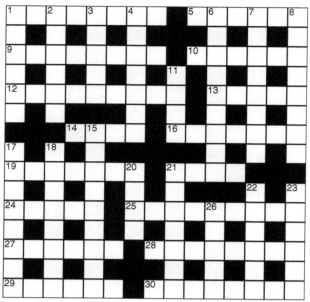

ACROSS

1 What an athletic clever student hopes to be in (4,4)
5 Put away the map and collapse with laughter (4,2)
9 Incorrigible rogue a barrister would find difficult (4,4)
10 Don't retire—remain cheerful (4,2)
12 An advantage for golfers wanting a secluded residence (4,5)
13 GP yet to be reappointed in Africa (5)
14 Did he get his colours for playing right-wing? (4)
16 Stacking away a shilling adding to salary (7)
19 Casually mention how to withdraw one's support (3,4)
21 Before last month a hundred formed religious sect (4)
24 Subject for article by yours truly (5)
25 Make sure time is right to mount a guard (3,1,5)
27 My robe being designed for an expected baby (6)
28 Distributes call for workers to strike (5,3)
29 Sailor needs secure object to aim for (6)
30 Senior laymen take on boy destined to succeed (5,3)

DOWN

1 Observed to be under arrest (6)
2 Recoil from a vulgar psychiatrist (6)
3 Confronted being beaten in court after first of February (5)
4 Relaxation I have despite being unrelaxed (7)
6 Sore spot if touched when literally seething (2,3,4)
7 Sir Robin's autobiography—in regular instalments (3,2,3)
8 In labs they are used for tube test transfer (8)
11 Hugh's heard what a woodcutter does (4)
15 The big sort used for headlines (5,4)
17 They inhibit walking from accommodation to parts of the yard (4,4)
18 Rest able to shape metal rod (5,3)
20 An ambitious drive to peddle drugs (4)
21 Cry of derision summoning Whittington's panto partner (7)
22 Razor edging belts up sports (6)
23 Snapshot negative needs only a bit of light (6)
26 Number 10 club secures Western border (5)

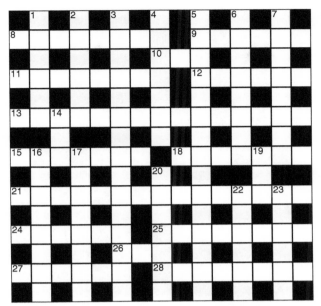

139

ACROSS

8 A Mexican overhead? (8)
9 Came to a similar conclusion, we hear (6)
10 Past a green light (3)
11 Charmed beloved (8)
12 Persuading second mate to leave whilst steering a boat (6)
13 Match overstatement? (7,8)
15 Broadcast serials that are stuffy (7)
18 Provided ornamentation placed at intervals (7)
21 Words of encouragement parliamentarian has for a Scottish pastor (7,8)
24 Prepare again rush item (2-4)
25 The last part in the act was fully described (8)
26 Fuel record (3)
27 Quality of character of eg iron, say (6)
28 Articulate lot queen removed (8)

DOWN

1 Carried nothing to a Pacific island (6)
2 Jack to get under way as mentioned and let himself down the rock-face (6)
3 Sheer pleasure having a drink with the game (4,3,8)
4 Plan for one who doesn't know which way to turn (4-3)
5 Timely thief, so it is said (15)
6 Cat looked, having keen sight (4-4)
7 Indicate hours spent in the intervening period (8)
14 Beware, internal strife (3)
16 Colourfully in debt (2,3,3)
17 One said in France to have been included by the girl with clarity (8)
19 The point on which one is punctual (3)
20 Sergeant-major and I had the information, a very small amount (7)
22 Blunder with students rising (4,2)
23 They go out during play (6)

140

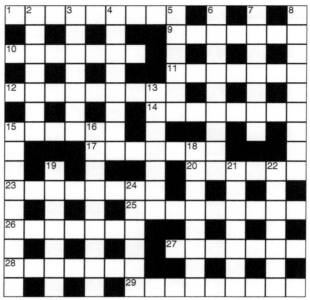

ACROSS

1 Veronica appears in good shape after race (9)
9 All rude characters can be so charmed (7)
10 Returned for meat left—a contrivance to avoid waste (4-3)
11 Seeing that a worker accepts many a useless entry (7)
12 An indication the directors meant to take notice (9)
14 Security devices for hair cutting blades (8)
15 Payment required with order (6)
17 Getting out—anger is let loose (7)
20 Larger-than-average game bird (6)
23 It's ready money only for expensive stuff (8)
25 Guidance given—may be cautioned (9)
26 Real estate involved in ups and downs (7)
27 A criminal getting in at the back of the house (7)
28 Engendering respect for the royal staff (7)
29 Mortified by underworld facility with a note (9)

DOWN

2 Smooth figure is given his head (7)
3 Some spare, lean, or even skinny girl (7)
4 Ramble on? Sure thing! (8)
5 Many a doctor and lawyer in America gets a letter from Greece (6)
6 Asks about shortfall money for those still working (9)
7 Defeat a catty individual after leading two of trumps (7)
8 Hard times, modern times—it's very disturbing (9)
13 Settled down and got established without direction (7)
15 The crowd not favouring progress? (9)
16 Start to grow grain and meet requirements (9)
18 There isn't anything about the cold causing cuts (8)
19 A seaman's got in by the book (7)
21 This bone has more than one name (7)
22 A woman admits a medico turned it up, giving rise to strong feeling (7)
24 The way to lie in the tall grass—relaxed (6)

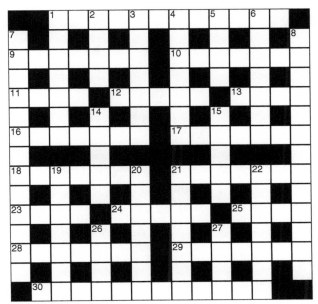

141

ACROSS

1 A prehistoric Dove Cottage? (4-8)
9 Dismissed team beyond the limit (7)
10 Nameless hoodlum a comedian? (7)
11 Grand first half for you, once (4)
12 Unruly Roman police-district (5)
13 Skipper, for example, is trapped in fire hydrant (4)
16 Silly place to play cricket ... (7)
17 ...and run, risking being caught (7)
18 Stunt of former pilot in a spin (7)
21 Behave like a happy dog, or bird (7)
23 One of the first men prepared to go to hospital? (4)
24 Notices stays back to front (5)
25 Hooligan damaged hut at midnight (4)
28 Nine for putting out great fire (7)
29 How people appear on Ilkley Moor, going by air? (7)
30 This track-coach may be dropped on the way (4-8)

DOWN

1 Discharges with pardons (4,3)
2 Make stitches to heal (4)
3 Inflexible stamp, difficult to affix? (3-4)
4 England's openers get 144 and entertain (7)
5 Pulls worms (4)
6 Lacework is showing clear profit (7)
7 Is it crewed by a holding company? (9,4)
8 Lothario's age, about a hundred? His life is in ruins! (13)
14 Look in marsh for this criminal (5)
15 Great wave certain to engulf girl's head (5)
19 Charity, we hear, not entirely generous—sorry! (7)
20 A copita ordered to make a pudding (7)
21 Cockney greeting we hear from bedside observer (7)
22 Tee-halt arranged for field competitor (7)
26 Catch 'flu, say? (4)
27 Hotly-tipped mount? (4)

142

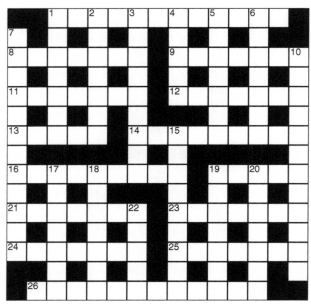

ACROSS

1 Much-reduced fare for a Birmingham MP going to the House (5,7)
8 Openly display a barley gruel (3,4)
9 Retired player who demands payment (7)
11 Leave the room quietly if one's petticoat is showing (4,3)
12 Loud gas explosion in the Isle of Man (7)
13 Each light pistol was his invention (5)
14 London resident finds purpose in Holy Week (4,5)
16 Advocate surrounding street with a roadblock (9)
19 Tax-free investment proves a recurrent boon (5)
21 Mark of mourning by a company of marines (7)
23 Visit oil-rig in North Africa (7)
24 Emotionless poem by Elizabeth Barrett Browning (7)
25 An element in getting information on headlight (7)
26 Made uniform flag with embellished side (12)

DOWN

1 It is in fashion to be a religious recluse (7)
2 Rhetorical skill conversely shown by a right-winger (7)
3 Nottingham banker consumes meat stew as medication (9)
4 Appeal to study spirit of the mountains (5)
5 Act to ascertain the length (7)
6 Irritated at having taken home only about a pound (7)
7 Ceiling liner used for sticking strip on flooring plank (12)
10 Qualms about making bookings (12)
15 Withdrew from the race with skin abrasions (9)
17 Don't batter ALL the embankment! (7)
18 Going round in circles—while performing aerobatics? (2,1,4)
19 Toys prove to be unimportant things (7)
20 Thrashed, despite having toiled like a Trojan (7)
22 Fellow upset an Italian lady (5)

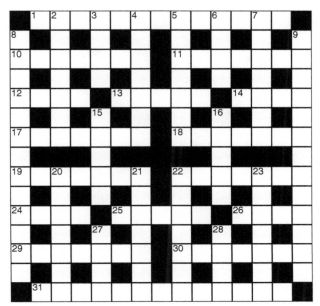

143

ACROSS

1 Down with psittacosis? (4,2,1,6)
10 Plunder piled so haphazardly (7)
11 Elegance given a trial in US city (7)
12 Terrible ruler of vain disposition (4)
13 Point of view that may be right (5)
14 Animal quarters, perhaps (4)
17 I'd turn awkward on a point and butt in (7)
18 Women's work for girl employees (7)
19 Two ways to fasten a male adornment (3-4)
22 Ran round in the commotion caused by the storm (7)
24 Famous ship is short of freight (4)
25 Nerve—but not of steel (5)
26 Wide smile gives support (4)
29 Fire—or part of one (7)
30 Fabulous supporter of royalty (7)
31 They're not the type to settle for one pop group (7,6)

DOWN

2 This month a worker's dependent on tick (7)
3 Boss sounds a toff (4)
4 One hears it being broken (7)
5 Preserved and drunk (7)
6 Sound rule for bad weather (4)
7 Like an egg, it's blown (7)
8 Is in control of distant armies abroad (13)
9 It's said to get things done in the army (4,2,7)
15 Fine for a playground tyrant? (5)
16 There's a lot of interest taken in it (5)
20 Did he paint in an attic studio? (2,5)
21 Strait-laced girl enters into the joke (7)
22 Papers—the first editions (7)
23 Sea creature in flower (7)
27 Pass the word to William (4)
28 Swimming pool with nothing under cover (4)

144

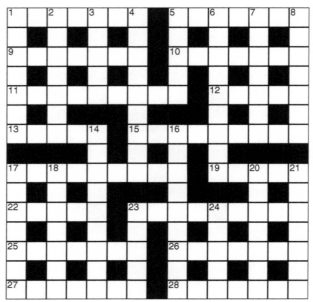

ACROSS

1 A 'familiar' spiteful woman (7)
5 Trestle fabricated by colonist (7)
9 Nickel, oxygen, bismuth, uranium and many another element (7)
10 Not inclined to be honest (7)
11 Finished incontestable evidence when very high on alcohol (9)
12 Upper-class investment in government bond leads to remorse (5)
13 Enquire in a back street for jobs (5)
15 Ahead, when it comes to identifying source of water poisoning? (2,3,4)
17 Serious tidings in the obituary column (5,4)
19 Out with a bad report on Cornish mine production (3,2)
22 Dad's army joined by short military Sri Lankan (5)
23 Steps taken in time to get tea by three (3-3-3)
25 Invasions from where ships lie offshore at anchor (7)
26 Giving out a writ presumably (7)
27 Performed including old instrument broken down (7)
28 Apparently West is ahead of the Orient (7)

DOWN

1 Put the washing on the line wherever one happens to live (4-3)
2 Leo sins mauling his mother (7)
3 Primate writing letter in Greek to a politician (5)
4 Time to get up and argue evasively (9)
5 Material to introduce a farce (5)
6 Join the environmentalists to show envy (4,5)
7 Ship's diary put on sack burning in the open hearth (3,4)
8 Pole going round art gallery went round and round (7)
14 Get by undetected with crib on history (5,4)
16 Scrap what cricket captains first do with a team (4,5)
17 Hear a rumour and suffer indigestion (3,4)
18 Fleet leader of terrorists in year 1050 (7)
20 Diplomacy on French island needs a sense of touch (7)
21 Cow catcher needs spirit undiluted (4,3)
23 Put in the box for having made a criminal survey (5)
24 They entertain great crowds (5)

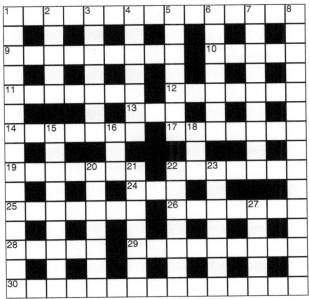

145

ACROSS

1 Rogue in a red suit (5,2,8)
9 Cave needs to be relocated, it disappeared! (9)
10 It is topping for a bishop (5)
11 Distributed ration, nothing else in Canada (7)
12 Ski comes unstuck, after a fast time, at the tree (7)
13 Dress trade journal? (3)
14 Unobstructed passage of course (7)
17 A wearing process, naturally (7)
19 Liverish chap with tie out of place (7)
22 Particular esteem (7)
24 How many were involved in the prison escape? (3)
25 At end of evening, Merlin removed the small creature (7)
26 High level prize, gold (7)
28 Inability to co-ordinate movement in a vehicle, we hear (5)
29 Play an even better card in a tricky way? (9)
30 Vessel on dry land? (4,2,3,6)

DOWN

1 Pedestrian warning to take the hard way (4,3,3,5)
2 A bit separate (5)
3 I'll be surprised if I raise it (7)
4 Plant agent with priceless spy (7)
5 Give way to a whim and drink excessively (7)
6 It serves to remind fellows to put me first (7)
7 Nourishing fruit girl (not Anne initially) and I have (9)
8 Megaphone needed for making oneself heard over a loud instrument (8-7)
15 I'm taking prince eastern garment for the showmen (9)
16 On the way up I left a girl (3)
18 About to include duck eggs (3)
20 Cry Holly could give after a word of thanks? (5-2)
21 Study wrong legal twist (7)
22 Charged in full (7)
23 Begin with left foot out to take another by surprise (7)
27 The Spanish due to make another escape (5)

146

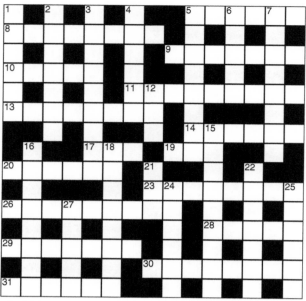

ACROSS

5 Poles note it's in short supply (6)
8 Soldiers drink, so he says (8)
9 Possibly the first to get a service book (7)
10 August would be great! (5)
11 Touching submission caused by a downturn (9)
13 The country's always behind this artist (8)
14 Public officer having yarn to spin (6)
17 Fitting for a drill (3)
19 A footnote backing a venomous creature (3)
20 The queen's place in Canada (6)
23 An indication of concern is doubly precious (4,4)
26 The punctilious person giving pain cries in distress (9)
28 Some actresses never dress their own hair (5)
29 Sanctimonious bounder or bull-fighter (7)
30 Turning out looking just right (8)
31 The self-centred individual for example is to reform (6)

DOWN

1 Push to support the Spanish (6)
2 Choose a quiet spot (7)
3 For the shopkeeper, having to dash back means trouble (9)
4 Many a bore supplies 5 *across* (6)
5 They cut people working in the theatre (8)
6 A young woman found to be at fault (5)
7 The main directors? (8)
12 Trip to take right after the end of December (3)
15 Being frank about relation's employment (9)
16 The trainee meriting instruction (8)
18 A fool rising to show his travel document (8)
21 Some sad and lonely girl (3)
22 Re-timed maybe, causing offence (7)
24 Desired completion without struggle (6)
25 Singer going to pieces given leave (6)
27 A little beast's covering one (5)

ACROSS

1 Circumvent Kansas City, say? (5)
4 Album for autumn > (5-4)
9 Coal-hole short of energy, perhaps? Try this spirit (7)
11 Fairly old tree, extremely lovely (7)
12 That fellow announced the song of praise (4)
13 What may be felt by leaders of any new government starting talks? (5)
14 Make fast run to be level (4)
17 Fair ride from the Big Dipper, one could say (6-7)
19 Essential to have spaniel's bed in good order (13)
21 Dead astern? How silly! (4)
22 Pines used for a box that does not open (5)
23 Lose one's balance knocking back half of lager (4)
26 Calf country? (7)
27 Set square laid down according to Mosaic Law? (7)
28 He a smoker, surprisingly, who may work in 26? (9)
29 Second vegetable is glossy (5)

DOWN

1 One may pull pints with sorry head, possibly (4-5)
2 Recurring medical disorder? (7)
3 Response comes from the chorus-line (4)
5 Exaggeration of the bowling figures? (13)
6 Destroys ambitions (4)
7 More noble-sounding in the past (7)
8 Her Majesty's entrance-hall? (5)
10 The grandfather in Jarndyce v Jarndyce? (8,5)
15 Buckles troubling divers (5)
16 Hide away residue below street (5)
18 Economical means of raising Hawker, say? (9)
19 It can be hell to conclude Japanese play (7)
20 Accept or contradict, for the most part (7)
21 Public rallies of a nation's people (5)
24 Film of Spartacus opens with Roman in support (4)
25 Profits by customs? (4)

148

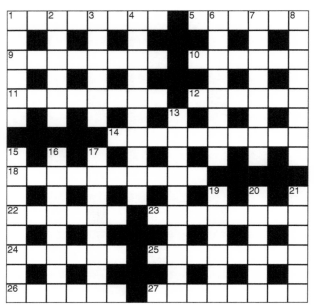

ACROSS

1 Sacked a politician for threat to mineworkers (8)
5 Composer exhibits work in a feature (6)
9 Do large percussion instruments cause depression? (8)
10 Anne is awfully mad (6)
11 Guess the gun was fired some time ago (4,4)
12 Giving dry champagne to a novice is cruel (6)
14 U-boat operation requires total obedience (10)
18 Service manual for restructuring poor bakery (6-4)
22 Runs in to stop the batsman reaching it! (6)
23 Reside in a basement to repair one's reputation (4,4)
24 No backtracking by a patient man at work (2,1,3)
25 Want bath and a weak drink (4-4)
26 Small change for one who effects a cure (6)
27 Airman to be redeployed as a film cartoonist (8)

DOWN

1 Row about two coppers exposing a case of fraud (6)
2 Become more amenable for about forty days (6)
3 Compulsion to be fashionable in formal clothing (6)
4 Married boss appearing on an elephant? Stuff and nonsense! (5-5)
6 She joins the chase for a German lock (8)
7 Shrub for industrious worker in low-lying area (8)
8 Has Heather got to be aggravating? (8)
13 One minute job, but it's a burden (10)
15 Gambling debts are deceptive (8)
16 Game played at a vulgar dance (8)
17 Man's house has style. That's the crux of it (8)
19 Fresh bacon can be found in East London (6)
20 Culinary skill in Tasmania (6)
21 To stabilise a ship is an endless task (6)

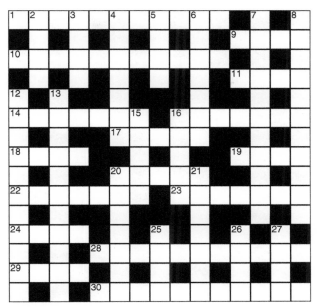

149

ACROSS

1 Deal involves a constraint (11)
9 When it falls, it has the cheek to go on (4)
10 Oversight the foreman's responsible for? (11)
11 Turn over at leisure (4)
14 Listen to a number cheer (7)
16 A go-slow which could be at an end (7)
17 Sort of track not in need of repair (5)
18 Agrees to one result of decimal coinage (4)
19 Broken oar left for examination (4)
20 Wild revel in the bar (5)
22 Ready for fuel he'd ordered (7)
23 In a way, Marconi was of Latin descent (7)
24 Topless wind or string instrument (4)
28 William's heart makes him a pasty fellow (4-7)
29 Chief part of the foot (4)
30 Nobody but Ed involved, that's certain (6,5)

DOWN

2 Playboy with nothing to feel sorry about (4)
3 Born in Paris, died in penury (4)
4 Tips guides (7)
5 Try at an international match (4)
6 Duck, plump and mouth-filling (7)
7 A band, bond or bind! (7,4)
8 Used for building a wind break? (6,5)
12 Country's cold in the interior—furs needed (11)
13 Supporter of something wicked (11)
15 Book for a boy about five (5)
16 Old car doesn't start, causing exasperation (5)
20 Fear of redundancy drove him to breaking point (7)
21 How a bird slept with toes round a perch outside (7)
25 Singer improved a lot (4)
26 She loved Narcissus, it's recalled (4)
27 One step up from the gutter (4)

150

ACROSS

7 Resolve argument about advice on chronically decayed tooth (4,2,3)
8 Totally unacceptable result of heavyweight metrication (3,2)
10 A real bargain for a fair quantity (4,4)
11 Is it possible for US lawyer to be found further North? (6)
12 Many going to health resort for processed meat (4)
13 Touch a sore spot and suffer distress (4,4)
15 Former Shetland feudal tax on land used for grazing (7)
17 Inclined to give advice to punters (7)
20 Bet London police HQ dig it up in search for the body (4,4)
22 Army and military police pack it in (4)
25 Softly has snow-leopard to leap on its prey (6)
26 A harbinger of spring turned over by a reformer (1,3,4)
27 A response to cold disdain (5)
28 Maybe spades usually worn out in the graveyard (5,4)

DOWN

1 Not a bare-headed fowl (5)
2 Delayed because threatened with a gun (4,2)
3 Hard disc backup for a full-width headline (8)
4 Add certain conditions to become eligible (7)
5 Where migrants settle for less than a 'floating city'? (8)
6 Weather forecast endured by one with his back to the fire? (4,5)
9 Land area given by Sacred Heart (4)
14 Chief modern equivalent of Pegasus? (9)
16 A bowler should be if made a mockery of (5,3)
18 How the stage criminal was caught (2,3,3)
19 Theoretically best if aquarium fish has a friend (7)
21 A Roman law promulgated by the young Alexander (4)
23 Doctor in case telling what criminal solicitors do (6)
24 Deeply buried entrance (3,2)

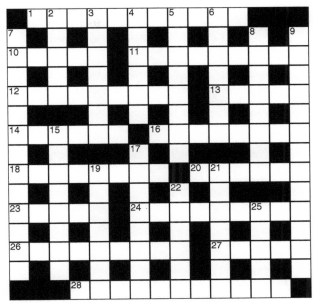

ACROSS

1 Premier court official (11)
10 Man protecting the French female to become less tense (5)
11 Salesman with a tale to tell? (9)
12 Impair validity of preconceived idea (9)
13 Drink he included was cold (5)
14 Fraudulently fitted the sails? (6)
16 Repeatedly listen to words of encouragement (4,4)
18 Another lion used 6 (8)
20 Summon everybody in a sporting contest (4,2)
23 Outsize vehicle gets an award (5)
24 You, you or you? (9)
26 Action due to be transformed having been warned (9)
27 Ooze from crushed limes (5)
28 Horribly dented, agree it grew worse (11)

DOWN

2 He includes as many as there are in the orchestra (5)
3 Combination of nine in the mountain above the river (7)
4 Necessarily involve turning in late (6)
5 Depart before Edward has made the dough rise (8)
6 Mistakenly Ron and I are about to sin (2,5)
7 Ready to do something in a dramatic way? (8,2,3)
8 Depressed girl said to be found in the wood (8)
9 Journalist getting all the bad stories (5,8)
15 Driver possibly found at the nineteenth hole (4-4)
17 Win over the boy after study (8)
19 Tree work (7)
21 Is unable to recall mental trouble (7)
22 Promise to put a penny on the shelf (6)
25 Does he go a quarter of the distance? (5)

152

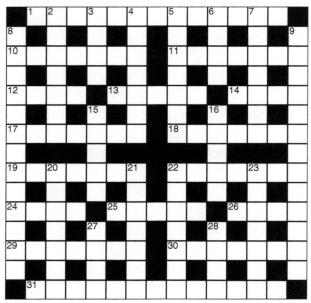

ACROSS

1 Scatter edible stuff—grass (5,3,5)
10 Country music composer (7)
11 Time is pressing (7)
12 Linked with bad diet (4)
13 Husband unkind about nothing (5)
14 Secret letter written on the quiet (4)
17 Competitive activity for an artist to draw (3,4)
18 Man turning over a gun? That's wet! (7)
19 Appear imprudent and the French cheer (4,3)
22 Wine from China—it's far form good (7)
24 Cut some of the best, absurdly enough (4)
25 Before the fifties sport in winter is an art (5)
26 Called back to snarl (4)
29 Causing a riot on a lake (7)
30 Modish and flighty creature accompanied by egghead or medico (7)
31 No automatic transport for coppers! (5-8)

DOWN

2 In attendance to demonstrate (7)
3 Grassy areas—not all are pleasant (4)
4 The little toad! (7)
5 Pointed remark of one beast in retirement about another (7)
6 A quarter say may be altered. It's not difficult (4)
7 Get half done before a trial, being most systematic (7)
8 Past learning (7,6)
9 Judges traipse inside to change (13)
15 The philosopher would make a scholar read (5)
16 Mock the Bohemian girl with a large figure (5)
20 Let rats free to shock people (7)
21 Drop 16 (4,3)
22 The painter's dog runs (7)
23 There's no need for the press to be involved! (3-4)
27 10 taking royalty in (4)
28 City-centre church causing some irritation (4)

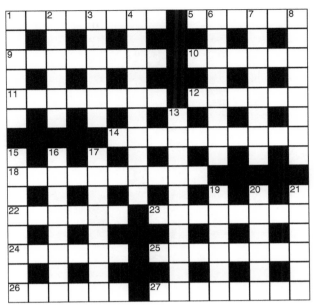

153

ACROSS

1 Miss your footing now winter has come (4,4)
5 Run aground a ship on leaving The Fleet (6)
9 Lake which provides a monster attraction (4,4)
10 Flinch from a backlash (6)
11 Tattered shin broken by Bolsheviks (2,6)
12 Get there in time to put together an article (4,2)
14 Salesman whose turnover is of outstanding volume? (4,6)
18 Avon still a place for a top football team (5,5)
22 Possibly Egyptian going to small capitals thought it sacred (6)
23 Water producer obtains water crop very expensive to buy (2,1,5)
24 Lie and contrive rejection of accusation (6)
25 Heavenly food supplied by Frenchman with brother in Asia (8)
26 In a card game Rex proves a real pig (6)
27 Reckoned to be a stupid fellow being followed by daughter (8)

DOWN

1 Line up on parade—and collapse? (4,2)
2 Hopper supplying food for the Baptist (6)
3 Positions worsen for men of property (6)
4 Novel midshipman succeeds in giving a warning to be careful (4,4,2)
6 Radio family visited by Yorkshire tourists (3,5)
7 Especially applicable to a supreme commander (5,3)
8 Tardy cover-up supported by a Conservative (8)
13 Always a somewhat unbelievable quality paper? (2,3,5)
15 Request was referred to higher authority but ignored (6,2)
16 Single coach used to clear stock (8)
17 All dressed up and showing oneself off? (2,6)
19 Spears thrown but thinly scattered (6)
20 Regrets the absence of the girls (6)
21 Send back into custody a chap in debit (6)

154

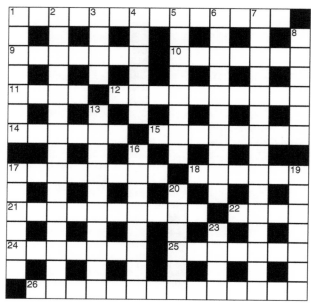

ACROSS

1 Father—he's not quite disposed to press his suit (3,3,8)
9 Bring back a necessity like some citrus fruit (7)
10 Aromatic flavouring found recurrently in a grain (7)
11 Vessels held by taciturn sailors (4)
12 Where landlords serve ale in jug (6,4)
14 When immersed in a river Henry has to breathe out (6)
15 Receive credit for negotiating a long tea-break (3,1,4)
17 Piped down when Sidney was about to call (8)
18 Singular characteristic displayed by a channel (6)
21 Every now and then casino is involved in coal production (10)
22 Overcharge for a castle (4)
24 Sugar and crisp lettuce put into a paste (7)
25 Weary cry from Egyptian imprisoned in tall house (5-2)
26 Buy the product which is superior—or worst! (3,3,6,2)

DOWN

1 East German in spotless carriage (7)
2 Informed that one was included in the photo-call (3,2,3,7)
3 Criminal spoils gold in the Upper Chamber (4)
4 Friend who trembles with terror (6)
5 Inspector upset woodcutter and collier (8)
6 The other man or woman from the Liberal Democrats (5,5)
7 By some method palindromes can thus be read (3,3,2,7)
8 Includes a divine child (4,2)
13 Dandies take to wine and hunting (5,5)
16 One reeks terribly of paraffin (8)
17 Small Irish lake and marsh (6)
19 Set out to become a spectacular success (4,3)
20 Pulp that is produced from iron (6)
23 Move up 17 yards (4)

155

ACROSS

7 It may make one smart, top or bottom (9)
8 Clergyman wants caviar, not a pie (5)
10 Quietly object to a small portion (8)
11 Bury someone—because of the wrong note given to the doctor (6)
12 At liberty to be generous (4)
13 Stay well away form work (8)
15 He makes a practice of seeing complaints (7)
17 The attendant's not responsible for it (7)
20 Sweet disorder in the bed (5,3)
22 They marked the passing of the horse-drawn vehicle (4)
25 An egg I scrambled, obviously not new-laid (6)
26 Girl thought to be like Queen Victoria (8)
27 & 28 Time to settle final accounts? (3,2,9)

DOWN

1 Boat's the same even when capsized (5)
2 Device for making bits smaller, or larger, we hear (6)
3 Nuts go well with cheese (8)
4 Values seem set for a change (7)
5 A length boxers go to—to avoid KO? (8)
6 Mabel gets entangled with chap in US resort (4,5)
9 Not the sole order dogs learn to obey (4)
14 He's given unwarranted responsibility (9)
16 A sticky sweet (8)
18 Private quarters (8)
19 He leaves his country to be protected by another (7)
21 Quiet time for a hotel employee (4)
23 It doesn't describe the present schoolboy (6)
24 Threatened strike that doesn't come off (5)

156

ACROSS

1 Hot drink is simply divine when swallowed by flirt (5)
4 Get up quickly or refuse to budge (5,4)
9 Immediate? No, just a moment (7)
11 Criminal hang-out calls for a swoop (3,4)
12 Bow depicted in a banknote (4)
13 Knocked up a highball at Klosters? (5)
14 Go ahead actor's role (4)
17 Shade of blue, not dark, used for brightening the room (8,5)
19 Their relation gives one the shivers (8,5)
21 Low cloud formation used by Saddam for air attacks (4)
22 Give a share of the profits from two metals (3,2)
23 Fifty first catalogue (4)
26 Henry joins the Met and is given rope (7)
27 Dejected despite having bought fine feathers (3,4)
28 Minor actor got his fangs into a sportsman (3,6)
29 Sack carried by an infantryman (5)

DOWN

1 Dope producing a hangover (9)
2 So bride managed to take off her finery (7)
3 Time enough for 525948 minute units (4)
5 Manoeuvre leading all in about D Day (6,7)
6 Crow on a pole, when it's time to crow (4)
7 In mental disorder one needs nourishment (7)
8 Scottish banker provides Scottish material (5)
10 What local washerwomen do—and housewives too if it rains (4,2,7)
15 Take off for a journey to the South (5)
16 Stone fence usually has one in it (5)
18 Maybe the perfect way to suggest times are not now so jittery (4,5)
19 A short rhyme describing a married pair to a T (7)
20 Left alone when made redundant (4,3)
21 Urdu gentleman from Lhasa hibernating (5)
24 Autumn trip over (4)
25 Wake up and cook the porridge? (4)

157

ACROSS

1 It lets you know there's a rough time ahead (5,6)
9 Surprised expression about hard butter (4)
10 Power from a heavenly body available on all but the dullest days (5,6)
11 Trousers Patrick's wearing hid the gaiter (4)
14 One side of Liverpool (7)
16 End so cruel a revolution (7)
17 Inquisitive one's confused by youth leader (5)
18 Agent crosses eastern river (4)
19 Potentially vile low-lying marshy ground (4)
20 Deadly plump boy (5)
22 Willing rider (7)
23 Umpire right, he's wrong to give new life (7)
24 Palm from E India, Northern Ireland and Pennsylvania (4)
28 In a way like principal male chauvinist in a stupidly obstinate way? (11)
29 Group taking first letter home (4)
30 Crooked pastoral lady! (11)

DOWN

2 It became you (4)
3 Horse hastened round ring (4)
4 Boy tramps (7)
5 Song of mirth (4)
6 Any girl distraught could react this way (7)
7 Erector found in dock (11)
8 Realise what one should be able to do at the end of the tunnel (3,3,5)
12 Deep indisposition (11)
13 Plunge into calm way of making lucky discoveries (11)
15 Friend, on returning, first found the cactus (5)
16 Large plant 'e'd found in the tram (5)
20 Sounds like the end of the race (7)
21 Escaping water forming lake before time (7)
25 Has relocated Penny on the fell (4)
26 Tennis star going to ground (4)
27 Positive advantage (4)

158

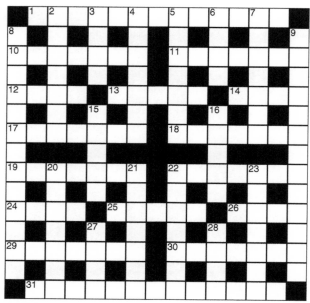

ACROSS

1 Metropolitan commission makes a deadly accusation (7,6)
10 Money is a typical feature in light entertainment (7)
11 To County Council a word of thanks for work of note (7)
12 Spots an expert coming about noon (4)
13 University man is taken in by retired fellow traveller (5)
14 Register nothing but a company trademark (4)
17 Restate treaties endlessly renegotiated (7)
18 Generous Socialist of similar character (3,4)
19 To surmount the difficulty, communicate (3,4)
22 An old blade snubbed the girl (7)
24 Submit appeal to Turkish governor (4)
25 A grand primate exhibits Christian love (5)
26 Passes for senior Army officers (4)
29 Unspoilt ancient city in S African province (7)
30 Notice a new kind of poison (7)
31 Punter personally has to climb the ladder (6,7)

DOWN

2 Go ahead and get a loan (7)
3 A centre of passionately devout monks once (4)
4 A school with Anglican investment is solvent (7)
5 TUC needs to reduce staff (3,4)
6 Superior spanner (4)
7 Note the French love physical attractiveness (7)
8 Knocking the top off a pencil is the last straw (8,5)
9 Catastrophe leads PM to arrange sad rites (5,8)
15 Put by about a pound for ointment (5)
16 One result of federalism (5)
20 The territorials sent up sappers to the ops room (7)
21 Professional soldier found, for instance, in rural setting (7)
22 Adam's son is innately suitable to be a leader (7)
23 Not wanting company to produce coal is a mistake (7)
27 Determination to make icy roads safe (4)
28 Give orders to South African security men (4)

ACROSS

1 A fine lawn—though it's never mown! (7)
5 Tick immediately available (7)
9 View duck taking wing (7)
10 A holy man goes on horseback or walks (7)
11 Financial expert effecting some difference to incomes (9)
12 Mean with a woman (5)
13 Reporters in force? (5)
15 Vehicle adapted for lame Cuban's use (9)
17 Snappy devil, a social worker—has to join in! (9)
19 Courses for various groups of people (5)
22 Judge getting a line about 23 *down* (5)
23 Dire scene created in a home (9)
25 Making observations about hospital of little importance (7)
26 Fifty say with minor following—lacking proper support (7)
27 Points put in broadcast aren't sincere (7)
28 Tough guy having a certain skill in bridge (7)

DOWN

1 Photograph sporting couples (5-2)
2 One party got in more money at one time in Portugal (7)
3 A Greek character set about trendy beast (5)
4 Frank fed an applicant (9)
5 Isn't rattled about the egghead not being on the level (5)
6 Cash received by an unknown assassin (9)
7 A firedog with 13 (7)
8 Willing to examine a note (7)
14 Pole having a go in the Orient, the outcome is grave (9)
16 Toiletry for city sailing men (4,5)
17 May be sent in with a key, which would be great! (7)
18 A guide dog (7)
20 "Green" after study gives cause to change (7)
21 Failing no tests, this is to go ahead (7)
23 Correct title (5)
24 Closely follow a well-qualified person's teaching (5)

160

ACROSS

7 Poor brothers' garbs given up by New Year reformers (3,6)
8 Fanatical bishop in surprise attack (5)
10 Badly-dressed woman, but strict about Latin (8)
11 Combine to shelter a Slav Catholic (6)
12 Money voucher for a pert young lass (4)
13 Guide leader needs a hooter (5,3)
15 Henry hankered to get hitched up (7)
17 Bad temper leads to a serious complaint (7)
20 Street warden gets more rum (8)
22 Complain about one form of transport (4)
25 Key in form of Algol found worldwide (6)
26 It benefits the complexion to confront a lot of wolves (4-4)
27 Information about a literature class (5)
28 Finish telephone conversation and have a lucky escape (5,4)

DOWN

1 Sudden outburst by Southern confederate (5)
2 Roofing the church over there (6)
3 He's away when article about mad cow disease gets green support (8)
4 A reserve has to be loyal (5-2)
5 To restrict Albert's consumption is sensible (8)
6 Deception is a filthy business (5,4)
9 A small car for oneself (4)
14 A manufacturer of spirit, yet in dire trouble (9)
16 Medical man hesitates to o to tea rooms (8)
18 Difficult to change cheque given by MO (4,4)
19 Couple love to do clerical work as a sideline (7)
21 Sore cheek (4)
23 Influence one Frenchman by agreement (6)
24 Climb up and balance (5)

ACROSS

1 It's not well organised to keep a pet in the pig's house (6)
4 Find that the record has finished (8)
9 Short plant with purple flowers—alternatively, long! (6)
10 Alarming perhaps when a member has to fight for this seat (8)
11 Thanks given temporarily for innate ability (6)
12 It gives directions on how to put a name a the bottom of a letter (8)
14 Want an opportunity to take a holiday (4,1,5)
18 He might jog one's memory, like Quasimodo perhaps (10)
22 One girl I converted to the faith (8)
23 Soon, what is mine will be returned, by someone whose name I don't know (6)
24 Ascertained that they were away from home (5,3)
25 Gives out, for example, directions about the way (6)
26 Give pike to the fellows who fought hand to hand (8)
27 Dog set about the suet pudding (6)

DOWN

1 Pus got in via the drainpipe (8)
2 A couple of pages by a top journalist without everybody being horrified! (8)
3 Fewer than a dozen looked around on the cutter (5,3)
5 It's conceivable to think in untidy lab (10)
6 Firm man needed, to be convincing (6)
7 Dealer drove in the point somehow (6)
8 Tell how the Spanish speed around! (6)
13 Half hearted rule Tories have broken (10)
15 It's a dim thing to be out so late (8)
16 Worried about nothing in a strange design (8)
17 One's given a guarantee, I see, following the concert (8)
19 Uses influence to transplant (6)
20 So blue about her crumpled chemise (6)
21 Some might try to bag a direct flight to Moroccan resort (6)

162

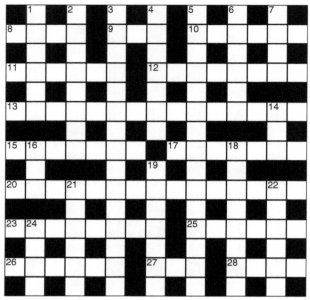

ACROSS

8 Company accountant provides a powerful stimulant (4)
9 Card game appreciated by tired workers (3)
10 Inspect rent forming small hole in fabric (6)
11 Maybe a pony tail knot worn by those with tails (3,3)
12 View—the cliff face from the precipice? (4,4)
13 Where both submarines and colliers ply their trade (5,3,7)
15 Prohibit female oriental wailer from Ireland (7)
17 Sanctimonious types take to allspice (7)
20 Show-case cathedral takes in one leading statesman (7,8)
23 It guides a sailor to the ends of the earth (8)
25 A stupid sloven carried by the Pied Piper (6)
26 Total recruitment that is needed to surround tank division (6)
27 What players wait for in the billiard saloon (3)
28 Pronouncedly miserly manner (4)

DOWN

1 With lumpy swellings medicine has not been prescribed (6)
2 Decide by chance to advise eager fly fishermen (4,4)
3 Where to find the met forecast when feeling low (5,3,7)
4 Attaches a second footnote containing misleading statement (7)
5 Insurgents gather once around the Sign of the Ram (15)
6 Lease part of the premises—free? (3,3)
7 In short we are what we used to be (4)
14 Pointedly ignore a knife wound (3)
16 Moslem title used sagas (3)
18 Not a difficult beat for one who is off duty (4,4)
19 States a claim to be Heath (7)
21 It should help to keep a cool head when one is... (6)
22 ...on top of the world having put story up to editor (6)
24 Has snow settled? (4)

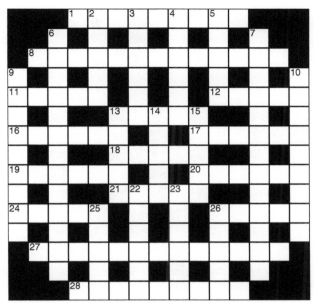

163

ACROSS

1 Painful affliction one might have to face (9)
8 & 11 Spree on the roof? (5,3,2,3,5)
12 Large number were changing at the station (5)
13 Grass snake perhaps (5)
16 Some fifteen ought to be about the right amount (6)
17 In Paris, questioned about what was bordering on indecency (6)
18 A fragment, one from the main artery (5)
19 It is difficult to squeeze into the northern shaft (6)
20 A trail coming from a star (6)
21 Staunch ally could accept nothing (5)
24 The continental salesman first to drive back (5)
26 Is to rebuild a city in Italy (5)
27 The highest bidder at the art auction will understand the situation (3,3,7)
28 Leaving out fashionable number in embrace once previously (9)

DOWN

2 The dreadfully large character (5)
3 The said Brazilian city bird must begin again (6)
4 Nameless valiant eccentric coming from the country (6)
5 Not right in being sarcastic about a Greek style (5)
6 Compiler is second-class, maybe a horrible pig (13)
7 Sportsmen who are six-pinters? (5-8)
9 Pass the dog (2,7)
10 Usual practice in the theatre (9)
13 Mum puts everything, say, under the loose cover (5)
14 Too soon? Almost lost a point (5)
15 Old boat up-ended by gangster in the village (5)
22 We will follow alternative author (6)
23 Associated with £1 in the new deal (6)
25 The French American has some milky sap (5)
26 From among a number found at short intervals (5)

164

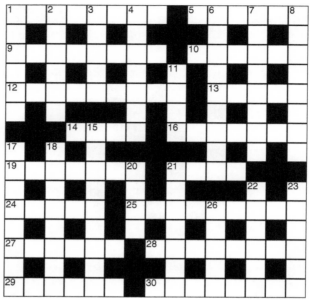

ACROSS

1 Undertaking to read a brochure (8)
5 Judge the blockheads will accept direction (6)
9 Getting into "green" tin production (8)
10 He could well make a good bowler (6)
12 Gets hot under the collar, seeing decay in sea-going vessel (9)
13 Game to write small child a letter? (5)
14 The place having the best turnover (4)
16 Polish spirit range (7)
19 These days few Irish are hostile (7)
21 A type of grass fly (4)
24 It takes just seconds to pack for leave (5)
25 Coming by water shows enterprise (9)
27 Contemptible cheat going back on promises to pay (6)
28 Air trite differences to cause annoyance (8)
29 Give the fellow a note (6)
30 Building for the workers in principle (8)

DOWN

1 Fold, though allowed credit still (6)
2 People not in a mess (6)
3 Backing some popular urbanisation scheme in a country area (5)
4 Cheat over examination and there'll be a fight! (7)
6 The main pictures (9)
7 Constituents relent—so that's the story! (8)
8 Underlined courses to be taken up (8)
11 It's a new kind of drink (4)
15 Standard volume, but quite outstanding (9)
17 Money for a weapon that could ensure access (8)
18 A certain form giving rise to animosity (8)
20 Forced retirement in the Netherlands (4)
21 Back touching lines (7)
22 Murmur an egghead can be benevolent (6)
23 Grieve for military personnel deprived of freedom (6)
26 The sound one is to be used (5)

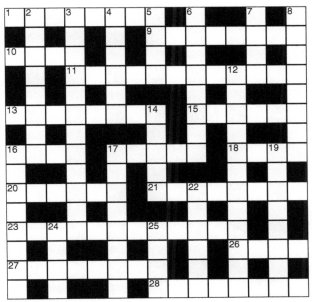

165

ACROSS

1 The last day for shaping mahogany? (8)
9 Decoration of books with gold title at front (8)
10 Fertility goddess currently in Oxford? (4)
11 Savoy, for example, immaculate for the summer visitor (7,5)
13 Spring roll, say, from good stock (4,4)
15 Greedy fish, given new head, would be capital! (6)
16 For hill shaped like this, take me to South America (4)
17 Longest support for a walker? (5)
18 Relief from sea-serpents (4)
20 Constable, say, approaching mole with a sword (6)
21 Suffers us to carry blemishes outside (8)
23 Silent monkey, jumping about in new town (6,6)
26 Headlight of type that can not go wrong (4)
27 One makes a killing with a pair of donkeys, past the post? (8)
28 "A Shropshire Lad"? (8)

DOWN

2 Ancient old boy alone, note! (8)
3 As writer of various essays, Scillies man comes out on time (12)
4 Two, for example, make knock one senseless (6)
5 Year ago, retired for meditation (4)
6 Former member of the house... (8)
7 ...house in home counties, next to motorway (4)
8 Time to support guide providing cheapest accommodation on board (8)
12 Competence up? (12)
14 Composer of a spirited French trio? (5)
16 Instruments of African wood-tappers (8)
17 Resolution of company head (8)
19 Beach-jumper? (4-4)
22 Wicked, almost entirely, after Sunday (6)
24 Cobbler works at one to stand up (4)
25 Nose resection takes ages (4)

166

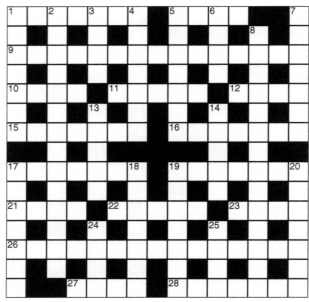

ACROSS

1 Small motor hired out to cardinal (7)
5 Fellow-doctor needs tidy hair (4)
9 Not in service. Cashiered? (3,2,10)
10 Male representative needs fibre (4)
11 Suddenly discover that a pop song is playing (3,2)
12 Tax firm in small street (4)
15 Train about to return military group to the East (7)
16 Not as plain to a pigeon enthusiast, maybe (7)
17 To get a match is the very devil (7)
19 Such a sale is fashionable indeed (7)
21 One is carried in a gun carriage (4)
22 I pine for Platonic perfection (5)
23 Lots of trousers (4)
26 Fault-finding when there are problems using a horn (15)
27 A county where people retire (4)
28 After last month encyclopaedia displays propriety (7)

DOWN

1 Son and parent take one's breath away (7)
2 George, Otto, Paul, Tim involved with CIA (9,5)
3 Abandoned port (4)
4 Couple use a stopwatch to deceive (3-4)
5 Happen to get detached (4,3)
6 Mould in the grape juice (4)
7 Drive around Islington to get a TV screen (7)
8 Record border before one country exhibits ethnic prejudice (14)
13 A nicotine addict would die without it! (5)
14 Reserved for skating (2,3)
17 Will beneficiary give note to ambassador? (7)
18 Correct uniform for sappers (7)
19 Disconcerted a wicked woman within (7)
20 Something one should smell in merry mood (7)
24 Some of the Arab leaders are talented (4)
25 Necklace with a Catholic dedication (4)

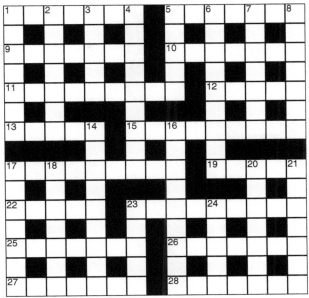

167

ACROSS

1 Begin to strike the lady over there (7)
5 One of a pair of airlines (7)
9 Agrees with Tom's first friends (7)
10 Get the aspect right for splitting up the light colours (7)
11 Simple phraseology used to encourage an impoverished customer (4,5)
12 Preside with gravity within the constraint (5)
13 One lass tied up with fibre (5)
15 At the wicket for 500—but got more (9)
17 Tramping around with a game bird (9)
19 Brush up on the area of bushes (5)
22 Take out lease to support the picture (5)
23 Very good speed, at the beginning (5,4)
25 I shall send a note to girl although this is not permitted (7)
26 Let Tory group arrange a national one (7)
27 Round about ten stumbling on the railway hoping to find the way in again (7)
28 No moss is harmed by the diffusion of liquid (7)

DOWN

1 Staggers about with small animal in a back street (7)
2 Treats bad habits very badly (3,4)
3 Lift up one in an enormous crowd (5)
4 Keeping a bit back for making a booking (9)
5 Detects a direction among those voting against (5)
6 The clarity of a Kent town (9)
7 Keeps a nastier mixture (7)
8 Found out how the student got paid (7)
14 I'll get him moved into the public gaze (9)
16 She is happy with only a low score (9)
17 Support round about a thousand—that's first class (7)
18 Grant forgiveness to the sailor and provide a solution (7)
20 They learn about adders but don't take note (7)
21 Sleep on what sounds like items for sale (3-4)
23 The weakness of a useless structure (5)
24 Symbol to have met up with (5)

168

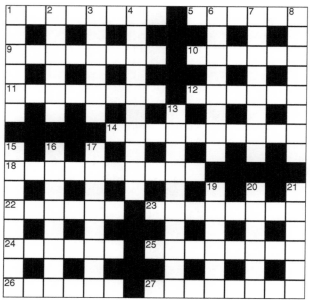

ACROSS

1 Discuss and study poetry (8)
5 Start out to ignite the fireworks (3,3)
9 Get the message that summery material is being worn (6,2)
10 Blackhead gets a pressing invitation! (6)
11 Price a lute broken by Senora Peron (8)
12 Exhausted when employed at high level (4,2)
14 Put simply, it means to read the letters one by one (5,2,3)
18 Exaggerate what harpooners do (5,1,4)
22 He foils a paling workman (6)
23 Rich oil-sheik's property leads to altercation (4,2,2)
24 Castle that is suitable for raw recruit (6)
25 What visitors do to meet the telephone charge (3,1,4)
26 Sentimental New York maid (6)
27 Dissolute merry age means she ain't what she used to be! (4,4)

DOWN

1 According to him it is reliable as a spaniel (6)
2 Good and acceptable (3,3)
3 Revised ox dues lead to mass emigration (6)
4 An abbreviation for a brief period (5,5)
6 Short letter upset court case deciding school uniform (4,4)
7 Butler's task was to provide a free trade policy (4,4)
8 Pavement leading to the podiatry lab (8)
13 Goldilocks? (6,4)
15 To request sex appeal is to invite trouble (3,3,2)
16 A pyknic type begins a bout of fisticuffs (5,3)
17 Attic reveals three different articles containing nickel (8)
19 Not clear barley soup (6)
20 Noted work by boy joining reserve force (6)
21 Not cordial that is meant for a native worker (6)

ACROSS

6 Playing one's cards right necessary to solve it? (6,7)
8 One not still sitting (6)
9 Poisonous alkaloid made into nice mixture! (8)
10 Own Scottish one is available (3)
11 A heap of snow becomes loose (6)
12 Gradually slackened on rough sea taking direction on the farther side about 1st December (5,3)
14 Do teach going round the terminal (7)
16 Walter's disposed to become a good-for-nothing (7)
20 So sanctimonious to rave over a candidate (8)
23 Spread the odds on a raw beginner (6)
24 Back at sea (3)
25 Indicate weapon first used under threat of injury (8)
26 Go to a much visited place (6)
27 Does this stairway have a magic carpet? (6,2,5)

DOWN

1 It could be food for a bird without hesitation (8)
2 A boy with wobbly gait first was excited (8)
3 Revolutionary worker? (7)
4 Portion of dry fruit that breaks up into a bacterium? (6)
5 Criticised what the top worker did? (6)
6 Screen fellow's used that's a light yellow in the game (9,4)
7 Chap with a limited vocabulary presumably (3,2,3,5)
13 Measures some of the broken specimens (3)
15 Over to the linesman (3)
17 Bats sure badly, it is hard to understand (8)
18 Conquered the spots inside on day one (8)
19 Position of one intending to travel? (7)
21 I'm not one to weaken (6)
22 Get off, it's on fire (6)

170

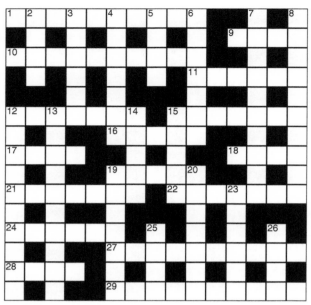

ACROSS

1 Totally idle, but nevertheless fills up the cash-box (5-5)
9 Capital seen as very large—and left nothing! (4)
10 Contracting for the production of a string net (10)
11 Hot rock, outstandingly big, got free (6)
12 Lord returning fish losing its freshness (7)
15 Clarets should of course be a bright red colour (7)
16 An archbishop's address and prayer (5)
17 The team has some ambitious ideas! (4)
18 An artistic person after silver in India (4)
19 A good man, and so getting support (5)
21 Glace in translation—in English (7)
22 Dull club for evening out (3-4)
24 Monstrous woman with a stony stare (6)
27 High-rise accommodation built by workers for their own occupation (10)
28 There's no holding a few sailors! (4)
29 The fellow organising an event's most fortunate (6-4)

DOWN

2 Thanks to some keen beginners, there's work here (4)
3 A neat enclosure (6)
4 Settling for the wrong man at the top (7)
5 Innovative time piece (4)
6 Slow admitting twitch is grating (7)
7 Starry-eyed forecaster (10)
8 Honest over the effort needed to get transport arranged (5-5)
12 The loss of legal representation meant birds being set free (10)
13 She wasn't dressed for riding (4,6)
14 Note value and so cause irritation (5)
15 Closely examines a container put on board (5)
19 Mark's to withdraw (7)
20 The eccentric may diet only between sunrise and sunset (7)
23 Single trade agreements—models of perfection (6)
25 Short article about a certain region (4)
26 Humble-sounding manner (4)

171

ACROSS

1 Amusement-park is not just loud at first (7)
5 Trains dolphins in groups (7)
9 Basic inside fare? (7)
10 The Red Queen seen in Amritsar in April (7)
11 One who denies profits always right? (9)
12 Is such a steamer a drifter? (5)
13 Stay to see dayspring (5)
15 With it, people cannot keep off the grass (9)
17 Thick, black and totally dry (9)
19 Hero in a plainly wet country? (2,3)
22 For soil-condition, list to Henry! (5)
23 Add a dash, as in gin-fizz (9)
25 Planet difficult to pick up? (7)
26 Joy—one member of family who does not open up (7)
27 Ann Turner anxious to find cotton fabric (7)
28 Classification of tars? (7)

DOWN

1 Given the cat, fellow recorded at sea (7)
2 Dark journey, say, to find chemical compound (7)
3 Helps wild beast (5)
4 Track event in which career lay in ruins (5-4)
5 Is back on pitch, as it is played in India (5)
6 Cardialgia, Keats' first symptom? (9)
7 Artistic paper folding, you could say (7)
8 Keen England openers raise the tone a little (7)
14 Pine-cabin, a communal dwelling? (4,5)
16 Shredded paper said to leave no trace (9)
17 The pitch of the roof? (7)
18 Banking flap—no lire exchanged after the first of August (7)
20 Organ-stop, that is clear! (7)
21 Spanish gooseberries? (7)
23 Composer's handy variation (5)
24 Make Bill work in the house (5)

172

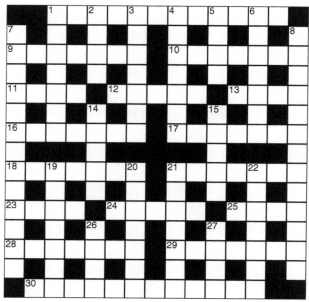

ACROSS

1 Horseman drawn by English novelist (5,7)
9 A quantity of anaesthetics (7)
10 A thin paper is under consideration (2,5)
11 Total defeat for a large party (4)
12 Prepare to fire first (5)
13 Small car—a minute one (4)
16 A diversion in Daddy's day (7)
17 Ode is composed about Anglican division (7)
18 Cut and clear the lawn of leaves (4-3)
21 Possibly where father and boy accommodated one (7)
23 Thanks to yours truly, it's no longer savage (4)
24 Anxiety caused by heteromorphic gnats (5)
25 Assemble for a service (4)
28 Fellow follows Judah's son unceasingly (2,3,2)
29 One I included in Latin translation first (7)
30 The French don't interfere (7,5)

DOWN

1 Spirit attributed to us is mere gossip (7)
2 Is sufficient for venison producers (4)
3 Husband reveals lack of sociability (7)
4 Lear mad, distraught and very apprehensive (7)
5 George I married, despite being humourless (4)
6 Brief delay occasioned by cryptaesthesia during ceremony (7)
7 Getting ready to give popular president compensation (2,11)
8 Clearly not alone in being overwrought (6,7)
14 Mayfair party attended by Welsh woman without husband (5)
15 What one may pay for a pen (5)
19 Friend absorbed by Hindu love god in Uganda (7)
20 One engaged to take in new funds (7)
21 Hound a lettered man full of pomposity (7)
22 Just think—one pit is filled with silver (7)
26 So upset about theologian taking chances (4)
27 A New Zealander in khaki windcheater (4)

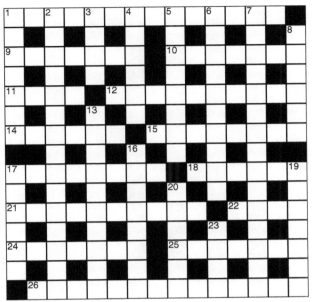

173

ACROSS

1 Getting on train for college (8,6)
9 One may peg out playing it out of doors (7)
10 He looks after a dog on a hill (7)
11 Place, it is within the borders of Singapore (4)
12 All-star casts? (10)
14 More unfortunate choice in the marriage ceremony (6)
15 Insect immature at first then finally with it (8)
17 I'm set back with a succession of wretched experiences (8)
18 There's a change in the Old Testament (6)
21 Devote to re-writing scene or act (10)
22 Boring makers of laws (4)
24 Characters that are inclined to be distinctive (7)
25 Promenade concert performer (7)
26 A healthy comparison (2,3,2,1,6)

DOWN

1 Supports people have when annoyed (5,2)
2 Advent is a very long time to go (1,5,2,7)
3 As a container it can't be beaten (4)
4 Thought it will turn up in time (6)
5 Helps those who have been had, we hear (8)
6 He crashed awkwardly at the end of the race—bad luck! (4,6)
7 Feeling extremely happy, having reached the N Pole? (2,3,2,3,5)
8 Responsible for a convict getting privileges (6)
13 Almost the end of a union dispute? (6,4)
16 A banker's order in mid-America (8)
17 Share jobs equally when there's dirt at home (4,2)
19 Favour shown to the electorate (7)
20 More work here—or less, many hope! (6)
23 I follow through with spirit (4)

174

ACROSS

7 Fall in love only to be discouraged (4,5)
8 Tincal gunners go in to fight with fists (5)
10 Somehow is around? Not for 60 million years! (8)
11 Can top cutter be first man to bat? (6)
12 Meadowland and river he gave his ungrateful daughters (4)
13 The Dutch spirit which provides Dutch courage (8)
15 In a wild party he gets the treatment (7)
17 Genuinely juxtaposing two articles with skill (2,5)
20 Wise old man embraces peace for the astronautical era (5,3)
22 BSI mark of quality bird (4)
25 Relative from America in the money (6)
26 Ban a coil designed to be energy-storing (8)
27 Cipher needed to glance over ancient Italian language (5)
28 Stop telling how to dispose of an irreparable old banger (5,2,2)

DOWN

1 Apparently broke out broke (3,2)
2 If you can't beg or borrow an item go away (6)
3 Prepare to catch and dismember a rat pest (3,1,4)
4 A leaner Frenchman caught in police detention (3,4)
5 Be fond of grouse etc, so walk over at Wimbledon (4,4)
6 Accept role as a dismantler (4,5)
9 Well I never call for silence (4)
14 Take axe to dwelling where meals are served (4,5)
16 Search I'm making for a thick vein of mine (4,4)
18 Choose a street for fast food cafe (4,4)
19 Great age produces a fury (7)
21 Bill born with a dermatological problem (4)
23 Also relatives provided accommodation (4,2)
24 Drunk started smoking (3,2)

175

ACROSS

1 Element man left out sometimes hard in winter (5)
4 Shipmates rioting on board this? (9)
8 Cast entered the wrong way round (5)
9 Pure but has not been seen (9)
11 Carry endless pole (4)
12 What worshippers are about to do (5)
13 Northerner initially takes wrong key (4)
16 Figure that cannot be improved on (7,6)
19 Stuff in a stable? (3,4,1,5)
20 Put up with a little sugar (4)
22 Frank's on time (5)
23 She followed Eliza to the throne (4)
26 What could be nicer, song about a brightly-coloured flower? (9)
27 Striker to make light of (5)
28 Bird changes colour (9)
29 He got the measure of an old king (5)

DOWN

1 Measurement that goes up and down in women's fashions (9)
2 Dangerous situation to be in when drunk? (5,4)
3 Speed estimate (4)
4 Reliable fence for radio equipment? (5,8)
5 African wasteland (4)
6 How heats are contested (5)
7 Priest had to shave round back of head (5)
10 patient gets carried away (9,4)
14 A girl redesigned the platter (5)
15 Dish served to surly fellow on the railway (5)
17 The warder is no vegetarian apparently (9)
18 Not wearing smooth footwear? (5-4)
20 It is allowable, having landed to go round the islands (5)
21 the reported style of a country house (5)
24 One who loved to be in the rose-garden? (4)
25 Expression of dissatisfaction of speed after a bend (4)

176

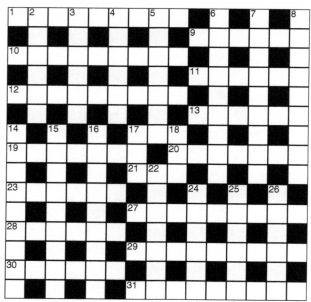

ACROSS

1 They give some thought to the rolls, being perfectionists (9)
9 Protective wear that's split—look into this (6)
10 Deception of a rogue sure to go wrong (9)
11 Quickly reacting to the French Right (6)
12 Urge to study and make an effort (9)
13 One has to drive around such a vehicle (6)
17 The main points put by African leader (3)
19 Sort of coal left to burn (7)
20 May 3 and have a good time (7)
21 A small bird, in fact it is really tiny (3)
23 Fights waste (6)
27 The allegatio made in a store's found to be false (9)
28 A metal drawer (6)
29 In a bad way—it's the bally fuel misuse! (9)
30 The military show thanks, the non-male included (6)
31 Moving with all speed when without cover (9)

DOWN

2 Fruit and nuts set up the boy (6)
3 A trick to hold the ring and so cause excitement (6)
4 In promoting his work the painter never shut up (6)
5 One of may six-footers engaged in high-rise building (7)
6 A player on the fiddle (4-5)
7 Famed for taking no nonsense over financial liabilities (9)
8 Mum, appallingly treated, is devastated (9)
14 School friend seen about with a girl before tea (9)
15 A great egg concoction to get together (9)
16 The fool, being given direction, told about 26 (9)
17 Make ready for company (3)
18 An exploit to imitate (3)
22 Stylish way a worker get pressing (7)
24 Withdraw in accordance with new decree (6)
25 Stopped work, being beat (6)
26 Bad spirit could well make one go almost totally blind (6)

177

178

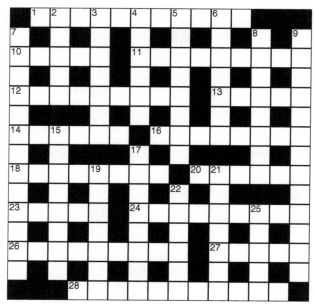

ACROSS

1 Tense situation for an abseiling enthusiast (5-6)
10 Large limousine gains Academy Award (5)
11 Bill is hostile about returning it (9)
12 Fashion model glad to win first prize (4,5)
13 Long poem initially inscribed 1942 years ago (5)
14 Making a mistake by hesitation to call (6)
16 One rightly ridiculed hoop-la, for instance (4,4)
18 Australian sheep-farmer is comparatively short and fat (8)
20 Composer expresses approval of a knight (6)
23 Additional article carried by ordinary soldiers (5)
24 An oil is to be blended in a place apart (9)
26 Make English ceilings a different way (9)
27 Depicted with gaunt features (5)
28 Alter a chit to get some silver (6,1,4)

DOWN

2 See airman in the neighbourhood (5)
3 Supervisor runs into an enemy (7)
4 Stores— vast numbers, by the sound of it (6)
5 A month before Fitzgerald's stories appear (8)
6 Former nobleman I introduced to King Edward (7)
7 Also sensoring resolution of the US legislature (13)
8 Security services inflamed by worker from Trotskyite group (8)
9 Going blind taking a mortality count (4,9)
15 Era of violence requires real fibre (8)
17 Single issue leading to anti-government agitation (8)
19 Dull seaman getting up in silence (7)
21 Leave with one's hair tied back? (7)
22 Man in the middle has to be consistent (6)
25 To sleep in it is not appropriate (5)

179

ACROSS

1 Keeping watch (11)
9 Measure of daytime temperature (4)
10 Not the end one's prepared for (6,5)
11 Poet Laureate's heard, making appearances (4)
14 The only luggage that one needs? (4-3)
16 Treatment mother's wise to have (7)
17 He breaks an oar (5)
18 It can be taken in a bank (4)
19 Stick together in a difficult situation (4)
20 Letter that is circulated around the Orient (5)
22 Bows were made from it, yet were wrongly formed (3-4)
23 A number making a noise in an examination (7)
24 Loss from a strike (4)
28 Criticise space in Army accommodation (7,4)
29 A man for one season (4)
30 Feel trained to be submissive (11)

DOWN

2 Unhappy choice of colour (4)
3 The aims of termini (4)
4 House holding an orchid (7)
5 Restrictions imposed for cup matches (4)
6 Old Empire, lacking arms, lacks backing (7)
7 Orders translation of rousing tale (11)
8 Newly leased building for sheep (11)
12 One more makes a soldier a sailor (6-5)
13 One who's out and about (11)
15 It's used for turning a French article to an English one (5)
16 Tom's turn to prove a saying (5)
20 Examine a note with a will (7)
21 It's meant to be read, so make it clear (7)
25 Available, if the price is about right (4)
26 Harry on the guitar (4)
27 Nothing in it, a mere tittle (4)

180

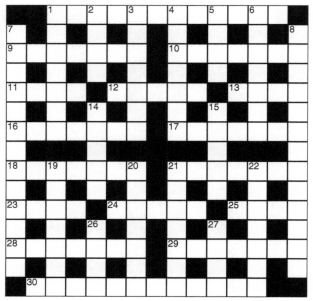

ACROSS

1 With little room do heat somehow when terminally ill (5,2,5)
9 Disconcerts disconcerted starlet (7)
10 Chlorophyll producer in Switzerland (7)
11 Lincoln died, but certainly not here (4)
12 Don't waste water (5)
13 Computer language everyone can summon up (4)
16 Ancient mariner told Sal differently (3,4)
17 Highly offensive racket in which retired doctor is caught (7)
18 Suffer humiliation if wrongly attired (3,4)
21 Understand the pistol cannot be fired (5,2)
23 Minor part of lock (4)
24 Namely how one should move a caravan (2,3)
25 Black mark for a group of second-raters (4)
28 Also going back into boxing arena cheering (7)
29 I'm going in to chatter to a high churchman (7)
30 When many a heart is broken fielding (5,3,4)

DOWN

1 Snootily ignore to perform an autopsy (3,4)
2 Ring railway to famous international airport (4)
3 Relaxation prohibited, so withdraw cautiously (4,3)
4 On and on about unruly sly sole male heir (4,3)
5 Scratch out a living as an engraver? (4)
6 To the navy much trouble! (7)
7 What strong fencer once managed to do to prove untrustworthy (5,4,4)
8 Bed-time-story-lover's plea? I don't believe it! (4,2,7)
14 Dickensian spiv whose lips were never without a cigarette (5)
15 I'd try tidying up if in this condition (5)
19 Put out at the road junction (4,3)
20 An idea nevertheless needing time initially (7)
21 Cut a pastry dish for the conductor (7)
22 Case suggests none should be granted bail (7)
26 Be about it and get your teeth stuck into it (4)
27 Upset keen prima donna (4)

181

ACROSS

1 Sway to and fro, leave office about to be unwell (9)

8 Furniture seen on more than three hoardings? (4-6,3)

11 Important person to return into the grips of Greek character by third of July (5)

12 Single actor (5)

13 Airman is liberated—sharp (5)

16 Whopper perhaps from German chemist (6)

17 Started batting (6)

18 Note a concoction made of cereals (5)

19 A Wren's redesigned suit (6)

20 Surpass in ingenuity without possibly losing aspiration (6)

21 Hears about an old tribe (5)

24 Sweet smell of a foreign city (5)

26 Overshoots the line (5)

27 Relatively unpleasant row? (6,7)

28 One in the centre of business perhaps (9)

DOWN

2 April in Paris (5)

3 Sneering at one boy in charge (6)

4 Fruit from sunlit China (6)

5 Engineers in the small group (5)

6 Female representative? (13)

7 Advancing by degrees towards 19 (7,6)

9 Suspiciously detect vermin (5,1,3)

10 Sweets on a bunch of threads found in the garden (9)

13 An attempt by artist at the market-place (5)

14 Chart movement of a toothed rack (5)

15 Way-out name included of a benevolent person (5)

22 Remained sober by the sound of it (6)

23 Get up late! (6)

25 A politician, one making a plea (5)

26 One is in revolt, spending year in the country (5)

182

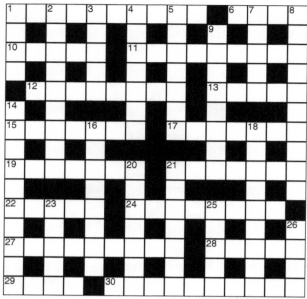

ACROSS

1 Bribe a worker to come in second (10)
6 A border meant to attract attention (4)
10 It's dogma, no matter how it's regarded (5)
11 In idleness maybe one will find extra sources of income (9)
12 Stuff obtainable for ready money only (8)
13 A few in the Tyneside area find this simple (5)
15 Combine read about in bed (7)
17 Bag left by cheats in a mix-up (7)
19 Having to let about a thousand cause anguish (7)
21 Notes the time (7)
22 Decoration can be a drawback (5)
24 Paid ransom for certain military personnel held (8)
27 Wind about in say turning right due to drink (6,3)
28 Tot presented with foreign article is confused (5)
29 Sound way to employ sheepish creatures (4)
30 The paper-seller never downs rum (4-6)

DOWN

1 Clean city (4)
2 This will hold for certain—no wobbling (9)
3 Beaten over church problem (5)
4 An ascending aroma is now being produced (7)
5 Non-stop, totally without purpose (7)
7 Some may well fall behind in learning a language (5)
8 With no top man, male stress may result (10)
9 Sea-food makes the board put on weight (8)
14 A charming invader is never on the square! (5,5)
16 Incurred indebtedness which may be exaggerated (8)
18 Feeling the effects of fever and rash (9)
20 Offering a suggestion about the queen's residences (7)
21 To crowd around back end would be sheer folly (7)
23 Her get-up's inane! (5)
25 Cancel because having entered before (5)
26 Drink requiring bottle-opener always (4)

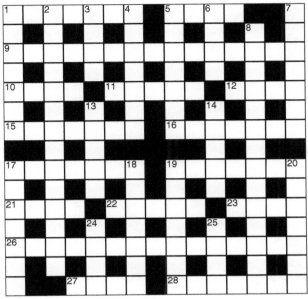

183

ACROSS

1 Savoy, for example, needs a number of keys (7)
5 Home fixture for Avon City (4)
9 Air of schoolboys (N.B.—not going to sea in a storm) (4,7,4)
10 Comply with honour at year's opening (4)
11 Gold sovereign? (5)
12 Tax some disco takings (4)
15 Land-express that carries the queen (7)
16 Surgeon's assistant with his back to the wall? (7)
17 Security-device for bundle holding old assortment (7)
19 Place for driving off to China is full of people (7)
21 Term to express contempt for strike-breakers (4)
22 Type of conference, long (5)
23 Governess out east unaffected by retirement? (4)
26 Time-taking thief of the saw? (15)
27 Mark of musicians in the street (4)
28 Multiply without going forth? (7)

DOWN

1 Cigar dear in France? Too bad! (7)
2 Representation of Dorian G to abide? No! it is breaking up naturally (14)
3 A reading-desk for a doctor on round (4)
4 Joy—niece, perhaps, who loses her head (7)
5 Pirate's kit carried by players (7)
6 Planned go at encircling ancient Rome (4)
7 Sirius put shadows on pitch (7)
8 In season, Cicero turned out to be a license holder... (14)
13 ...in a type of Roman police-district (5)
14 Number observed around Civic Centre (5)
17 Bank to protect soldiers—standard tape put out (7)
18 This kosher diet brings saint to knees, in a way (7)
19 Better half takes car to the very limits (7)
20 Good tag, perhaps, for a satyr? (4-3)
24 Dead spirit one can beat (4)
25 Dress-ring lost by old film-idol (4)

184

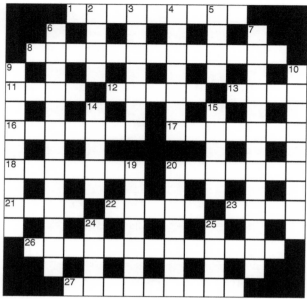

ACROSS

1 Criterion which judges observe (9)
8 Capable of taking note of meeting with it (2,2,3,6)
11 Schubert song gave a false impression (4)
12 Daggers drawn when alumnus confronts Hebrew high priest (5)
13 Independent sovereign is in charge (4)
16 Brief agreement (7)
17 Form of art with spirit and propriety (7)
18 Great fortitude needed if lady-love is married (7)
20 To clarify matters is no longer simple (7)
21 A pain in the trachea (4)
22 Finish with one's tail in the air (3,2)
23 An Egyptian god has the last word (4)
26 An admired gent, unusually popular (2,5,6)
27 Notable bishop is in haste (9)

DOWN

2 School where oriental gains score of one hundred (4)
3 To live together is a firm, established practice (7)
4 Mother, on being miled of cash, was incoherent (7)
5 To classify in hierarchical order is offensive (4)
6 Drug pusher who enjoys life in the fast lane (5,8)
7 Handling of astronomical subjects requires special attention (4,9)
9 Only a half-wit would obstruct the boss (9)
10 Woman's 'usband in confined accommodation is constant (9)
14 Saw unknown man coming in badly hurt (5)
15 Opportunity to get small ceremonial vestment (5)
19 Order partner to come around as well (7)
20 Eurocurrency Dora changed in S. America (7)
24 Native Americans about to enter Anglican church (4)
25 Stomach is upset by cereal fungus (4)

185

ACROSS

1 A choice of courses or delicacies (10)
9 Deliveries completed (4)
10 Date stumps in an evenly contested game (5,5)
11 With a new clue I'd find the mathematician (6)
12 Withdraws a direction on grants (7)
15 Not a change for the better (7)
16 Box holding Eastern weapon (5)
17 She writes a reflective article (4)
18 Musical group get port after the end of the concert (4)
19 A capital ring from one's lover (5)
21 Used in making her kind of pickle (7)
22 Type of magenta identification label (4-3)
24 Nectar may produce a state of ecstasy (6)
27 In French, France for example (3,2,5)
28 Stand torture (4)
29 To lead on is wrong, causing great distress (10)

DOWN

2 Great Chinese build-up (4)
3 Possibly run and see to make certain (6)
4 Well preserved Egyptian parents (7)
5 A number given to someone to sing (4)
6 Plot developer (7)
7 The demon drink? (4,6)
8 Early form of rock music (6,4)
12 Dispatches produce merriment on board (10)
13 Legal document that could be a trap (10)
14 Club that has lofty aims (5)
15 It flies a welcome in the British fleet (5)
19 I write in red—not green (7)
20 Porridge going round at breakfast? (7)
23 Peephole for viewer to lease (6)
25 Politician is about to see mischief-makers (4)
26 Short of ammunition (4)

186

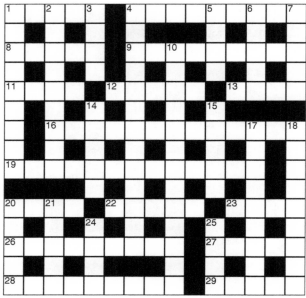

ACROSS

1 Why the matador had to become embarrassed? (5)
4 Exhibit—ability as an impressario (3,2,4)
8 In charge of the situation at a summit (2,3)
9 Able bodied British composer who has signed the pledge (9)
11 Jaw employed in machinery (4)
12 Dead queen's return proves carthartic (5)
13 Herb in perfect condition (4)
16 Briefly endorse communication to the first landlord (7,6)
19 Tory wants to lambast union's fundamental freedom (5,2,6)
20 Ancient Ethiopia border for those snookered (4)
22 Elicit information from eastern Fascist leader (5)
23 What accounts for dame being drunk? (4)
26 Smoother shoe preserver lining London streets (5,4)
27 Stone I met an ancient, ancient man a-sitting on (5)
28 Arrange no USSR aid for extinct species (9)
29 Drug which is major cause of motorway accidents (5)

DOWN

1 Happiness is what popular winners deserve from their fans (4,5)
2 Telling work for a shop-keeper (9)
3 Stupid fellow used to strengthen fabrics (4)
4 Properly arranged to be assigned as a novitiate (6,2,5)
5 Flood survivor apparently declined throat inspection (4)
6 It is spoken in south India (5)
7 Best or least best (5)
10 Unmarried parasite set out to get one-way passes (6,7)
14 Accompany about 500 from one side to the other (5)
15 Admit to being unexpectedly involved (3,2)
17 The ones here confront ante-revolutionary legislature (3,6)
18 Portly principal parliamentary supporter (9)
20 Copper, copper, one old copper pagan god (5)
21 Single man on board gets fish eggs (5)
24 Man's house could be opened by them (4)
25 Deep sea fish (4)

ACROSS

6 Near accommodation in which one makes contact immediately (5,8)
8 Cat right behind a timid person (6)
9 Landing at the end of the flight (8)
10 Water hardly used as a drinks additive (3)
11 Energetic part of play I have to conclude (6)
12 Dream run produced as a result of illegal bowling (8)
14 Didn't allow free speech (7)
16 Pesos I'd arranged to distribute (7)
20 Defective hearing (8)
23 Reason it was substituted in turn (6)
24 Trouble with an old copper ring (3)
25 Press man with regard to beer (8)
26 Does it drive one to drink? (6)
27 Another sane patriot is one who favours disunion (13)

DOWN

1 Girl to jam the control lever (3-5)
2 Rescue dog losing its tail (8)
3 Step into line with others (5,2)
4 Got rid of unwanted letters (6)
5 Go and get married again? (6)
6 Note one point of short-temperedness (13)
7 Call when one least expects it (8,5)
13 One of 26 in procession (3)
15 Particularly content in finding a deity (3)
17 Moving a fashionable proposal (2,6)
18 Girl not quite a hereditary noble (8)
19 Lucidity of the French rebel leader in a large town (7)
21 Actors moved to Peru (6)
22 One after another hospital doctor was heard (2,4)

188

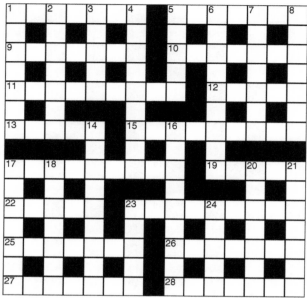

ACROSS

1 Pals upset by jerk being so easily influenced (7)
5 There's many a drinker sound as a bell, using this (7)
9 Some left—no-on returned (7)
10 Serious matter of security (7)
11 Photographer's concern revealed by an informer (9)
12 She shows great potential (5)
13 The fibre used in evening dresses is a lustrous synthetic (5)
15 A hold-up for the viewer's benefit (9)
17 An angry expression could baffle one (9)
19 Finding a note enclosed in listening equipment, he'll scoff (5)
22 Follow directions and initiate legal action (5)
23 A natural slip of landladies lacking a bent for it (9)
25 An entitlement to beef? (7)
26 Second parking in a test (7)
27 The rate fixed for entertainment (7)
28 Row about a way that's slower (7)

DOWN

1 Pages in the Lords—they're hot stuff! (7)
2 Writing article to support the ordinary seaman, as is fitting (7)
3 Double issue (5)
4 A woman never scored highly (9)
5 The mating game (5)
6 Contempt shown for car with no gear-change (9)
7 Give now! (7)
8 Once more go over touching evidence (7)
14 The boor imbibing a drop got aggressive (6,3)
16 Turned and made off when not needed (9)
17 Provided at one time for pitch illumination (7)
18 Keep taking notice (7)
20 Blunder over oil-production in North Africa (7)
21 Beasts offered eggs rush up (3-4)
23 Left an engineer to make a cut (5)
24 Taste drink with some hesitation and find it excellent (5)

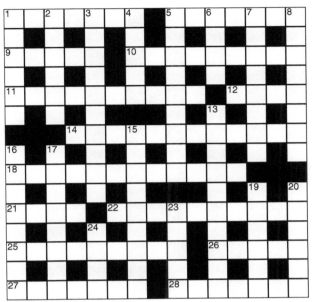

189

ACROSS

1 Fun race organized by stifling place (7)
5 Paul's letter-record is let out (7)
9 Stroll in Lakeland town, showing no side (5)
10 Instrument not available to Canute, presumably? (4-5)
11 Tiniest amount taken from a roll? (10)
12 Lid to protect baked beans? (4)
14 Running a ranch and bringing up a family (5-7)
18 Wire-tapper? (12)
21 Stone jar (4)
22 Jack—standard partner? Not in the regular way (10)
25 Wind light? That will produce blasted heat! (4-5)
26 Bearing of former PM (5)
27 Creek is French, alongside university and a railway (7)
28 Send forth spring issue (7)

DOWN

1 Extremely fitful baby, perhaps, is rather overweight (6)
2 Teased wife on couch (6)
3 Old gags altogether (10)
4 Apple taken from a tree? (5)
5 Modern hop tricky for a dumpy type (9)
6 Scandinavian girl popular with Georgia (4)
7 Starting to turn out nice for the German (8)
8 Late papers? Just sing out! (8)
13 Declines nothing—kind of frenzy in compulsive drinking (10)
15 Little credit goes to Barney R., perhaps, as fruit-jelly maker (9)
16 Can be kept in a warehouse (or in reliable setting) (8)
17 Shortage in battle brings news stoppage (8)
19 Closely-woven material of hymn-setting (6)
20 Caerphilly cheese contains this exotic fruit (6)
23 Chore, spreading colour (5)
24 Way round a portico? (4)

190

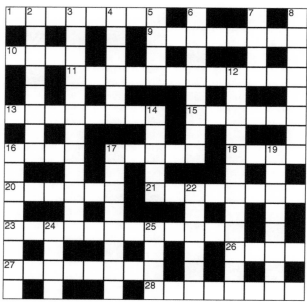

ACROSS

1 Wearing a hairpiece to add excitement (6,2)
9 Work by post office location over the road (8)
10 Visual handicap appearing in the middle of last year (4)
11 Fear of arrest (12)
13 To be honest, it's a quiet song with a loud melody (4,4)
15 Stern oarsman has apoplexy (6)
16 Shed is reduced by five hundred (4)
17 Had to be admitted (5)
18 One of the family is in Majorca until Sunday (4)
20 Where car travellers take their luggage as well (2,4)
21 Suspicious about grandiloquent language in covenant (8)
23 Arrive with a harvester, only to meet disaster (4,1,7)
26 His latin love verse I had briefly rephrased (4)
27 Government leader in Arab state made to quit home (8)
28 Financial outlay leaves son still undecided (8)

DOWN

2 A battle later settled in court (8)
3 Are yet to form revised EC agreement (6,2,4)
4 Housework left to go to a game (4-2)
5 Observe that the subtonic was omitted (4)
6 A parish priest relaxed and satisfied (8)
7 Situated between small island and the south of France (4)
8 Have to settle fashionable socialite in punt (2,2,4)
12 Publicise a foreign banquet (6,6)
14 About noon we returned to start afresh (5)
16 In retirement Edward longed to be free of ties (8)
17 He provides glasses for IPA and tonic cocktail (8)
19 Symbolic signs are to be set up in the country (8)
22 Model once again needs rest (6)
24 Servant I discovered in wild embrace (4)
25 Nothing is written on some French poems (4)

191

ACROSS

7 Recovery results in delight round the City (9)
8 He takes the animal out what's left (5)
10 Sweet that scores highly? (5-3)
11 Pounds of sultanas? (6)
12 It is thought to be almost perfect (4)
13 Pushed the boat out in Paris? (4,4)
15 Vessel—lacking stabilizers? (7)
17 Overweight boy's tie pulled out (7)
20 Christmas present drawer (8)
22 Peter is out of danger (4)
25 Go over undulating track (6)
26 Put up with the closed shop (8)
27 A bit of an act? (5)
28 His plight might possibly warn sailors (9)

DOWN

1 Information given us in class (5)
2 Naughty ladies went to sea (6)
3 In the main it's the cheapest way to travel (8)
4 insect settled on the cheese for a short while (7)
5 Assigns to a berth in stormy seas (8)
6 End for miner injured in gallery (9)
9 Heartless head cook (4)
14 It's sensible to have a break and a joke (9)
16 Contradict, using a mild expletive (8)
18 The bogus arrangement asked for (8)
19 Club money that is short (7)
21 Looked over carefully? I'd say (4)
23 Thief's unusual charm (6)
24 Exhaust pipe (5)

192

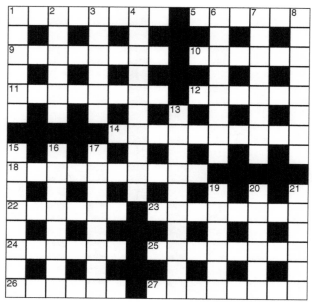

ACROSS

1 Give up suggesting how to include item in a suitcase (4,2,2)
5 Call to account for what windlasses do (4,2)
9 Slug has now been made always to play a similar role (8)
10 A black mark awarded to drunk (6)
11 Shows relatives evidence of Nordic descent (4,4)
12 highlight single lock of hair (6)
14 Play a leading role to put on a show of bravado (3,3,4)
18 What Mrs Sprat liked to do was argue (4,3,3)
22 Run twice (6)
23 Who would ever have thought both twins were in perfect health? (4,4)
24 For one sultana it is the capital grape (6)
25 Flatter way to load high a luggage trolley (4,2,2)
26 Boat that should slice through the waves (6)
27 Tries to entice in wartime army girls (8)

DOWN

1 Lost interest because postponed (3,3)
2 Select Sidney for England team despite being a pest (6)
3 Where the barrister was employed and kept his brief (2,4)
4 Laughing one's head off just after a surgical operation (2,8)
6 The whole fleet has sailed but is totally lost (3,2,3)
7 Application to view but I need time to think (3,2,3)
8 The indigent exhibit a lamentable effort (4,4)
13 He plans street to speed the general idea (10)
15 Current confusion of media about nature of education (8)
16 Rise from bed ready to become disquieted (3,5)
17 Newly settle around Los Angeles like the stars (8)
19 Complex legal point to imply in court (6)
20 responsible motorist's first request to back seat driver (4,2)
21 150 units all identical (6)

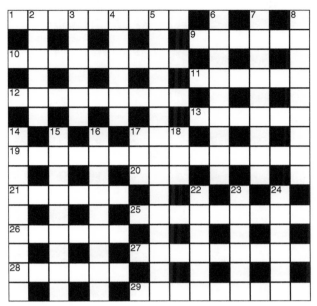

193

ACROSS

1 Pretty poor arrangement, not right, for the first of its kind (9)
9 Metallic blue (6)
10 What the tree did before it produced fruit? Flourished and prospered (9)
11 In obtaining this instrument, I spent out (6)
12 Green record, cost ie unfortunately enveloping (9)
13 In fun really it was imaginary (6)
17 Love of French verse (3)
19 Blooming fighting? (6,2,7)
20 French word test (3)
21 Troublesome animals not starting by end of June to produce fur! (6)
25 Showing affection in a roundabout way (9)
26 To have a regular girl-friend up to now (2,4)
27 In foreign trip, get on with the attendants (9)
28 Devoted adherent to go back in and change (6)
29 Bucks ducks (9)

DOWN

2 Widow, about 51, on court (6)
3 Lets us get beaten up in a scuffle (6)
4 Nevertheless hesitantly leaves the uncut grass by the fairway (6)
5 What the valet did when hard up? (7,3,5)
6 Honourable friend? (9)
7 Illegally handled money while A1 endured torture (9)
8 Say fewer have no nationality (9)
14 Aim I have at goal (9)
15 Tax to be paid at the Post Office? (5-4)
16 Scheme by extra-terrestrial going over a number of lines of certain heavenly bodies (9)
17 Nothing is on order for uncle (3)
18 Little creature abandoned having been decapitated (3)
22 Long hollow circle in the wood (6)
23 A crab's wandering round a beatle (6)
24 Wild ass or small horse 'e found inside (6)

194

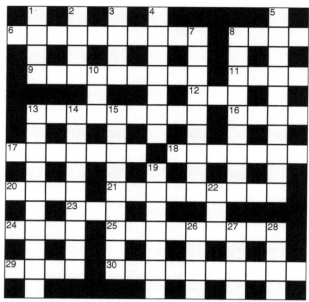

ACROSS

6 Woman over-order (10)
8 The team that's not ahead (4)
9 Bear with an ill-disposed dancer (9)
11 Against interrupting supporter when keen (4)
12 The retired seaman is a little beast (3)
13 Temperate land mass (9)
16 He's put royalty in charge (4)
17 Pole having to pay for room (7)
18 A story about bovine creatures being ruled (7)
20 A pound's nothing as an extra (4)
21 It's wrong to rag Ivan the pilot (9)
23 Whisky or port? (3)
24 Taking part in a guessing game, get the shivers (4)
25 "Use of grinder" is to include in French translation (9)
29 A record the old-fashioned desire (4)
30 A hero—one going in left and right with hot blood (4,6)

DOWN

1 A larva representing food to some people (4)
2 Game 3?... (4)
3 ...or only 2? (4)
4 Dreams of making a point about a section of the church (7)
5 A key government official's in control (10)
7 Support without cutting, which is most surprising (9)
8 Account for preparation of testament (9)
10 The fate of a great many (3)
13 On the way to barbecue the steaks? (6-4)
14 Woodland home with directions for its occupation (3,6)
15 Popular officer on the whole (2,7)
19 Time for getting uniform (7)
22 Music that's inspired! (3)
26 The hearing devices are adjusted—start speaking (4)
27 An island shows a certain amount of coastal erosion always (4)
28 A song can give great pleasure (4)

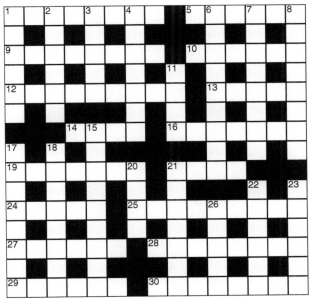

195

ACROSS

1 Faith I learn about at church (8)
5 First major profit declared (6)
9 See animal go wild in the bush! (8)
10 Well-turned out daughter takes paper round (6)
12 Silent pictures being shown here in Scotland (9)
13 Slackened, as in river that backs up (5)
14 Evidence of damage in second vehicle (4)
16 Portable stand for thingummy? (7)
19 Monastery bugle-call? (7)
21 Lines of people waiting, we hear, for signs (4)
24 Game in which 6 may appear? (5)
25 Likely place for tennis elbow—mind out! (9)
27 Temple of a deity in Pennsylvania (6)
28 Hasty games of tennis behind hedge (8)
29 Heart-breaking, coming to end of blown capital... (6)
30 ...needy, all going about in dispirited manner (8)

DOWN

1 Specific solution? (6)
2 Vegetable glue used in shelter (6)
3 Israeli money in Greek market-place? (5)
4 Uncle Sam's pet name? (7)
6 Draw at Maltese resort (9)
7 August trespassing? (8)
8 Constitution of DIY there is different (8)
11 Cocaine used in surgeries nowadays? (4)
15 Dry places ruined this old-timer, we hear (9)
17 Eccentric champion on grass? (8)
18 Advantage of muscle? (8)
20 Square now re-designed in Helston, for example (4)
21 Converse intimately in kibbutz? (7)
22 Name of inventor noised abroad (6)
23 Having lumps on trunk can be difficult to sort out (6)
26 Beaming, copper retires in informal hat (5)

196

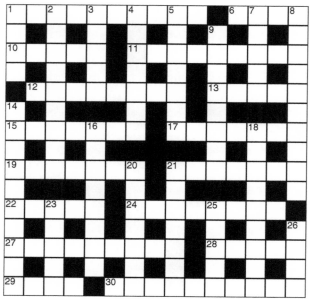

ACROSS

1 Served only with ice if penniless (2,3,5)
6 Stop up for an advertisement (4)
10 Sweet wine—clearly a gift for Catherine (5)
11 Disorderly protest about Common Market is kept under wraps (3-6)
12 A WW2 fighter—one with a hot temper (8)
13 Get decked out for a celebration with sailors (5)
15 A priest sprightly but delicate (7)
17 Top-quality French salt is rejected in Poland (7)
19 Pull fish around away from the wind (7)
21 Ordered to accommodate retired gent, despite notoriety (3,4)
22 In Mexico we resolve to eat quail (5)
24 Bound to be short of cash (8)
27 Vote in CIA reforms for a probationary period (9)
28 About to give entry to honourable French banker (5)
29 making the Queen head scientific association is wrong (4)
30 Poison a beautiful woman in Italy (10)

DOWN

1 A pledge to hearten the goatherds (4)
2 Happen to be a squatter (4,5)
3 "I am dying,—, dying" (*Antony and Cleopatra*, Act IV) (5)
4 Without a fielding team (7)
5 Have they dropped off some fish? (7)
7 Slow passage in large, fabulous Greek ship (5)
8 Promised to wed when given a job (3,7)
9 The German got sick of being put off the track (8)
14 Liquor store conceals $0.51 in breach of custom (3-7)
16 One certain to be replaced right away (2,1,5)
18 Settle into a makeshift bed (9)
20 Complaint received by seaside resort (7)
21 Time signal for local customers in the weightlifters' gym (7)
23 Hesitate to give a perm to Regina (5)
25 Top secretary embarrassed when cut down to size (5)
26 The female answer to Zeus? (4)

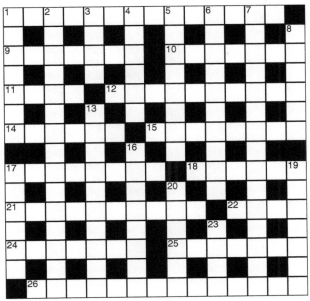

197

ACROSS

1 One who's given up (5,9)
9 A warning to the introvert (4,3)
10 Motorist waiting for a chance to pass (7)
11 A drawer of money (4)
12 Contests in which no one goes the distance (5,5)
14 Look upon with respect (6)
15 Box smart during trial (3-5)
17 Possibly relating to the whole (8)
18 Orders a transfer of credits without right (6)
21 Pet of a girl, perhaps, but recklessly extravagant (10)
22 She has them shortened to a degree (4)
24 Unpaid companion in a biblical city (7)
25 Adopted and raised (5,2)
26 Neither arrival nor departure is a problem (4,4,4,2)

DOWN

1 It's worn with one's arm inside (7)
2 Mother accepts soothing tonal composition is by Beethoven (9,6)
3 Lighting the gas? (4)
4 Head branch (6)
5 Let out or let out again (8)
6 Tried if car smash results in manslaughter (10)
7 Guilt-edged security? (10,5)
8 Port is used in making a toast (6)
13 Picture-house (3,7)
16 Jumper having a pocket in front (8)
17 Skill at the billiard-table or on stage? (2,4)
19 The head cleaner (7)
20 Liberty, for example (6)
23 Bird seen when others rise (4)

198

ACROSS

7 Sturdily built oil installation now completed (4,3,2)
8 Cry of joy from those identified getting work (5)
10 First task when staffing new school is to improve on schedule (3,5)
11 Sailor takes overland route to get overseas (6)
12 Market speculator representing Russia (4)
13 Joker allowed to compete without qualifying (4,4)
15 Stocking fabric likely to catch on board (7)
17 Discuss French water and wine source (7)
20 A teach-in arranged for caddies maybe (5,3)
22 What the murderer takes and gets (4)
25 Tell how an athlete should be if he is to win (2,4)
26 Clasps providing 'em with trouser supports (8)
27 Payment includes us for the big match (5)
28 Highly praised despite having broken under the strain (7,2)

DOWN

1 Revel overturned the bar (5)
2 Stick to split along the grain (6)
3 Practise with gun-carriage used at sapper's funeral? (8)
4 Commit to paper a humiliating rebuke (3-4)
5 Bob finds a less circuitous route than... (5,3)
6 ...the queen's highway (5,4)
9 A sleuth finds a dog-end (4)
14 Judge if it be not what an insulted duellist wishes to defend (3,6)
16 The morning after it becomes an anachronism (8)
18 Don't go on if you are suffering from lumbago (4,4)
19 Compelled a provisional organisation to supply wine (7)
21 Book dedication by egocentric autobiographer? (4)
23 Roman priest employs Flemish prayer ending (6)
24 Cheer increase in value of tax-saving investment (3,2)

199

ACROSS

1 Have force to take the ship (7)
5 Girl takes cover from a worm! (7)
9 Seconder, of course? (6,9)
10 The man's taking a second to express disapproval (4)
11 Maybe laid back initially at pleasure (2,3)
12 To fit, it must be slightly more than a foot long (4)
15 Highly arrogantly (7)
16 George, youth leader, holds record on earth study (7)
17 Sole support for a jockey (7)
19 Island celebrates eradication of vermin (7)
21 Attorney with the Italian at another country's parliament (4)
22 Organised tour right into the city (5)
23 Last character in a long time with the priest (4)
26 Fruits of the meeting (10,5)
27 Pen found on catalogue of clothes designer (7)
28 One taking a former ring-road first during the beginnings of the speeches (7)

DOWN

1 Father takes Sarah round the Church of the Passover (7)
2 No company has such independence (4-11)
3 Drain doesn't begin to hold water (4)
4 May does come round eventually (7)
5 Count up the fish that are going bad (7)
6 Wriggly line in the map of Africa (4)
7 Artist gets the bird in Bedfordshire (8,7)
8 Although indecisive, I had gone up to the railway (7)
13 Young children, that is to say, inside are impetuous (5)
14 Cheerful sailor on board (5)
17 Without aspiration, duchess 'e misleadingly tempts (7)
18 Flawless finish (7)
19 Officer has clear break on the boat (7)
20 As new as another city (7)
24 Half of the academics? (4)
25 Capable of being put out with oxygen (2,2)

200

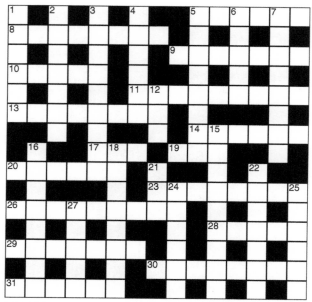

ACROSS

5 Pay for resolve (6)
8 Gets no quack remedies (8)
9 Judge to be without honour—and smarter (7)
10 Spoke repeatedly (5)
11 Left a company, having done badly (9)
13 Carried in the main (8)
14 The individual renting pasture with little hesitation (6)
17 Girl in need of aid and advice (3)
19 Cage-bird (3)
20 A vindictive person setting one sailor against another (6)
23 He'll support the woman in a depression (8)
26 Small daughter is proceeding to talk (9)
28 Jolly man, no longer a high-flier (5)
29 Raising a cheer maybe about a complaint made (7)
30 The usual range of colours (8)
31 Underwear for matches (6)

DOWN

1 Goes easy on husbands (6)
2 Warm drink prepared from fruit (7)
3 Where lots of people pay sound attention (9)
4 Managed to retain record left and make changes (6)
5 Sort of grants the French put an end to (8)
6 Play time (5)
7 Loyal 22 fellows? (5,3)
12 Sleeping accommodation for a university man (3)
15 In the finish the listener is winning (9)
16 Jocularity elderly folk find unacceptable (8)
18 Men on the board air unrest (8)
21 Used to be cut up (3)
22 Bengali settled in Northern Europe (7)
24 Note land scarcity (6)
25 Abuse from one in the business (6)
27 A Scot upset by the sea (5)

ACROSS

1 Straightforward quality of tin, hard and inflexible (7)
5 Permanent rule, bad to break (7)
9 Call forth for a late service? (5)
10 Modern dance sure to spoil conversation (9)
11 Underwriter with a telephone? (10)
12 Rolled oats in the Painted Porch? (4)
14 Gymnastic summons, in that case, by Olympic finalists (12)
18 Not in favour of a shooting-brake, say? (7-5)
21 Where to land in France coming from Bognor, Lyme Regis etc? (4)
22 Demonstrative girl coasting freely (10)
25 Finland back in line in such a big car (9)
26 Master sailors on mixed ale (5)
27 English can, in French street, form an entourage (7)
28 Current news? No, it is rather old! (7)

DOWN

1 Superior vessel found in earth (6)
2 Barney breaks out close at hand (6)
3 Rush, say, having completed attack (10)
4 More than one spoke of circle-lines! (5)
5 Indigestion, Pepys said, miserably (9)
6 Starting-point for ferret? (4)
7 Male voice to forbid one accent? (8)
8 Polish review of EEC angle? (8)
13 No longer fresh in stock (10)
15 Idle vicar, running wild, will polish off the grub! (9)
16 One who takes constitutional wave below street? (8)
17 Sporting plaid, Tom is a tactful sort abroad (8)
19 Procure a dry article at home (6)
20 Science articles that go like hot cakes? (6)
23 Scotsman's cry in salute (5)
24 Char from stream (4)

202

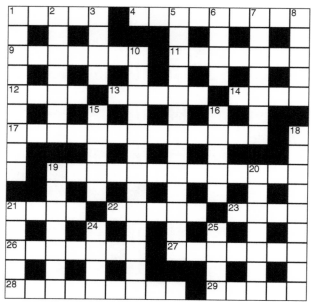

ACROSS

1 Bill brought in my French wine (5)
4 Mafia supremo returned to hound stout lady (9)
9 Drive mad grandee all over the place (7)
11 Digressed to say what happened when
Abraham spared Isaac (7)
12 Beams when presented with flatfish (4)
13 Standard requirement for a good soup (5)
14 River behind low tract of open land (4)
17 Language spoken impudently and insincerely
(6,2,5)
19 The garden is in disarray. How depressing! (13)
21 Married master from the staff (4)
22 Head cook is egocentric (5)
23 Is able to take in one marked man (4)
26 A clipper in comparatively good condition (7)
27 Historian understood by you and me (7)
28 Henry gets depressed even on 31st October (9)
29 Maureen took a partner and got a cut (5)

DOWN

1 Fashion criticised and so toned down (9)
2 Continue to make a fuss (5,2)
3 The sisters of Joshua's father (4)
5 Supervise present-day power supply (6,7)
6 Service which must always accommodate
marines (4)
7 I shall lay in German wine, despite slight rise (7)
8 A signal invention, however one views it (5)
10 Champ needs to have gargantuan meals
(3,4,1,5)
15 Wanton woman with a yen to follow Bohemian
heretic (5)
16 Father has to live and acquire possessions (5)
18 Grandiose design put into effect (9)
19 Censure Scottish landowner upset about the
Common Market (7)
20 Worried about where oysters should be reared
artificially (2,1,4)
21 Contest the marriage (5)
24 Boss gets stuck into the rum bottle (4)
25 Film employing a hundred in total (4)

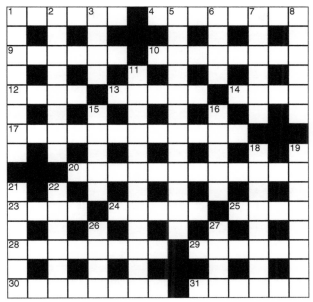

203

ACROSS

1 Emigre beaten up by the authorities (6)
4 Opening for a photographer (8)
9 How often models that have lost their shape are employed? (6)
10 Passing place (5-3)
12 One form of trust (4)
13 A fascinating woman about to be detected in depravity (5)
14 It may be the making of a man! (4)
17 Something bound to appeal to the less affluent readers (5,7)
20 Rest centre or perhaps a place for hanging about (6,6)
23 Whaler's cry of surprise touches sailor (4)
24 Get down to dividing bribe (5)
25 Where the workers may strike to make less money? (4)
28 Measure appropriate for Londoners (4,4)
29 Unbridled lust, an essential for an Eastern ruler (6)
30 Suspicion of corrosion after condensation (8)
31 A game on which the captain rules (6)

DOWN

1 Military informant shows initiative (8)
2 Swift traveller (8)
3 Emotional state low, with onset of depression (4)
5 Nearest point at sea for the launch (12)
6 Speed charge (4)
7 Straightened things out and became more friendly (6)
8 Son wed, perhaps, presents required (6)
11 Bows and scrapes to obtain marks of approval (12)
15 Sees one vessel inside another (5)
16 Small firms get together over a drink (5)
18 Shown to have a deficit and charged (8)
19 False profession (8)
21 Disorder for a month on the border (6)
22 Changing planes in Italy (6)
26 Structure ripe for conversion (4)
27 A stroke of the cat may produce it (4)

204

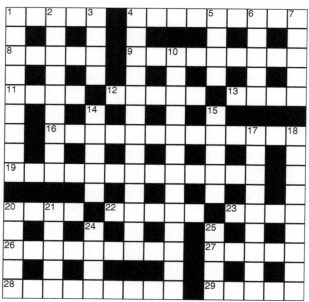

ACROSS

1 County flags (5)
4 Dolly is a girl who never says 'No' (4,5)
8 Sempstress finds it a drain (5)
9 Informed of how the mantelpiece vase came to be broken (6,3)
11 He was belted only when he succeeded (4)
12 Provide entertainment and encouragement for Macduff (3,2)
13 Perform a little movement (4)
16 New cocktail is stirred widdershins (13)
19 Mob of cows kept on village land? (3,6,4)
20 Wise men suggest personalised number plate for Lady Thatcher (4)
22 An exponent providing a list of references (5)
23 Speed at which a boat goes to tie up (4)
26 Model media man has to use a keyboard (9)
27 What a skin diver takes to explore south Caribbean island (5)
28 Diana shouted wildly but worked in the servery (6,3)
29 Scandinavian vegetable (5)

DOWN

1 Faded and jaded (6,3)
2 Small letter let down the legal argument (5,4)
3 Nimble man of intelligence is about right (4)
4 Charm and wealth buys one's way in (8,5)
5 Breaking the code of single-sex education? (4)
6 Norwegian dwarf fish (5)
7 Heavyweight caught in a theft yesterday (5)
10 Part of wedding ceremony which binds 'him' and 'her'? (13)
14 Tried to get a seat unsuccessfully it would seem (5)
15 Made a big hit at the winter sports (5)
17 Documented articles found in plate used for eating (9)
18 Demand food required by changeless bus conductors (5,4)
20 Pined for a low-powered motor cycle (5)
21 Polish comment inserted by editor (5)
24 Part of earth providing carbon and mineral deposit (4)
25 Employs American naval vessel around the East (4)

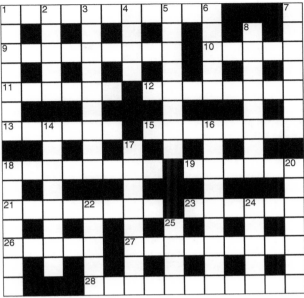

ACROSS

1 Gambler's mistake? (7,4)
9 Curious Nigel finds the fellow is careless (9)
10 Night-shift article (5)
11 A dog is lost? (6)
12 Talk two I arranged about power (8)
13 The choice included being onomatopoeic (6)
15 New fastener for the window (8)
18 First-class pupil (8)
19 Remnant, a discontinued part (6)
21 What the drug addict did added new life (8)
23 One needing help retrospectively for listlessness (6)
26 Shy boy I had trailed (5)
27 Time-honoured practice that can be passed down (9)
28 Prominent figure carrying the Olympic flame (5-6)

DOWN

1 Players get on with dressing (7)
2 Drawn close (5)
3 Not an original take-off (9)
4 In the jungle noticed a narrow valley with a stream (4)
5 Went first round upper room with a network of crossed bars (8)
6 Girl I love and court (5)
7 Target was moved before a race meeting (7)
8 Enormous grotesque carriage leading (8)
14 One might be for it in athletics (4,4)
16 Causing something powerful (9)
17 One finding out what might be activated by smoke (8)
18 Port or sherry? (7)
20 Coach with one shoe? (7)
22 Tom goes round employment department for trainee (5)
24 Rider came unstuck using this machine (5)
25 City club with aspiration (4)

206

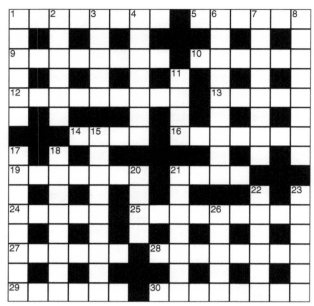

ACROSS

1 Not altogether content about English standard (8)
5 A story a member has to finish (6)
9 Intimidate heart-broken 'X' (8)
10 Sections of the camp without aspiration (6)
12 A note accompanying furniture for the restorer (9)
13 His aim is always to improve the pitch (5)
14 The attitude of fellows receiving one (4)
16 To declare before time can appear mean (7)
19 A dreadful strain for a worker (7)
21 Quick-growing type of grass? (4)
24 Fall off, causing a spill (5)
25 It's drier in Kent (4-5)
27 A little hyperactive rascal medically quietened down (6)
28 What tops sporting by water? (3-5)
29 Such mistakes are holding a sailing man back (6)
30 They'd soon divest people of capital! (8)

DOWN

1 It's a play about sardonic wit (6)
2 Having to recompense outside staff is a travesty (6)
3 Learned Oriental writer (5)
4 Double-dealing, but aren't so bad (7)
6 Foreign princess who could be a choosy woman! (9)
7 A European schoolboy can get round the school-head (8)
8 Complaint of the underworld class (8)
11 Some land is in a really good state of cultivation (4)
15 The revolting individual crookedly ruins a man (9)
17 A little soft thing (8)
18 The person painting in a dotty sort of way (8)
20 Recess for which approval is not to be granted (4)
21 Refund of holiday cash for some travellers abroad (7)
22 Practice, that's what tradesmen want (6)
23 Sound mind—but so near madness (6)
26 He would work inside, being trusted (5)

207

ACROSS

1 Blind poet a big hit in baseball (5)
4 "Turkey on a plate"—an ode to pass over? (8)
10 One who takes stock of others... (7)
11 ...without the capacity to be eminent (7)
12 Short pair always make petition (4)
13 Suspicious if backward and retiring (5)
14 Tarry rope (4)
17 E German partner involved in advance organization (3-11)
19 Trickery of firm putting £500 up front? (6,8)
22 First-class quarter in which to drink a lot (4)
23 Clergyman curtailed the right-hand pages (5)
24 Jetty ripe for reconstruction (4)
27 It can be difficult to prove, the more tricky it is (7)
28 Excitement of Elgar's first movement (7)
29 Faction in Split living there? (8)
30 Ignited high-explosive that is flexible (5)

DOWN

1 Steps taken in following sea-air (8)
2 1000-1 bet could be an error of judgment (7)
3 Annoy one whose easy life is cut short (4)
5 Suffer in the hit-parade? (3,3,8)
6 Disallow tove that gyres? (4)
7 Teases heavyweight with an apple (7)
8 All taken separately, continually over a year (5)
9 Reason dairyman ordered common salt? (8,6)
15 Means to stop an estate-car (5)
16 Compass? A doctor needs it... (5)
18 ...is French compass separate? (8)
20 Harry using work force (7)
21 One involved with titles (only)? (7)
22 Coach tour, perhaps, around head of Thirlmere (5)
25 Guide's first to deliver map-reference (4)
26 Defeat with sword (4)

208

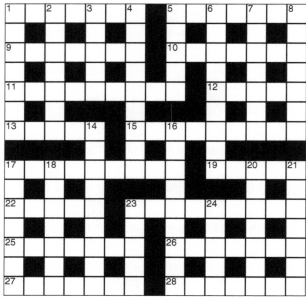

ACROSS

1 Socialist in era of prosperity displays weary indifference (7)
5 Charged a couple of hundred and exploited (7)
9 Anglican in singing ensemble is better selected (7)
10 Agitate to include registered riding accessory (7)
11 Put back in office to curb civil government (9)
12 The common man's knucklebones (5)
13 Mother Augusta and the Sorcerer (5)
15 Tell how to roast suckling pig alfresco (4,2,3)
17 Performed in a musical group without inhibitions (9)
19 More loyal trustee filled with regret (5)
22 One of the greens must look at tax (5)
23 Stripped down? Anything but! (7,2)
25 A born saint resolved not to imbibe (7)
26 Locals separated by a road need guts (7)
27 In taking industrial action he's forward (7)
28 Typical example of the first Epistle, in my view (7)

DOWN

1 Material and butter under a dollar (7)
2 Getting plants established is cheering (7)
3 Love, love, love (5)
4 Isn't moral disintegration the result of it? (6,3)
5 A detachment mainly found in church (5)
6 It charges exorbitantly to trim a piece of meat (4-5)
7 Baronet confronting two senior officers gets the wind up (7)
8 Store silicon in a warehouse (7)
14 Divert team to the racecourse (9)
16 Diet menu I produced at the appropriate moment (2,3,4)
17 Eager to learn how Midas felt when turned into an ass? (3,4)
18 One who recommends making a commercial sun-screen (7)
20 Submit oneself to one drug treatment (7)
21 Outwardly mature East German makes a come-back (7)
23 He gives a party, but has no right (5)
24 A Muslim given backing in student body (5)

209

209

ACROSS

5 Address for delivery? (6)
8 Rehearsal for a ventriloquist (5,3)
9 Mother's in the outhouse, drunk! (7)
10 Determined to fight (3-2)
11 Results of changes at the farm (9)
13 A lovable disposition may be most important (5,3)
14 Take on work (6)
17 A small whisky for severe cold (3)
19 Fuss made by a dog losing its tail (3)
20 Dim sun, when out, will hardly encourage it! (6)
23 Guard sent to breached line (8)
26 A harvest on new soil in ancient Greece (9)
28 Praises the upper house in speech (5)
29 It can be made to display china (7)
30 Angry about dress getting wet (8)
31 Escape of fifty during battle (6)

DOWN

1 Lines up a ship in port (6)
2 No one book could raise this feeling (7)
3 Definitely not many bones broken (2,2,5)
4 Common sort of friend Dickens wrote about (6)
5 Immersed, cooked and gently boiled (8)
6 Course involving the translation of poems (5)
7 The making of Haydn's oratorio (8)
12 Travel the smart way (3)
15 People in serious offence (6,3)
16 A local tour (3,5)
18 Swirling mist hides the way forward (8)
21 Footnote one added to letter from Greece (3)
22 "Bony" ran Gaul in style (7)
24 Company car (6)
25 He is taken in by a girl—who fluttered them? (6)
27 Outstanding result of love taking wing (5)

210

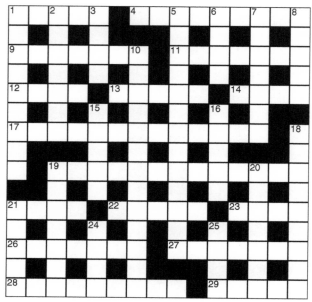

ACROSS

1 Take notice, but don't retire (3,2)
4 A visit to the pub which is not a long distance (5,4)
9 American deer going to Virginia make tracks (7)
11 Joined with crowd having gone first to old Chinese rulers (7)
12 Sail back to the Jurassic rock (4)
13 Post Christian chap needs a publicity agent (5)
14 New star returns for current run in Stratford (4)
17 Rule frequently leading to mistake in revolutionary France (5,2,6)
19 Be careful to guard your threshold (5,4,4)
21 Fought, so it is said, to get the stronghold (4)
22 Mass of people welcome temperature forecast for Wessex area (5)
23 Very little can with yttrium (4)
26 No heart broken woman sought by wayward husband (7)
27 Short cut along the beach (7)
28 Feverish rash (3,6)
29 Island upset by fellow finding ancient Phoenician city (5)

DOWN

1 It suits Londoners to have a wicked argument after Sunday (6,3)
2 Drums of scattered paint in which I'm immersed (7)
3 Arab insurgents need time to plan (4)
5 Infant Communist becomes a fellow fighter (7,2,4)
6 Come down to earth (4)
7 Finished the steeplechase without any mishaps (3,4)
8 How the full cargo ship left a Yemeni port (5)
10 Doomsday for one of the Poles? (3,2,3,5)
15 One an only goal of ecumenicism (5)
16 Get up wage demand (5)
18 Jolly miserly but gratifying compromise (5,4)
19 Find the answer to a spell in the gym (4,3)
20 Caught on, like a burgeoning sapling (7)
21 Ostentatious arm patch (5)
24 Once you name the first letter of 10 (4)
25 Voice contempt for American atom spy (4)

ACROSS

1 With pioneering ideas beating the clock? (6,4,4)
9 Doctor taken in by girl on African xylophone (7)
10 Stanley accepts equality, being very strict (7)
11 It's a foreign wine (4)
12 Despicable person has low-priced fish (10)
14 In part undrained treeless zone (6)
15 He included, after lunch time, two beginners and Sidney on the slope (8)
17 Hat, it could have been placed on a Scotsman, an islander (8)
18 Explosive noises about demand for political union (6)
21 I name an inquiry that's under consideration (2,8)
22 Shed a tear (4)
24 Unpack, but have nothing to write while away from home (4,3)
25 Fictional school subject? (7)
26 It's a job not to be working for someone else (4-10)

DOWN

1 Brag about physician in inflated luggage (7)
2 Front liner (5,2,3,5)
3 It isn't steep, pram can make it (4)
4 In the manor, a chewy vegetable (6)
5 London area still in a state of rapture (8)
6 It has been given to one with a change of heart (10)
7 Reciprocal contract in which policyholders are shareholders (6,9)
8 After inspiration suddenly expire (6)
13 Had sent an order in the post that had been cancelled (7-3)
16 Handyman, fellow to perform outside with hesitation (8)
17 One suitably employed? (6)
19 Is it wise, having removed panties? (7)
20 Unendingly seek information from a foreign agent (6)
23 Neat sum to fine a litter lout? (4)

212

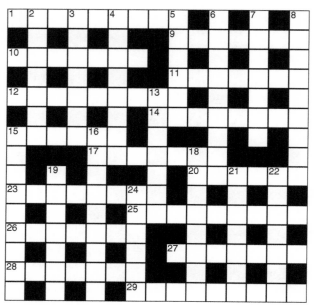

ACROSS

1 The collection of curios may appear barbaric to many (9)
9 A failing to accept a never-ending greed (7)
10 The grassland beyond the river (7)
11 A little support accorded to a fellow creature (7)
12 Great painting? Far from it! (9)
14 Compromise to cut short acrimony (8)
15 Material to northern school (6)
17 Old soldier opposing neater arrangement (7)
20 A key is left also (6)
23 The retiring person wants lustreless hair! (8)
25 A top man's sound tribute to the dead (9)
26 The current turbulence exercises one in dire trouble (7)
27 Cricketer presenting 10 to the queen (7)
28 The woman in the star role is restricted (7)
29 Tan with a dress specially made for the beach (3-6)

DOWN

2 Capitalise on savvy (7)
3 Cash in the kitty growing? (7)
4 A singer, a Brit, unhappily single (8)
5 A number get ready to do battle in French opera (6)
6 Keeps writing about a tin in a different way (9)
7 Gathering for pressing reasons (7)
8 Prepared to play (9)
13 Free service given with rent (7)
15 A girl more affected by long-winded talk (9)
16 Viewing to excess is a mistake (9)
18 A Scottish town (small) eliminates dampness naturally (3-5)
19 Makeshift draught-excluder? (4-3)
21 There's money in refuse—but less of it (7)
22 A woman full of enthusiasm for cotton fabric (7)
24 A ship must carry a great many pieces of pottery (6)

213

1 Ancient length of copper piece (5)
4 Beach-jumper that irritates the skin? (4-4)
10 Bird given drink at end of garden (7)
11 Liberal spoke to admit Conservative (7)
12 Set down on terra firma (4)
13 Athenian doctor in the money, commonly (5)
14 Midnight quarrel to develop (4)
17 Good word or term no comedian used? (14)
19 Treatment currently given to the bad (14)
22 Tennis in parks (4)
23 Racecourse tax after the first of August (5)
24 Beware of schoolboys in grotto! (4)
27 On father's head be it! (7)
28 FND announced as educated man (7)
29 Greta Lee thrown out, put in lower class (8)
30 Carried out, having played? (5)

DOWN

1 These drinks are working at last! (8)
2 New action to support British gardens of this kind (7)
3 Huntsman returning with pelt (4)
5 Inspiration-aid for song arranger? (3-11)
6 Bird dead, with no tail? You can say that again! (4)
7 Swiss resort packed, we hear (7)
8 Authorize everybody to ring women (5)
9 Something to cheer up suffering patients instead? (14)
15 Small-sized dummy displaying blouse (5)
16 Excessive soak (5)
18 But this Australian flier should not be plucked (4-4)
20 Dull part of elite rally (7)
21 Con brings a profit on street (7)
22 Drab robes embroidered (5)
25 Sunday, day in Germany set aside for men (4)
26 Dyke-builder's tender announced (4)

214

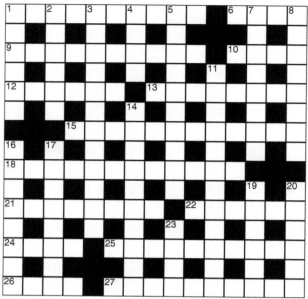

ACROSS

1 Male nanny and market gardener (10)
6 Nothing should be added to a blue dye (4)
9 Little time to produce a few charming words (5,5)
10 Convict returns to a celebration (4)
12 Repugnant swindle over promissory notes (6)
13 President establishes many links around Sandhurst (8)
15 Striking example of the stripper's aim? (6-6)
18 Central heating has a social function (5-7)
21 Prelate of sensual nature holds back primitive instincts (8)
22 Rip off a woollen coat (6)
24 Fail to award honour to Italian (4)
25 Child's paper has five Irish limericks, perhaps (5,5)
26 Flavour which can be put into a stock (4)
27 Printer should be kind to author (10)

DOWN

1 Wise old Greek provides home for fledgling soldiers (6)
2 Castle that is constructed by new recruit (6)
3 To show repentance, consume only modest fare (3,6,3)
4 Talks complainingly of small salary rise (4)
5 A little hem needs repair constantly (3,3,4)
7 Lucky escape from a parsimonious young lady (4,4)
8 Taking home under a pound in one's apprenticeship (8)
11 Luxuriate when about to be embraced by resident boyfriend (4,2,6)
14 Graduate fed-up with a right-winger being vituperative (10)
16 Leave one's pension by the supermarket counter (8)
17 One in charge of a minor paper (8)
19 Ruth and Rex pursued by a heron (6)
20 Facade displayed by archdeacon perpetually (6)
23 Rabbi least likely to harbour ill-humour (4)

215

ACROSS

1 They have suffered from offhand relationships (10)
9 Turns up with a mother cat (4)
10 Point to one duke or another (10)
11 Demonstrate an early form of motion (6)
12 Horsemen surround a group of attackers (7)
15 Fruit and nut, alas, all mixed up together (7)
16 Was off for the rest of the night (5)
17 One effect of gravity on a monkey is to yawn (4)
18 Agreed, but not about being old (4)
19 Animals in spasm is dangerous (5)
21 A piece of current conflict (4-3)
22 Bitterness associated with an age old craft (7)
24 Quick, the doctor's in the river! (6)
27 Their union offers security (4,3,3)
28 Settle in the country (4)
29 Going for acquittal (7,3)

DOWN

2 A point we take up, once more (4)
3 Take articles from a magazine? (6)
4 Dance for soldiers and surgeons (7)
5 One gets no thanks for this small item (4)
6 Fresh suet not exported (4,3)
7 Prison dispute heard in the exercise area? (10)
8 Manager we'd ordered to run the wild life reserve (10)
12 Corner at 90 (5,5)
13 I'm in prison without money, that's the snag (10)
14 Boat causes waters to rise (5)
15 Shoot for almost the whole season (5)
19 Get mail, perhaps, but not without delay (4-3)
20 Settle out of doors with fresh air and a drink (7)
23 Pet greyhound? (3-3)
25 Short way round company tax (4)
26 When the buzzer gets loud, complain (4)

216

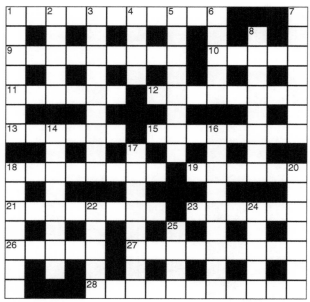

ACROSS

1 Brought into bright focus with a beacon (11)
9 A brainy subject (9)
10 He leads you and me to the woman (5)
11 It may finish up in the soup if oil tax is renewed (6)
12 A papist contracted nettle rash in the muniment room (8)
13 Gully where Rex is caught by a ruffian (6)
15 OED written in code (8)
18 Soft-soled shoes for climbers (8)
19 Method of surveying sports grounds (6)
21 Umpire employing phrase "Not out" in answer to appeal (8)
23 Manage to get the feel of things (6)
26 Gunners retreating before skirmish get an old projectile... (5)
27 ...straight from a barrel (2,7)
28 Submitted to wages being paid on demobilisation (8,3)

DOWN

1 Live only to put the laundry to dry (4,3)
2 Bony and emaciated son of Edward III (5)
3 Referring to a reference book for astronomical observation (7,2)
4 Harp for a character like Harpo? (2,2)
5 Ain't Tory disposed to be a little loco? (3,5)
6 Bread ought to include it (5)
7 Read by Scottish Education Dept attached to S American state (7)
8 Shattered by the cold presumably (8)
14 Start blazing away—that's what one hopes it will do (4,4)
16 Strike and demonstrate for a record programme (3,6)
17 Effect caused by a follower with hang up (5,3)
18 Litigation applied to auto body (7)
20 Design art Lely presented with eyes wide open (7)
22 We'd support it even though all cut up (5)
24 Find how to eradicate weeds (3,2)
25 German flower with a pronounced fragrance (4)

217

ACROSS

1 Sneak giving indication that it is an obvious clue (4-4,4)
8 Aspiration to have a woody area as shelter (7)
9 One complains with anger or excitement (7)
11 Movement of cattle is unexpected on Sunday (7)
12 It may be for each hasp has been replaced (7)
13 It is used to season in season, so it is said (5)
14 Carry out a tool (9)
16 Record symbolised said registration (9)
19 Landed outside motorway boundary (5)
21 Set of rules in the finish was put into a less clear form (7)
23 Naive young woman smashes engine about the middle of January (7)
24 Motoring in this rain? (7)
25 Moved not by a Brazilian city but a lake (7)
26 Powerful man finds his way in the capital (6,6)

DOWN

1 A terrible reign? (7)
2 Views making a brief inspection (4-3)
3 Roundabout way to gain admission (9)
4 Assistance for dog at lamppost (3-2)
5 Second commander to drive a whip (7)
6 One in France weak during strong wind on the side of the ship (7)
7 Give no indication (5,3,4)
10 Achieved a blooming high ambition! (4,2,3,3)
15 Sounds an insignificant garment for a girl to wear (9)
17 Rest from another liner are going round the market (7)
18 Wrecker having diluted concoction (7)
19 Will left it for his benefit (7)
20 Encountered rain-storm whilst in the tower (7)
22 Appreciate something on foot (5)

218

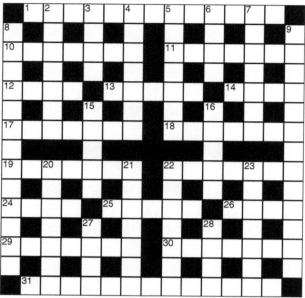

ACROSS

1 Possibly ten lads reforming encourage this professional person (6,7)
10 Jumpers for agricultural workers in the Southeast? (7)
11 Flap when grabbed by a foreigner—may be drunk (7)
12 Want heartless nurse and top journalist to get together (4)
13 Provisions made by the directors (5)
14 Stupid comeback causing shock (4)
17 Examine an assortment of pins etc (7)
18 Plant everything in turn (7)
19 Glare as key is demanded by youngsters (7)
22 Leaf-insect display (7)
24 Felt wrong, not right (4)
25 Flower trade improvement—there's money in it (5)
26 The man in management had ambition (4)
29 Moral support (7)
30 Pain-killing tablets one may take in pairs (7)
31 Read coming down—so pretentious (13)

DOWN

2 Quick to get out of a jam (7)
3 The direction to be taken next (4)
4 The French drink—and survive! (4,3)
5 Judges a member with some ill-feeling in America (7)
6 Sports spectators could well be barred (4)
7 Going round to take part in viva voce examination (7)
8 Speaking one's mind? (8,5)
9 Bringing back control, say, reportedly proposed (13)
15 A fight to get going (3,2)
16 The trainee on an old ship appears slow (5)
20 Draw a small number for the hell of it (7)
21 Tells some soldiers garbled tales (7)
22 Proof the head will have to steal in (7)
23 Too smooth for a firedog (7)
27 For example a small daughter's mild oath (4)
28 Did like to see the result of exercise in a large figure (4)

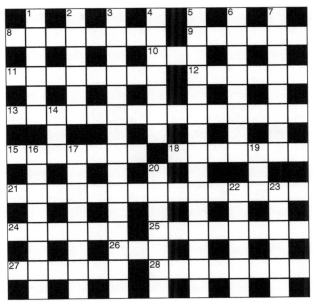

ACROSS

8 Greeting a double feature? (4-4)
9 Summary not entirely accurate (6)
10 Secure hamper (3)
11 Somehow saving energy at both ends? Fancy! (8)
12 Observe, no square diamonds! (6)
13 Threat of budding wild garden (9,6)
15 "Wary" clue far-out? (7)
18 National side on the ball in America (7)
21 The birds director, we hear—old king taking trouble with rooster (6,9)
24 Employed pole outside, being stirred up (6)
25 Stable part of unattached wood (5-3)
26 Sentimentality almost acceptable? (3)
27 Took meal at tavern—that's natural (6)
28 Eskimo in a boat, perhaps, is at once in trouble (8)

DOWN

1 This religion thins out approaching occident, initially (6)
2 Salad plant from garden, diverted (6)
3 Dip into "The Dartford Glue Mystery"? (3,6,6)
4 England's openers later trouble is intestinal (7)
5 Gave new business to bank, began a story (6,2,7)
6 Guard transported on new line (8)
7 Do they abandon farmworkers? (8)
14 Hill of tipped rubbish (3)
16 Nothing lost, presumably, in such a price (3-5)
17 Japanese polish, you could say, is one (8)
19 I would contract nothing in artificial language (3)
20 Pipe-bubble? Look close! (7)
22 Bright opening of cocktail-bar (6)
23 Company shoe design is select (6)

220

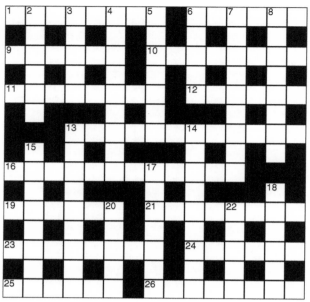

ACROSS

1 Hesitating to acknowledge one's marital status (8)
6 Remember to phone again (6)
9 Circle of light from a long cigar (6)
10 Where to find vehicles in transit (2,3,3)
11 Succeed in taking one's leave (8)
12 Say the same thing about an organic fertiliser (6)
13 Incorruptible Irish MEP uncommonly competent (12)
16 Bob chases Chinese bird (8,4)
19 Girl brings mother French salt (6)
21 Begin to attack (3,5)
23 Keeper to a monarch of riper years (8)
24 Smuggled Benedictine is always chancy (6)
25 Crazy painters take Indian port (6)
26 Keep one's head above water when it's no longer rising (4,4)

DOWN

2 Morning examination revealing total lack of standards (6)
3 Wear a bolero decorated inside (5)
4 Angry inmate distressed childless person (2,1,6)
5 Dog carriage (7)
6 Moving arm up and down (5)
7 Shoddy fellow clutching small English flag (9)
8 Fields able to be rented out (8)
13 Remedying dire pains is hopeless (2,7)
14 Speak in an outbuilding with covered windows (9)
15 A rail and cab link newly established in Italy (8)
17 The smell of sodium is beginning to rise (7)
18 Calcium deposit on mineral causes an outcry (6)
20 Coin for many a French king (5)
22 Crosby gains nothing from a gambling game (5)

221

ACROSS

7 Lengthens "The Lone Ranger" stage version (9)
8 Was first, for instance, to be drawn into Prohibition (5)
10 Meets and makes an impact on (4,4)
11 Stops and sees that everything's all right (6)
12 With open wounds, has internal injuries (4)
13 Standing for the president to greet, is infirm (8)
15 A travesty of a soft drink, based on tea? (7)
17 Some bars don't (7)
20 Make his curl and wave (8)
22 A second indication of one's satisfaction (4)
25 The divider is for show (6)
26 Thinks bees, perhaps, live in it (8)
27 Had looked about five, though older (5)
28 Rushed like crazy—the sea was going out (4,5)

DOWN

1 "Not vetoed," you say for all to hear (5)
2 In agreement with one over the child (6)
3 The servant, Nora, has fallen in a big way (4,4)
4 In a super manoeuvre the firm makes good its losses (7)
5 A gun for the teller (8)
6 As the patient is in hospital with the same old slipped disc? (4,5)
9 Be eager to get into a first-class hotel (4)
14 A kind letter (9)
16 Translated and gave to (8)
18 For once, rang and said something nice about (8)
19 A Teddy Girl? (3-4)
21 Island that's no good to hide up in (4)
23 Certain I missed out Greek (6)
24 The nippers understand that half (5)

222

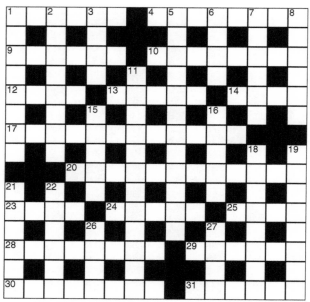

ACROSS

1 Knock back pill if you want a boost (6)
4 A single weapon kept by a reliable man (4,4)
9 Instruction for saving electricity (6)
10 In high glee because Euro group is making no progress (8)
12 Sort letters (4)
13 Frequently decimal (5)
14 Part of Pakistan's India (4)
17 What fed-up depositor did when penalised for early withdrawal (4,8)
20 Triplets essential to a full house (5,2,1,4)
23 Why beef-eaters cheer Oxfordshire? (4)
24 Odd number which minus one would be even (5)
25 Wave on a pool (4)
28 Cheat everyone but gamble away every penny (2,3,3)
29 Fail at bridge and sink (2,4)
30 Reserve as back up with army team (3,5)
31 Beer and lemonade for Tristram (6)

DOWN

1 Leaning over as far as one can go at top speed (4,4)
2 Military call to retire from previous job (4,4)
3 Press refugee organisation to take an indefinite number (4)
5 A source of current international threat (7,5)
6 It is found in south-eastern location (4)
7 Not in healthy clothing (6)
8 Wintry poem put in clear language (6)
11 Unattributed reason for stylus failing to pick up the music (3,3,6)
15 Diana is over timorous but very good looking (5)
16 Before morning a steamship reaches North India (5)
18 Occupy basement flat to overcome a scandal (4,4)
19 Change from outlandish currency (3,5)
21 Delay caused by armed robbery (4,2)
22 Walk all the way to pay the bill (4,2)
26 Islands small enough to fit into locks (4)
27 Sufficeth for hall of 28 (4)

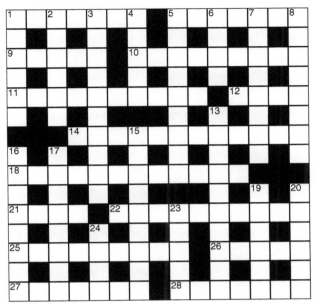

223

ACROSS

1 Flower spends a short time in the river (7)
5 Police department involved in transaction that had been settled (7)
9 Put up an objection about the Italian (5)
10 Occasionally I seem most upset (9)
11 Removing cover, one from Paris Heather had protecting hand-warmer (10)
12 Legal right of heartless doorkeeper (4)
14 Current fault that might appeal to tired racing drivers (5-7)
18 Woolly-headed embarrassment? (12)
21 Tallyman tentatively included the stake (4)
22 Spoke about one spirit that had come into existence (10)
25 One existing by the water in the city (9)
26 Just over four weeks with gold furnishings (5)
27 Heavenly cast? (3-4)
28 Give money to the boy holding none of the cargo (3-4)

DOWN

1 Henry leaves port for a shady place (6)
2 Variations in game! (6)
3 Not in good form (3,2,5)
4 Stand in the drawing-room (5)
5 Caribbean friar? (9)
6 Large town, it is within the county limits (4)
7 So copper's found under the embankment in Syria (8)
8 Girl's going over island that's consisting of distinct parts (8)
13 Current birthday? (7-3)
15 River rose turbulently and formed a lake (9)
16 One's post, first-class, brought up from Egyptian city (8)
17 Last five going to the feast (8)
19 Divides up firm plaster (6)
20 Loved to have a colourful party inside (6)
23 Georgia bound for the most part to have a dance (5)
24 Pine wood? (4)

224

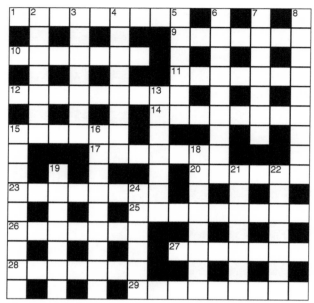

ACROSS

1 Taken to mean ten possibly will get compensation (9)
9 "Night owls!" they jeer (7)
10 Drug company accountant—popular Oriental (7)
11 A coin is not usually represented as capital (7)
12 Opening a French bistro with a small band (9)
14 Kiss the copper—none find cause to complain about that (8)
15 Observe some military men make an impression (6)
17 Diversifying is a real essential for viewers (7)
20 See about reversing ill feeling in a most odd way (6)
23 State for/against in church (8)
25 A fellow embracing a girl—one must make allowance (9)
26 Not a hearty eater, though she doesn't keep to a strict diet (7)
27 A woman's struggle to swallow a drink mid-afternoon (7)
28 Slips away—pleases constituents (7)
29 A number watched without anything happening (9)

DOWN

2 Counter-productive defeat (7)
3 Falls back repeatedly on the big guns (7)
4 Plant a large number with a tool designed for gardeners (8)
5 Objects—makes some scathing suggestions (6)
6 Meeting, though opposed to proceeding (9)
7 Sacking a man with some craft in a reorganisation (7)
8 Shady male reforming in conscience-stricken fashion (9)
13 Not frigid, so gets paid attention (7)
15 Note a point to consider and he'll find an answer (9)
16 Sending up tiptop car, heel appears prejudiced (9)
18 Old patriarch going to an art gallery to get a lift (8)
19 As to support, hold back (7)
21 Think much of detail (7)
22 Beastly row—about time! (7)
24 Demonstration of affection troubles the skinhead (6)

225

ACROSS

1 Girl who has to cut everything back (8)
9 Hat-maker upset when embraced by a pitman (8)
10 Nick with spur? (4)
11 Decide Thames position for a house (4-8)
13 Calf sore, injured in the open air... (8)
15 ...it could be tender in Spain (6)
16 Lines addressed to queen, flower of Europe? (4)
17 Show on board (5)
18 Rush of blood? (4)
20 Protein-catalyst in a frenzy, medically speaking (6)
21 Wealthy elderly ladies' parties include a risk (8)
23 Wistfulness of domestic trouble? (12)
26 Easy pace of David Copperfield (4)
27 How many to the dozen in fast delivery? (8)
28 Ready-to-wear? (8)

DOWN

2 Sold as cured farmhouse mice? (8)
3 Cursory, for example, like Simple Simon (7,5)
4 This paper may be read, we hear, in the laboratory (6)
5 Wanton maid in the middle of things (4)
6 Does one have a big bill, having let out the clutch? (8)
7 Elected church-leaders move cautiously (4)
8 Mark off to become a qualified student (8)
12 Tries charges out—that's what takes the money (4,8)
14 Mountain nymph takes Scandinavian money these days (5)
16 Beetle ended on deck (8)
17 Entry into account by editor is accepted as true (8)
19 New car—or wreck, showing signs of stress (8)
22 A cotton-picking nuisance! (6)
24 Reason to disapprove (4)
25 County no longer known (4)

226

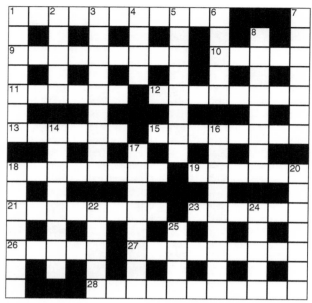

ACROSS

1 Surroundings in which Mr Doonican has mixed feelings (11)
9 Instruct class to get a requisition (5-4)
10 Treatment which puts years on you and me (5)
11 Prime time to make hay, by the sound of it (6)
12 Make way for pets (4,4)
13 To fix things up, change partners (6)
15 To increase pressure makes a market speculator sad (4,4)
18 Omit to mention having made a velouté (5,3)
19 Putting suet in pudding binds together (6)
21 Repertory company on tour is rejected (4,4)
23 Minor details right about one Roman road (6)
26 Charming little piece of self-indulgence (5)
27 I am beaten and held in custody (9)
28 Admonished for wearing informal clothing (7,4)

DOWN

1 A negative woman is quite different (7)
2 A good friend to Holly (5)
3 Articulate lines about an Indonesian isle (9)
4 Card game played quietly in a circle (4)
5 To gossip about civic honour is perfectly OK (2,6)
6 Supply piqué to order (5)
7 Administer discipline for burglary (5-2)
8 Georgia lawyer fit only to be a social butterfly (8)
14 Fiddle with a strongbox, but be very careful (4,4)
16 Manage to get a canon to chase to and fro (3,6)
17 Simple cleric without time for tea (8)
18 Caerphilly cheese stuffed with Chinese fruit (7)
20 Dan isn't suited to be a locum (5-2)
22 A week before Edward appeared with a beard (5)
24 See nothing but a recorder (5)
25 RAF officer returns to the States for work (4)

227

ACROSS

1 Fouled player retaliated (6,4)
6 Third man sounds competent enough (4)
9 Act the liar in a dramatic way (10)
10 A step up the ladder (4)
13 They're used to lift—or bring down (7)
15 There are doubts associated with this name (6)
16 It's best drunk or put in a sweet (6)
17 Two tools for a pound (6,3,6)
18 Brave father set back with pain (6)
20 A wool-gatherer perhaps (6)
21 Seat of Empire (7)
22 Awkward situation a golfer tries to get into (4)
25 Sets up organisations for education and research (10)
26 Bring down, strange though it may sound (4)
27 It shows the running total when a number embark (10)

DOWN

1 Take out a girl—a bit of a shrew? (4)
2 A short cut for sailors (4)
3 Ex-star replaced in crowd scenes (6)
4 Materials, of course (6,3,6)
5 Encourages firms that are about to make drastic cuts (6)
7 It's sad but courage is needed as a policeman (10)
8 Stevedores who don't carry as much weight as others? (10)
11 He's second mate, from a child's point of view (10)
12 Studies lists for the police (10)
13 Agree to start home without me calling in pursuit (5-2)
14 King of the sun and the new moon (7)
19 Racial description Elizabeth Nicholson takes to heart (6)
20 Worker goes in taxi from Cambridge (6)
23 Tourists see it in Sicily before rising (4)
24 Went under American name (4)

228

ACROSS

7 Encouraging cry to parched desert traveller from far in front (4,5)
8 Doctrine expressed by proven bitch (5)
10 Sounds as though it's not there. Not there to express approval (4,4)
11 It is said to be cold enough for making a hot meal (6)
12 Move cautiously to the border (4)
13 Repeal law which incarcerates monk in stone (8)
15 Notwithstanding a sandbank in the Solway river (7)
17 Walks or staggers past the street (7)
20 Take to the hustings to air your views forcibly (5,3)
22 Dance held by anglers (4)
25 A loose box maybe but it is quite steady (6)
26 Bankrupt to make a fast exit (5,3)
27 Too glib an explanation for oil pollution in the main (5)
28 Start dealing with anything you can palm off? (3,2,4)

DOWN

1 Hebrew gets Spanish article cut by lapidary (5)
2 The wide skirt was apparently not flame-proof (6)
3 Stop advising on how to preserve sour milk (6,2)
4 It is quite some distance between tee and putting green (7)
5 Arriving at a state of consciousness (6,2)
6 A little conversation leads to gossip (5,4)
9 Maple is a provider of unreturnable service (4)
14 Stay put and maybe bottle up your independent spirit (4,5)
16 Repeat record—against well-pitched up fast bowling? (4,4)
18 Gave up and went to bed (6,2)
19 Was proud—and still is apparently (5,2)
21 Ring up red banker on the Polish border (4)
23 Uninhibited and of hearty disposition (6)
24 Local American turns Muslim (5)

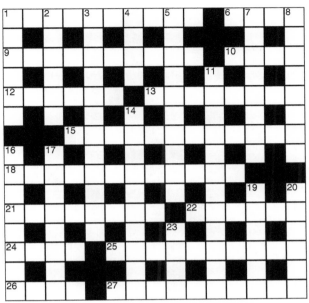

229

ACROSS

1 Wind instrument (10)
6 One in weak condition who is homeless (4)
9 It makes a change to study the translation (10)
10 Express grief over the law I broke (4)
12 Six-footer at school (6)
13 Twice as expensive, what a pity (4,4)
15 Religious song first by a medium (12)
18 Military man, a policeman in paid employment (5-7)
21 This year's wild uncontrollable excitement (8)
22 Starry artist found in the last resort (6)
24 River port unfinished (4)
25 Does he not enjoy night vision? (10)
26 Some popular kind of singer (4)
27 Sinking arrangement (10)

DOWN

1 Lorry that's cold inside—extremely cold (6)
2 Solemn-sounding fellow (6)
3 What appeals in the afternoon (4,3,2,3)
4 Formerly in another state (4)
5 Self-centred, say, with no money before one in church (10)
7 Of no practical significance to a don (8)
8 Runny tar I left to leak out (8)
11 Cause a commotion on stage? (6,1,5)
14 For 50 initially with 51 at the entrance are recklessly extravagant (10)
16 Lily's new shop deal (8)
17 Ignore the festival (8)
19 Weight of sheep held by Meg struggling! (6)
20 Girl has time for a drink (6)
23 An entrance of mine (4)

230

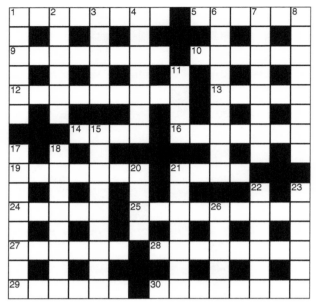

ACROSS

1 Grounds for changing men's diet (8)
5 Having written a note, break loose (6)
9 Put off by article about rest, scoffed (8)
10 Learners turning in error (4-2)
12 A policeman shows many over the horses' accommodation (9)
13 Doesn't concentrate on work, so is led astray (5)
14 The accountant backing the man will get hurt (4)
16 The politician may find a quarter are not affected (7)
19 Phone after a party, being a devoted admirer (7)
21 Proper contact (4)
24 A bird watcher, one gathers, must carry it (5)
25 Loathe serving mob in a tea-break (9)
27 Run to raise money and totter (6)
28 Charming rustic about fifty (8)
29 Concerned with the first lady's stewards (6)
30 A way to travel cheaply—always within a certain period (8)

DOWN

1 Panic about the cold if it's exceptional (6)
2 Sees fit and sound Europeans (6)
3 The artist met no models (5)
4 Ineffective as a VIP (7)
6 Trifling figure to a syndicate (9)
7 Having to lie maybe after trouble-maker is rude (8)
8 Attempt to contain a nuisance—that's material (8)
11 The French vessel is smaller (4)
15 Patrons of the establishment holding the right permit up (9)
17 Single music-man with backing role (8)
18 Griped or agitated in prison (8)
20 Not all big ladies are happy (4)
21 Illuminated at night— naturally (7)
22 Where a qualified individual accepts a bet (6)
23 Soft bait for the angler (6)
26 The first person to deserve being put out (5)

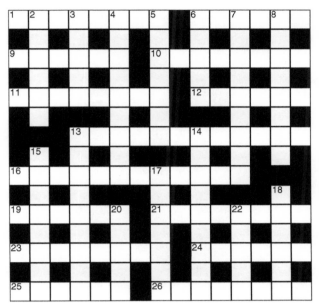

231

ACROSS

1 Title given to William's last book? (8)
6 Elgin's charge for an alley (6)
9 Shops for husbands? (6)
10 Slow, for example, to indicate on the way (4,4)
11 With its snare set, it needs two beaters (4-4)
12 Set features that are dangerous? (6)
13 One uses craft for cases (6,6)
16 They provide shock treatment (12)
19 Musician for each ballad included (6)
21 Glowing passion turning sour? (8)
23 Lighting up the car? (8)
24 Overcoat's unusual lustre (6)
25 Accent can bring anxiety (6)
26 Once red tongue of schoolboy swallowing last of cherries? (8)

DOWN

2 Lower, inferior batsmen in the soup (6)
3 Way of sending messages further round sun (5)
4 Ship-breaker? (9)
5 Metropolitan bobby not under cover as rail-worker? (7)
6 Intends wealth... (5)
7 ...in respect of Crusoe's exchanged capital (9)
8 Embassy has long tea-break about one (8)
13 The year of the pistol? (5-4)
14 Formal attire in which to treat hearts, say (5-4)
15 Victorian brilliance of Georgia Small? (8)
17 Quiet please for the rest of Hamlet! (7)
18 Bath's overspill produced this outcry (6)
20 Headless bears— features of Pompeii, for instance (5)
22 What makes bowing easier for 19 (5)

232

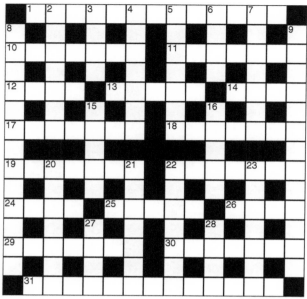

ACROSS

1 Shop has soft grain for next to nothing (4-4,5)
10 Post requiring erudition (7)
11 To render an account is no longer simple (7)
12 American pull (4)
13 Within 24 hours theologian will become a father (5)
14 Female pursued with fury and passion (4)
17 Not only after is it notedly slow (7)
18 Making an assault—on house modernisation (5,2)
19 Record a retired medic has to throw out (7)
22 Cleaner sea in France. That's wizard (7)
24 Eyes symbols of royal power (4)
25 Brief, but most important (5)
26 Small island returned to you (4)
29 Transport for alien to be arranged (7)
30 Herb adds nothing to orange squash (7)
31 Conversion following Dr Barnard's ministrations (6,2,5)

DOWN

2 Recited where the car that hit Edward went (7)
3 In Kiev entertainment is constant (4)
4 Loss incurred by Washington theatre (7)
5 Bore admitted defeat (7)
6 Cole—a king to copy (4)
7 Note wild desire (7)
8 Feign indifference if the drama is out of print (4,4,2,3)
9 Disorderly person I detain as a last resort (2,11)
15 A continental drinking place is open (5)
16 Essential to place teaspoon in medicine bottle (5)
20 Day when alumni return to southern university (7)
21 Make someone enraged (7)
22 Happen to fall (4,3)
23 Late spring is sunny in London (7)
27 Right to take a siesta before noon (4)
28 Present ambassador is full of hesitation (4)

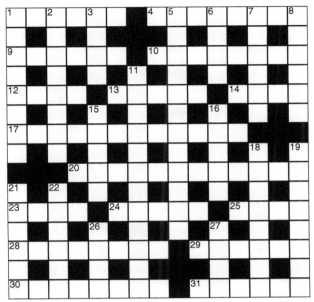

233

ACROSS

1 I'm lacking lustre in run through (6)
4 Single reed blown in the wind (8)
9 Used an odd dessert dish (6)
10 Not knowing what to believe and acting so strangely (8)
12 Study a book about publicity (4)
13 The car that creates records (5)
14 A mad race to get land (4)
17 Statement the cane's able to make (7,5)
20 Rising from the ranks? (12)
23 Will him to succeed (4)
24 Is about to compete for evergreen plants (5)
25 Monster note in Scandinavian currency (4)
28 Definite sign of an increase (8)
29 Point has a need to be put differently (6)
30 Hen, perhaps, spotted beetle (8)
31 Run out on the sand (6)

DOWN

1 Write letters in bed in quarters (8)
2 Magic Circle star? (8)
3 Idle, like many an awkward lout (4)
5 The price of a suit? (5,7)
6 Area said to be uncultivated (4)
7 It's possibly nice to see (6)
8 Untidy kit etc leads to army discharge (6)
11 The last fish in the sea (4,8)
15 Silly Annie gets confused (5)
16 Give instruction to companion after a meal (5)
18 A doctor might mix a gin in the medicine (8)
19 Profit from hobby (8)
21 Man goes over the Spanish place of worship (6)
22 Lady journalist not caught out (6)
26 Cut nuts up (4)
27 Measure for fitting, say? (4)

234

ACROSS

6 Swagger cane—the top brass (8,5)
8 Little Mo (6)
9 Like to hide by field beside the railway (8)
10 Airline serving double Scotch? (3)
11 Full scale autumn hail (6)
12 Dallied with girl wearing cosmetics and too outspoken (4,2,2)
14 Primitive pot-holer (7)
16 Plaid is popular as sign at hotel (5,2)
20 Cabaret turn an adept can adopt (3,5)
23 A comic star turn which is right up to date (4,2)
24 A bit of a twit in glasses (3)
25 Walker gets an American push-chair (8)
26 What the dishonest landlady did to guests (4,2)
27 Check a horse groom buttonhole for new life (13)

DOWN

1 Get on to Illinois America and abuse (3,5)
2 Greek letter about Crete settlement and so forth (2,6)
3 Roman candle giving a very bright light (3,4)
4 Obviously not sea! (6)
5 Accountant needs French cabbage as a cure for halitosis (6)
6 Hero gets most important letter (4,9)
7 Elementary calculation made by top football teams (5,8)
13 Alternating current in Devon? (3)
15 New Zealand bird Samoans take to heart (3)
17 What shot somehow had appeal to the umpire? (4,4)
18 Broad-minded Christian? (8)
19 Chairmen expressing hesitation amongst market speculators (7)
21 Call unexpectedly for the addition of a wee dram? (4,2)
22 Unlock combination but without success (2,4)

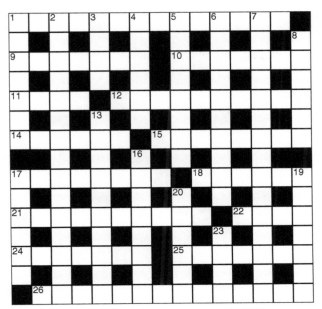

235

ACROSS

1 They have their points—could be a sensation (4,3,7)
9 Upset one in France never involved (7)
10 The run's organised by those in pursuit (7)
11 Donkey stops short of the prickly seed-case (4)
12 Giant struggling in the sea to get to the ship (10)
14 Better to put in another class? (6)
15 Herb having no end of Spanish port! (8)
17 Shipwrecked players abroad (8)
18 Temporarily appropriate (6)
21 Pair I'm following with an alternative had been laid back from the beginning (10)
22 A faintly illuminated retreat in the middle (4)
24 Inaccurate rugby formation? (4-3)
25 Type of sugar coming from various sources (7)
26 With synthetics, encourage one employed to restore one's features (7,7)

DOWN

1 Piper used in an emergency? (7)
2 Is such conduct acceptable from an amateur? (3-12)
3 Offhand when enchantress at the top of the tree loses her head (4)
4 A Derry medley is not very cheerful (6)
5 Record from Fleet Street area on two farm animals (8)
6 Messy place to eat? (6-4)
7 A late bloomer (7,8)
8 Back at sea (6)
13 Until the motive is contained, we object to being called disloyal (10)
16 Outlaws group with sex-appeal before half-time (8)
17 A couple endlessly damaging the dome (6)
19 Sort of winged duck? (7)
20 American sailors first coming from Paul's home (6)
23 One right under the tree (4)

236

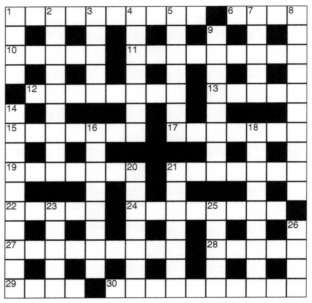

ACROSS

1 Having to trail one, make allowance (10)
6 Shindig in a jail-bird's retreat (4)
10 Refuse to drive before noon (5)
11 Progressive people, engineers—and past bearing! (9)
12 Given a little notice, work into shape for taking over (8)
13 He lunches in style, has maybe a terrine and fruit (5)
15 A period for getting all straight (7)
17 A remark with some point—point to more than one beast (7)
19 Defer pay out if America intervenes (7)
21 Having some influence, a fellow gets luxurious transport (7)
22 When no longer cold the Spanish do well (5)
24 Weary father retiring if there's little drink (8)
27 Block a view of the Syrian capital (9)
28 Danes getting involved in a fight (5)
29 Running water—runs unsatisfactorily (4)
30 A painter without an opening may well become a speculator (10)

DOWN

1 Not all want a skilled job (4)
2 She cleans many a strip (9)
3 Quickly made a hit embracing a Greed character (3,2)
4 Calling time in Gateshead (7)
5 Crime committed by a shady dealer? (7)
7 Keep off a green (5)
8 Romans test make-up selection (10)
9 Unrestricted choice of decoration receiving little back-up (4,4)
14 Those patronising him will be made the wiser for it! (4-6)
16 Fancy table for an impractical individual (8)
18 A person calling up about a balance (9)
20 Bad deed, and that makes further progress impossible (4-3)
21 Go before coppers give up again (7)
23 A large animal was brought and left (5)
25 Laid into trendy lot (5)
26 Standing up in a knot (4)

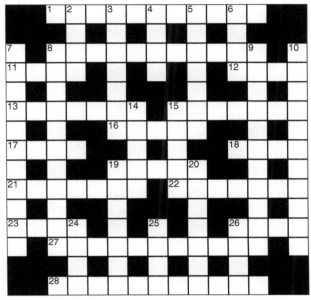

ACROSS

1 Volcanic lava to fashion into a ball perhaps (11)
8 Breathing in irregularly whilst asleep in Winter (11)
11 Beat around to 26 down (4)
12 Clothes to boast about (4)
13 When prophet is around, French nobleman leads people astray (7)
15 An extra 50 see red—cherry red perhaps (7)
16 Cut off ragged beard (5)
17 We French have intelligence! (4)
18 Live around a low lying swamp (4)
19 Put offer about, if it's in two parts (5)
21 Plead for an alteration in net rate (7)
22 A Catholic nowadays gets first class return to the land of rustic simplicity (7)
23 Spanish wine found in French abstainer! (4)
26 He will shortly reach a very unpleasant place (4)
27 Charge rates, otherwise someone will attend uninvited (11)
28 A literary forgery can be produced quietly with unlimited spare dough (11)

DOWN

2 The courage required on icy roads (4)
3 He's not an early riser, neither does he tell the truth on the plot (3-1-3)
4 I'm possessive about one article, or quite a few of them (4)
5 This goes round in both directions (7)
6 A sharp sound and a sharp smell (4)
7 One may accommodate a friend who encloses one short poem (11)
8 Go looking for workers who are chasing after froth! (11)
9 Found 10 somewhere to store a fluid which aids digestion (4,7)
10 Upwardly mobile graduate with monastic title got in with a friend and was found in the lower trunk (11)
14 How to transfer a clock back (5)
15 Mother provides musical backing for the girl (5)
19 Gang fetched water and bandage for the head (7)
20 Get ready, with some hesitation, to hold the cups and saucers (7)
24 Screw cutters were ejected backwards (4)
25 Riot organised by small music group (4)
26 The man who is on record as offering assistance (4)

238

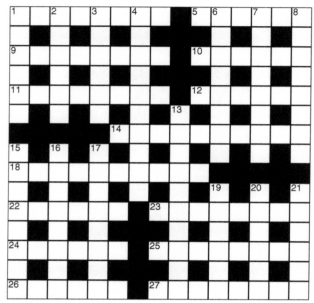

ACROSS

1 Telephotographic picture unlikely to succeed (4,4)
5 Illegal acts by a part of the Ukraine (6)
9 Returning fuel supply to a conurbation requires foresight (8)
10 A Ravel composition anglers consider gentle (6)
11 Explanations for wild geese in sex change (8)
12 More beautiful, but that's just comparative (6)
14 Noted local owner is antimonarchical (10)
18 Admit indebtedness and don't demand cash (4,6)
22 Forward child about to reach a conclusion (4,2)
23 Egotistic ex-student mirrored variety of faults (8)
24 Simpleton taken aback by a hard scrubber (6)
25 He sticks to a woman sunk in depression (8)
26 Pick of the Australian army! (6)
27 Thousands staked by scion of the family (8)

DOWN

1 Bent over to give heed to press boss (6)
2 Raised firearm to obtain a piece of gold (6)
3 Fall ill when neck is dislocated (6)
4 Not inclined to be honest (2,3,5)
6 Easily understood how to make bread and ale (8)
7 Michael about to declare his views are unorthodox (8)
8 But in Austria turgid talk is not the norm (8)
13 Made a monk get things straight (3,2,5)
15 Urges a young man to prepare a light meal (3,5)
16 Monotonous chant for a service (8)
17 Award for expert accommodating company junior (8)
19 A small sea bird following the ship (6)
20 Where to find the last seven letters of pudding (6)
21 Excess nut found in cereal grains (6)

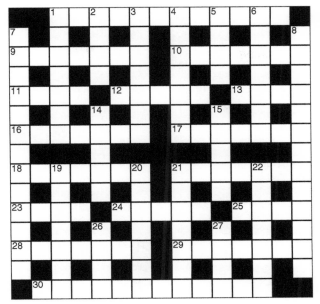

239

ACROSS

1 Ignores one as one browses (5,7)
9 Holding a large hat fished out of the water (7)
10 Joke responsible for a mountaineering accident? (3-4)
11 No trouble in vocalising the notes (4)
12 Slowly advanced to the void (5)
13 Search for the house doctor (4)
16 Like the bikini advertised as "50% off"? (7)
17 Go back to the asylum (7)
18 Favouring a charge in advance (7)
21 I'm leaving here. I arranged to go into business (7)
23 Write a letter and get nine letters back (4)
24 After all, that was it! (5)
25 Merely said "Attack" (4)
28 Makes it louder, one finds (5,2)
29 A dish breaker (7)
30 Does it get weaving on the bananas? (6,6)

DOWN

1 Finds in the directory and calls on (5,2)
2 He has to join the other without her (4)
3 Shows they're the cause of many separations (7)
4 An arm-rest (7)
5 She's roaming in the gloaming (4)
6 Stick something to eat inside to keep you going (7)
7 A funny article? (6,2,5)
8 Do they run the world? (5-8)
14 Go off for a month ever after that (5)
15 Further round to the right (5)
19 Some sailor brought it back and it's catching (3-4)
20 Is he careless when handling the dispenser? (7)
21 Gets as far as, when one wakens up (5,2)
22 Not exactly violently (7)
26 Old, but not on the shelf (4)
27 Second home (4)

240

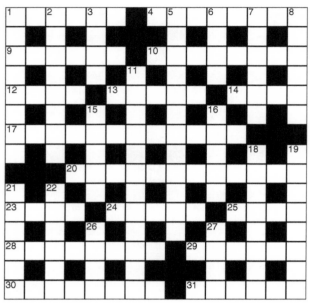

ACROSS

1 Lost interest when the matter was postponed (3,3)
4 Highly satisfactory method is quite some distance off (1,4,3)
9 Utter base calumny then hide (3,3)
10 Joker gets firm to adopt a middle line (8)
12 Famous contralto, the object of jokes... (4)
13 ...not stale, but impudent (5)
14 Fair pronouncement of one's doom (4)
17 Outpouring of this week's magazine (7,5)
20 Penny game enough to suffer the discomforts of sea travel (5,3,4)
23 Parched terrorists returned and then died (4)
24 Where I'm backing Bradman to hit the ball? (3,2)
25 Plea to woman to give orphan sanctuary (4)
28 Not a bad prison for healthy people to be in (4,4)
29 In days the Federalist dream falls to pieces (6)
30 He should provide a cue with less delay (8)
31 Brother Baker is devastated (6)

DOWN

1 Check a racehorse, place a bet, and retire (4,4)
2 They make films best seen through telescopic lenses (3,5)
3 Sell birch (4)
5 Complain over pepper and salt from August to December (6,6)
6 Ancient thorn in Australia started the old town crying (4)
7 In war I have made a renunciation (6)
8 One dry cocktail over there (6)
11 The Northern Line? (6,6)
15 Cotton on is the way to acquire sex appeal (3,2)
16 Damn'd healthy looking (5)
18 Quick reply by return (4,4)
19 In the same way clandestine troops wrong a murderous type (8)
21 To bang down the phone indicates an emotional problem (4,2)
22 Jungle boy has nothing on but an Eastern robe (6)
26 Cut price bargain? (4)
27 Equipment changed by motorists (4)

The Answers

1 _____
ACROSS: 1 Batch, **4** Espresso, **10** Dilemma, **11** Earache, **12** Nave, **13** Guide, **14** Mend, **17** Give up the ghost, **19** Ring the changes, **22** Cave, **23** Amman, **24** Bait, **27** Carmine, **28** Tonsure, **29** Identify, **30** Xylem.
DOWN: 1 Badinage, **2** Tel Aviv, **3** Home, **5** Speed merchants, **6** Rory, **7** Success, **8** Oread, **9** Law unto himself, **15** Buggy, **16** Cheap, **18** Isotherm, **20** Inverse, **21** Gradual, **22** Cacti, **25** Gist, **26** Onyx.

2 _____
ACROSS: 1 Redresses, **9** Asinine, **10** Upstart, **11** Imprest, **12** Protracts, **14** Omnivore, **15** Course, **17** Present, **20** Escape, **23** Starched, **25** Lemon sole, **26** Acreage, **27** Digital, **28** Condone, **29** Newmarket.
DOWN: 2 Esparto, **3** Rotator, **4** Streamer, **5** Sadism, **6** Misprints, **7** Firedog, **8** Sentience, **13** Topside, **15** Constance, **16** Spectator, **18** Nepotism, **19** Barring, **21** Cashier, **22** Pillage, **24** Eleven.

3 _____
ACROSS: 8 Pooh, **9** Ova, **10** Really, **11** Handel, **12** Regicide, **13** Conventionalist, **15** Figleaf, **17** Smidgen, **20** Parliamentarian, **23** Boss-eyed, **25** Ignore, **26** Salami, **27** Aga, **28** Stem.
DOWN: 1 Potato, **2** She-devil, **3** Bowling analysis, **4** Hairpin, **5** Trigonometrical, **6** Parcel, **7** Glad, **14** She, **16** Ida, **18** Darkness, **19** Headway, **21** Lascar, **22** Agreed, **24** Okay.

4 _____
ACROSS: 7 Take pains, **8** Pants, **10** Hospital, **11** Riling, **12** Memo, **13** Get about, **15** Crusade, **17** Poverty, **20** Play fair, **22** Titi, **25** Dry rot, **26** Presided, **27** Notch, **28** Put on airs.
DOWN: 1 Salon, **2** Kelpie, **3** Fast food, **4** Analogy, **5** Fallible, **6** Stand up to, **9** Brut, **14** Grill room, **16** Say grace, **18** On the hop, **19** Drop-out, **21** Acts, **23** Tribal, **24** Ferry.

5 _____
ACROSS: 1 Public property, **9** Tallies, **10** Tornado, **11** Left, **12** Punishment, **14** Aboard, **15** Felonies, **17** Antelope, **18** Snicks, **21** Ameliorate, **22** Agra, **24** Atlanta, **25** Martini, **26** Telephone kiosk.
DOWN: 1 Patella, **2** Bolt from the blue, **3** Ibid, **4** Pass up, **5** Obtained, **6** Earth-bound, **7** Travel incognito, **8** Routes, **13** Brilliance, **16** Approach, **17** Ararat, **19** Seasick, **20** Stamen, **23** Trek.

6 _____
ACROSS: 1 Second person, **8** Nearest, **9** Alfalfa, **11** Whopper, **12** Stinker, **13** Hit on, **14** Fat chance, **16** So let it be, **19** Pecks, **21** On trust, **23** Realign, **24** Erosive, **25** End game, **26** United States.
DOWN: 1 Seaport, **2** Creep in, **3** Net profit, **4** Pears, **5** Raffish, **6** Oilskin, **7** Know the score, **10** Air personnel, **15** The orient, **17** Let down, **18** Tourist, **19** Plaudit, **20** Cuirass, **22** Tweed.

7 _____
ACROSS: 1 Lamenting, **8** Traffic-signal, **11** Essex, **12** Learn, **13** Veils, **16** Single, **17** Metric, **18** Lathi, **19** Nereid, **20** Rascal, **21** Tweak, **24** Elfin, **26** Heart, **27** Take advantage, **28** Key worker.
DOWN: 2 Affix, **3** Edible, **4** Tassel, **5** Nigel, **6** Prisoner of war, **7** Cavalry charge, **9** Messenger, **10** Inoculate, **13** Veldt, **14** Istle, **15** Smirk, **22** Window, **23** Affair, **25** Niece, **26** Hythe.

8 _____
ACROSS: 1 Stockist, **5** Spread, **9** Apprised, **10** Dinant, **12** Distemper, **13** Train, **14** Gear, **16** Contest, **19** Eastern, **21** Inst, **24** Op art, **25** Adherents, **27** Upshot, **28** Emigrate, **29** Ernest, **30** Interest.
DOWN: 1 Stands, **2** Oppose, **3** Knife, **4** Sleeper, **6** Paintings, **7** Emanated, **8** Detonate, **11** Eric, **15** Elections, **17** Resolute, **18** Assassin, **20** Neat, **21** Inhuman, **22** Enrage, **23** Aspect, **26** Rogue.

9 _____
ACROSS: 1 Well-read, **6** Aghast, **9** Cleave, **10** Fielding, **11** Historic, **12** Domain, **13** Night-clothes, **16** Investigator, **19** Lesion, **21** Gargoyle, **23** Coverlet, **24** Listed, **25** Measly, **26** Royalist.
DOWN: 2 Eclair, **3** Least, **4** Eyebright, **5** Deficit, **6** Ahead, **7** Hodometer, **8** Sentinel, **13** Neediness, **14** Laterally, **15** Envelope, **17** Gagster, **18** Pliers, **20** Nelly, **22** Ousel.

10 _____
ACROSS: 1 Considerate, **10** Least, **11** Vacillate, **12** Thesaurus, **13** Banjo, **14** Flicks, **16** Play ball, **18** Has a chat, **20** Nordic, **23** Heave, **24** Gallipoli, **26** Nocturnal, **27** Radon, **28** Preliminary.
DOWN: 2 Osage, **3** Setback, **4** Divers, **5** Rock-salt, **6** Tallboy, **7** Flat of the hand, **8** Gainsaid, **9** Recollections, **15** Instance, **17** Marginal, **19** Chequer, **21** Omicron, **22** Slalom, **25** Order.

11 _____

ACROSS: 1 Pawnbroker, 6 Spar, 9 Experience, 10 Otic, 13 Tethers, 15 Appeal, 16 Eponym, 17 Hailing distance, 18 Nassau, 20 Fences, 21 Bleared, 22 Tool, 25 Stagnation, 26 Note, 27 Prosperity.
DOWN: 1 Peek, 2 Wipe, 3 Barrel, 4 Overhead charges, 5 Encore, 7 Put on an act, 8 Recompense, 11 Washington, 12 Spoilsport, 13 Taxi-cab, 14 Spotted, 19 Ulster, 20 Female, 23 Mini, 24 Envy.

12 _____

ACROSS: 1 Subsidiarity, 9 Reginal, 10 Supreme, 11 Seer, 12 Binge, 13 List, 16 Out cold, 17 Tempest, 18 Egghead, 21 Through, 23 Skip, 24 Screw, 25 Hump, 28 Indiana, 29 Artless, 30 Crossed lines.
DOWN: 1 Suggest, 2 Bank, 3 Ill wind, 4 Insight, 5 Rape, 6 The time, 7 Press one's suit, 8 Left at the post, 14 Lower, 15 Umbra, 19 Guilder, 20 Dictate, 21 The mall, 22 Usurers, 26 Baas, 27 Eton.

13 _____

ACROSS: 1 Proconsul, 9 Senile, 10 Ascertain, 11 Sledge, 12 Innisfree, 13 Oblige, 17 Ass, 19 Strings attached, 20 Ply, 21 Rag-bag, 25 Jerusalem, 26 Draw in, 27 Jet-setter, 28 Locate, 29 Pyongyang.
DOWN: 2 Rising, 3 Credit, 4 Notify, 5 Universal remedy, 6 Jellybean, 7 Hindsight, 8 Referenda, 14 Astraddle, 15 Fragrance, 16 Insatiate, 17 Asp, 18 Sty, 22 Bunsen, 23 Pastry, 24 Severn.

14 _____

ACROSS: 1 Indonesian, 6 Goad, 10 Caste, 11 Enteritis, 12 Releases, 13 Dinar, 15 Arabian, 17 Notable, 19 Tooling, 21 Derange, 22 Rabbi, 24 Ancestry, 27 Unsullied, 28 Addle, 29 Yeti, 30 Retrievers.
DOWN: 1 Inch, 2 Desperado, 3 Niece, 4 Stetson, 5 Artisan, 7 Often, 8 Disordered, 9 Predator, 14 Canterbury, 16 Initials, 18 Banbridge, 20 Granite, 21 Decider, 23 Beset, 25 State, 26 Bess.

15 _____

ACROSS: 1 Commonplace, 8 Herd of goats, 11 Hood, 12 Salt, 13 Rosette, 15 Augment, 16 Edict, 17 Ends, 18 Tyro, 19 Tepid, 21 Unarmed, 22 Deltaic, 23 Seer, 26 Scup, 27 Rabbit-punch, 28 Candleberry.
DOWN: 2 Owed, 3 Mediate, 4 Naff, 5 Lookout, 6 Cats, 7 Charge-nurse, 8 Horse-dealer, 9 Safety-catch, 10 Stethoscope, 14 Edged, 15 Acrid, 19 Test-bed, 20 Deplume, 24 Raga, 25 Stye, 26 Scar.

16 _____

ACROSS: 1 Artists' model, 9 Requite, 10 Tripper, 11 Unit, 12 Spent, 13 Ruin, 16 Heeltap, 17 Croydon, 18 Traitor, 21 Copycat, 23 Bach, 24 Scrap, 25 Clio, 28 Outlast, 29 Hosanna, 30 Achilles heel.
DOWN: 1 Acquire, 2 Trim, 3 Sweep up, 4 Satanic, 5 Ohio, 6 Expound, 7 Brought to book, 8 Grand national, 14 State, 15 Hoops, 19 Ascetic, 20 Recital, 21 Clashes, 22 Colonel, 26 Maxi, 27 Esse.

17 _____

ACROSS: 5 Infirm, 8 Chew over, 9 Screens, 10 Fawns, 11 Take a drop, 13 Seepages, 14 Scores, 17 Let, 19 Leo, 20 Wooden, 23 Ringside, 26 Top drawer, 28 Raise, 29 Pillage, 30 Serenade, 31 Demand.
DOWN: 1 Scoffs, 2 Seaweed, 3 Constable, 4 Debate, 5 Increase, 6 Freed, 7 Runs over, 12 Ash, 15 Conger eel, 16 Colonise, 18 Enlarged, 21 Ere, 22 Similar, 24 Ironed, 25 Eleven, 27 Delta.

18 _____

ACROSS: 1 Cape town, 5 Step up, 9 Pulled in, 10 Eraser, 12 Reindeers, 13 Evoke, 14 Lass, 16 Roomers, 19 Amusing, 21 Pitt, 24 Mulga, 25 Go on leave, 27 Stalin, 28 Salt mine, 29 Taking, 30 Taken out.
DOWN: 1 Capers, 2 Pulpit, 3 Trend, 4 Waiters, 6 Turned out, 7 Pass over, 8 Perverse, 11 Tsar, 15 Animation, 17 Marmoset, 18 Pull back, 20 Gags, 21 Pro rata, 22 Casino, 23 Defect, 26 Lathe.

19 _____

ACROSS: 1 Settle down, 6 Wand, 9 Off-spinner, 10 Stow, 13 Coterie, 15 Toucan, 16 Llamas, 17 Labour supporter, 18 Corpse, 20 Verona, 21 Trooped, 22 Slog, 25 Pianissimo, 26 Deed, 27 Begrudging.
DOWN: 1 Shot, 2 Tuft, 3 Lepton, 4 Dangerous corner, 5 Weevil, 7 Automation, 8 Downstream, 11 Italicised, 12 Cumbersome, 13 Casuist, 14 Elbowed, 19 Ermine, 20 Versed, 23 Hifi, 24 Tong.

20 _____

ACROSS: 1 Alienation, 9 Anna, 10 Tournament, 11 Innate, 12 Acclaim, 15 Serpent, 16 Caged, 17 Stay, 18 Able, 19 Doter, 21 Leander, 22 Redress, 24 Treble, 27 Re ection, 28 Oslo, 29 Shattering.
DOWN: 2 Loot, 3 Enroll, 4 Anaemic, 5 Idea, 6 Noticed, 7 Unnameable, 8 Talentless, 12 Absolution, 13 Clarabella, 14 Manor, 15 Sever, 19 Deserts, 20 Respect, 23 Raptor, 25 Offa, 26 Coin.

21 ____

ACROSS: 1 Red admiral, **6** Scan, **10** Novel, **11** Prejudice, **12** Greycoat, **13** Label, **15** Coinage, **17** Rainbow, **19** Omnibus, **21** Caterer, **22** Holst, **24** Transfer, **27** Betrothal, **28** Ridge, **29** Apse, **30** Gooseberry.
DOWN: 1 Rank, **2** Diversion, **3** Delay, **4** Improve, **5** Abetter, **7** Climb, **8** Needlework, **9** Duellist, **14** Acrophobia, **16** Ambition, **18** Bartender, **20** Satchmo, **21** Chablis, **23** Lotus, **25** Scrub, **26** Very.

22 ____

ACROSS: 1 Test pilot, **8** Avert one's eyes, **11** Acre, **12** Abate, **13** Fool, **16** Achieve, **17** Aimless, **18** Cobbler, **20** Hitched, **21** Norm, **22** Stage, **23** Snow, **26** Deliberate lie, **27** Birthdays.
DOWN: 2 Earn, **3** Trouble, **4** Inertia, **5** Owed, **6** Over the border, **7** Get one's hand in, **9** Damascene, **10** Close down, **14** Hello, **15** Smite, **19** Retreat, **20** Haggard, **24** Midi, **25** Bevy.

23 ____

ACROSS: 1 Telephone bill, **10** Rarebit, **11** Trawler, **12** Veer, **13** Match, **14** Gaga, **17** Fetlock, **18** Says you, **19** Uniform, **22** Pork-pie, **24** Test, **25** Brunt, **26** Dyer, **29** Inferno, **30** Chekhov, **31** Practice match.
DOWN: 2 Earnest, **3** Ebbs, **4** Hit back, **5** Notices, **6** Brat, **7** Lullaby, **8** Trevi fountain, **9** Treasure-trove, **15** Cocoa, **16** Hydra, **20** In so far, **21** Marconi, **22** Panache, **23** Psychic, **27** Eric, **28** Vera.

24 ____

ACROSS: 1 Pitch, **4** Up in arms, **10** Open cut, **11** Landing, **12** Prop, **13** Minsk, **14** Abet, **17** Retailer of news, **19** Cross reference, **22** Fags, **23** Barmy, **24** Mali, **27** Ram home, **28** Antigen, **29** Manifest, **30** Genie.
DOWN: 1 Prospero, **2** The post, **3** Hock, **5** Polish off a meal, **6** None, **7** Rainbow, **8** Sight, **9** Strike breakers, **15** First, **16** Snare, **18** Defiance, **20** Regimen, **21** Neat gin, **22** Forum, **25** Wolf, **26** Stag.

25 ____

ACROSS: 6 Fits and starts, **8** Biceps, **9** Inventor, **10** Ear, **11** Idlest, **12** Aesthete, **14** Houston, **16** Presume, **20** Walkover, **23** On hand, **24** Lac, **25** Condense, **26** Corrie, **27** Starting-price.
DOWN: 1 St Helens, **2** Falsetto, **3** Admiral, **4** St ives, **5 & 6** French fried potatoes, **7** Sportsmanlike, **13** Toe, **15** Two, **17** Reoccupy, **18** Spheroid, **19** Orleans, **21** Kidnap, **22** Vanity.

26 ____

ACROSS: 1 Goods train, **6** Plum, **10** Agent, **11** Depressed, **12** Peerless, **13** Overt, **15** Artless, **17** Exploit, **19** Forward, **21** Hidalgo, **22** Tibia, **24** Allusive, **27** Headlight, **28** Ozone, **29** Dies, **30** Sterilised.
DOWN: 1 Goal, **2** One better, **3** Sitar, **4** Redress, **5** Impasse, **7** Lisle, **8** Meditation, **9** Recouped, **14** Far-fetched, **16** Erasable, **18** Oblivious, **20** Draught, **21** Holster, **23** Brake, **25** Spool, **26** Lead.

27 ____

ACROSS: 1 Allspice, **5** Proper, **9** Handsome, **10** Spared, **11** Neap tide, **12** Armies, **14** Deliberate, **18** Rearranged, **22** Barrow, **23** Assassin, **24** Images, **25** Manicure, **26** Gneiss, **27** Tenement.
DOWN: 1 Athens, **2** Landau, **3** Peseta, **4** Comedienne, **6** Reporter, **7** Partisan, **8** Radishes, **13** Fire-escape, **15** Drubbing, **16** Carriage, **17** Prioress, **19** Malice, **20** Assume, **21** Intent.

28 ____

ACROSS: 1 Illiterate, **6** Scab, **9** Properties, **10** Alto, **12** Sliver, **13** Chairman, **15** On re ection, **18** Constraining, **21** Anisette, **22** Refuse, **24** Bias, **25** Delectable, **26** Even, **27** Attendance.
DOWN: 1 Impost, **2** Look in, **3** There and then, **4** Rate, **5** Toe the line, **7** Colombia, **8** Browning, **11** Disconcerted, **14** Department, **16** Scramble, **17** Intimate, **19** Durban, **20** Recede, **23** Here.

29 ____

ACROSS: 1 Dormant, **5** Hope for, **9** Non-stop, **10** Dresses, **11** Discharge, **12** Stiff, **13** Dopes, **15** Warm spell, **17** Bestirred, **19** Nears, **22** Trail, **23** Tea-leaves, **25** Million, **26** Penance, **27** Nowhere, **28** Trident.
DOWN: 1 Denuded, **2** Rings up, **3** Aitch, **4** Top-drawer, **5** Hedge, **6** Presses on, **7** Festive, **8** Restful, **14** Still life, **16** Red carpet, **17** Batsman, **18** Swallow, **20** Advance, **21** Suspect, **23** Tense, **24** Ennui.

30 ____

ACROSS: 1 Lancs, **4** Good catch, **9** Gestalt, **11** Step out, **12** Them, **13** Fairs, **14** Spin, **17** English master, **19** Taking on board, **21** Moan, **22** Astir, **23** Flap, **26** Tapioca, **27** Striver, **28** Firm offer, **29** Worst.
DOWN: 1 Light year, **2** Nest egg, **3** Siam, **5** Observatories, **6** Caen, **7** Trooper, **8** Hit on, **10** Teaching staff, **15** Dicky, **16** Stubs, **18** Bad spirit, **19** Trapper, **20** All over, **21** Motif, **24** Dodo, **25** Prow.

31 _____

ACROSS: 1 Knocked, 5 Comical, 9 Twenty-five years, 10 Haft, 11 Carry, 12 Into, 15 Needled, 16 Paddled, 17 Yearned, 19 Kindred, 21 Goon, 22 Scree, 23 Isle, 26 Unhappy memories, 27 Throned, 28 Trigger.
DOWN: 1 Kitchen, 2 One after another, 3 Kite, 4 Defraud, 5 Cover up, 6 Mayo, 7 Channel crossing, 8 Lassoed, 13 Fling, 14 Adana, 17 Yoghurt, 18 Decayed, 19 Keenest, 20 Dresser, 24 Open, 25 Topi.

32 _____

ACROSS: 1 Sparrow, 5 Chatter, 9 Realist, 10 Recline, 11 Abasement, 12 Ankle, 13 Set to, 15 Sage-green, 17 Posthaste, 19 Learn, 22 Astir, 23 Sediments, 25 Telling, 26 Wastrel, 27 Respect, 28 Redhead.
DOWN: 1 Surpass, 2 Adamant, 3 Raise, 4 Witnesses, 5 Carat, 6 Archangel, 7 Trickle, 8 Roedean, 14 Otherwise, 16 Glendower, 17 Psalter, 18 Settles, 20 Aintree, 21 Nestled, 23 Sight, 24 Mused.

33 _____

ACROSS: 1 Positive, 5 Tin hat, 9 Thorough, 10 Headed, 12 Ungallant, 13 Lie in, 14 Fist, 16 Mascots, 19 Reels in, 21 Bade, 24 Traps, 25 Macedoine, 27 Ranger, 28 Dumb-bell, 29 Siesta, 30 Seething.
DOWN: 1 Put out, 2 Sponge, 3 Troll, 4 Vagrant, 6 Idealised, 7 Hedgehog, 8 Tidiness, 11 Atom, 15 Insistent, 17 Arcturus, 18 Detainee, 20 Name, 21 Because, 22 Sileni, 23 Jet lag, 26 Debut.

34 _____

ACROSS: 1 Neath, 4 Good sport, 9 Gosling, 11 Embrace, 12 Teal, 13 Atone, 14 Eire, 17 Prepare the way, 19 Firm handshake, 21 Mood, 22 Alarm, 23 Spar, 26 Spinach, 27 Decline, 28 Deadlight, 29 Smelt.
DOWN: 1 Nightspot, 2 At stake, 3 Heir, 5 One in a hundred, 6 Sobs, 7 Opacity, 8 Theme, 10 Go the whole hog, 15 Harry, 16 Swish, 18 In earnest, 19 Florida, 20 Apprize, 21 Mused, 24 Pall, 25 Ecus.

35 _____

ACROSS: 7 Relay race, 8 Layer, 10 Baseball, 11 Eskimo, 12 Arid, 13 Terrains, 15 Colonel, 17 Off-hand, 20 Recently, 22 Lisa, 25 Maiden, 26 Overhaul, 27 Plonk, 28 Sectional.
DOWN: 1 Legal, 2 Career, 3 Organdie, 4 Acolyte, 5 Backlash, 6 Permanent, 9 Gear, 14 Tolerable, 16 Overdone, 18 Falsetto, 19 Bygones, 21 Tank, 23 School, 24 Susan.

36 _____

ACROSS: 6 Turn on the heat, 8 Allege, 9 Reigning, 10 Rat, 11 Potion, 12 Unhinged, 14 Stayers, 16 Therapy, 20 Keep it up, 23 Valise, 24 Ave, 25 Cool down, 26 Attain, 27 Nothing to go on.
DOWN: 1 Free city, 2 Governor, 3 Start up, 4 Jewish, 5 Pennon, 6 Talk of the town, 7 Tender passion, 13 Ice, 15 Eli, 17 Have a row, 18 Relation, 19 Apanage, 21 Pilate, 22 Tropic.

37 _____

ACROSS: 1 Processor, 9 Overall, 10 Patella, 11 Lattice, 12 Minuscule, 14 Eruption, 15 Amulet, 17 Cyanide, 20 Attire, 23 Dominion, 25 Well-being, 26 Headman, 27 Aground, 28 Press on, 29 Gastropod.
DOWN: 2 Realism, 3 Coequal, 4 Salacity, 5 Roller, 6 Sextuplet, 7 Pacific, 8 Alternate, 13 Leonine, 15 Amidships, 16 Economise, 18 Daylight, 19 Smeared, 21 Tiepolo, 22 Run into, 24 Owning.

38 _____

ACROSS: 1 Stepsister, 6 Asti, 10 Steep, 11 Eyebright, 12 Paradise, 13 Voter, 15 Railing, 17 Terrace, 19 Candace, 21 Prelate, 22 Salmi, 24 Overcast, 27 Intensive, 28 Agent, 29 Nuns, 30 Reiterated.
DOWN: 1 So-so, 2 Elevation, 3 Sepia, 4 Seeking, 5 Element, 7 Sight, 8 Interceded, 9 Traverse, 14 Procession, 16 Italians, 18 Amassment, 20 Erosive, 21 Present, 23 Let on, 25 Chair, 26 Stud.

39 _____

ACROSS: 1 Hercules, 9 Overcast, 10 Ossa, 11 Nationalised, 13 Brooklet, 15 Pelota, 16 Hypo, 17 Druid, 18 Roam, 20 Design, 21 Tea-party, 23 Noctambulism, 26 Eric, 27 Subtitle, 28 Dilating.
DOWN: 2 Easterly, 3 Craniologist, 4 Lentil, 5 Soho, 6 Decamped, 7 Pass, 8 Stud-farm, 12 Ill-treatment, 14 Trust, 16 Hedonist, 17 Dynamite, 19 Artesian, 22 Animal, 24 Cobs, 25 Used.

40 _____

ACROSS: 1 Go round, 5 Sacrist, 9 All-star, 10 Apropos, 11 Appealing, 12 Nasal, 13 Adept, 15 Get across, 17 Outskirts, 19 Expat, 22 Carpi, 23 Deference, 25 Amnesia, 26 Repaint, 27 Dissect, 28 Enlarge.
DOWN: 1 Granada, 2 Relapse, 3 Ultra, 4 Derringer, 5 Slang, 6 Chronicle, 7 Impasto, 8 Tussles, 14 Take issue, 16 Task force, 17 Orchard, 18 Thrones, 20 Pannier, 21 Theatre, 23 Draft, 24 Repel.

41 ____

ACROSS: 1 Southpaw, 5 Regina, 9 Absolute, 10 Script, 11 Flamingo, 12 Daniel, 14 Straight up, 18 Ten to seven, 22 Nearer, 23 Preserve, 24 Sign on, 25 Literate, 26 Parity, 27 Flinches.
DOWN: 1 Staffs, 2 Unseat, 3 Hold it, 4 Altogether, 6 Exchange, 7 Initiate, 8 Antelope, 13 Career girl, 15 Stands up, 16 Endanger, 17 Comes out, 19 Astern, 20 Breath, 21 Recess.

42 ____

ACROSS: 7 Royal mail, 8 Level, 10 Upper lip, 11 Intern, 12 Inca, 13 The dutch, 15 Caboose, 17 Rectory, 20 Stitches, 22 Soma, 25 Greens, 26 Limerick, 27 Smear, 28 Be on guard.
DOWN: 1 Coupe, 2 Take on, 3 Small ads, 4 Dispute, 5 Best suit, 6 New record, 9 Mine, 14 Last trump, 16 On the way, 18 Easy mind, 19 Psalter, 21 Hess, 23 Mark up, 24 Scarp.

43 ____

ACROSS: 1 Abide with me, 10 Helen, 11 Guerrilla, 12 New guinea, 13 Unite, 14 Lumber, 16 Quayside, 18 Sinister, 20 Bengal, 23 Tiger, 24 Ruritania, 26 Sensation, 27 Right, 28 Meaningless.
DOWN: 2 Below, 3 Denture, 4 Waging, 5 The hague, 6 Mercury, 7 Thankless task, 8 Claiming, 9 Farewell party, 15 Managing, 17 Georgian, 19 Serrate, 21 Enthral, 22 Cronin, 25 Negus.

44 ____

ACROSS: 1 Standard, 5 Ornate, 9 Rashness, 10 Elapse, 12 Concourse, 13 Tales, 14 Idle, 16 Protein, 19 Traffic, 21 So-so, 24 Actor, 25 Roundhead, 27 Goring, 28 Adhesive, 29 Eleven, 30 Gradient.
DOWN: 1 Spruce, 2 Absent, 3 Dingo, 4 Reserve, 6 Relations, 7 Appalled, 8 Evensong, 11 Keep, 15 Deference, 17 Strangle, 18 Parterre, 20 Carp, 21 Sounder, 22 Venice, 23 Advert, 26 Dread.

45 ____

ACROSS: 7 Skin int, 8 Fibre, 10 Prurient, 11 Action, 12 Brag, 13 Mayoress, 15 Ransack, 17 Top coat, 20 Proposer, 22 News, 25 Antrum, 26 Demerara, 27 Agate, 28 Schnorkel.
DOWN: 1 Skirt, 2 Snorer, 3 Allergic, 4 Anatomy, 5 Historic, 6 Groomsman, 9 Wary, 14 Patronage, 16 Separate, 18 Ornament, 19 Produce, 21 Same, 23 War cry, 24 Greet.

46 ____

ACROSS: 1 Handling, 9 A la carte, 10 Area, 11 Mean business, 13 Protract, 15 Towage, 16 Epic, 17 Oscan, 18 Boar, 20 Unclad, 21 Tumblers, 23 Play with fire, 26 Tuan, 27 Existent, 28 Endanger.
DOWN: 2 Airstrip, 3 Dramatically, 4 Iguana, 5 Garb, 6 Pass it on, 7 Free, 8 Menswear, 12 News bulletin, 14 Tacit, 16 Equipped, 17 Old-timer, 19 Abrogate, 22 Maimed, 24 Agin, 25 Hate.

47 ____

ACROSS: 1 Present company, 9 Ireland, 10 In range, 11 Opts, 12 Prosperous, 14 Frowns, 15 South-paw, 17 Spaniels, 18 Missus, 21 Red herring, 22 Dear, 24 Wreaths, 25 Vaulted, 26 Psychoanalysts.
DOWN: 1 Pair off, 2 Election address, 3 Edam, 4 Tudors, 5 Omission, 6 Perfect fit, 7 Non compus mentis, 8 See-saw, 13 Antiseptic, 16 Alfresco, 17 Straws, 19 Strides, 20 Uneven, 23 Bull.

48 ____

ACROSS: 6 Double dealing, 8 Mascot, 9 Polaroid, 10 Rut, 11 Pagoda, 12 Exchange, 14 Capered, 16 Obesity, 20 Hardware, 23 Apeman, 24 Dun, 25 Bluebell, 26 Charge, 27 Lepidopterist.
DOWN: 1 Quick one, 2 Flat race, 3 Adapter, 4 Gallic, 5 Sierra, 6 Draw a parallel, 7 Going straight, 13 Hie, 15 Row, 17 Blanched, 18 Scenario, 19 Red lips, 21 Dieppe, 22 Amends.

49 ____

ACROSS: 8 Complete, 9 Appeal, 10 Lar, 11 St helena, 12 Errant, 13 Marriage service, 15 Sixteen, 18 Psalter, 21 Sovereign remedy, 24 Wicket, 25 Feverfew, 26 Ill, 27 Lean-to, 28 Innocent.
DOWN: 1 Contra, 2 Appear, 3 General election, 4 Relaxed, 5 Careless driving, 6 Approval, 7 Barnacle, 14 Rex, 16 Idolised, 17 Trekking, 19 Tee, 20 Egg- ip, 22 Maraca, 23 Duenna.

50 ____

ACROSS: 1 Seating, 5 Tunisia, 9 Crown, 10 In a groove, 11 No love lost, 12 Stud, 14 Strike a light, 18 Reproduction, 21 Sash, 22 Ringmaster, 25 Baltimore, 26 Idiot, 27 Rostrum, 28 Tannery.
DOWN: 1 Second, 2 Apollo, 3 Innovation, 4 Grill, 5 Transient, 6 Nark, 7 Shortage, 8 Anecdote, 13 Allocation, 15 In uniform, 16 Crossbar, 17 Apostles, 19 Strive, 20 Pretty, 23 Ghent, 24 Liar.

51 _____
ACROSS: 1 Susan, 4 Maidstone, 8 Inner, 9 Statement, 11 Fell, 12 Knave, 13 Well, 16 Weather-beaten, 19 Territorially, 20 Lima, 22 Rivet, 23 Knot, 26 Midinette, 27 Kyoto, 28 Rock-plant, 29 Acton.
DOWN: 1 Skin int, 2 Sun ower, 3 Norm, 4 Misanthropist, 5 Shed, 6 Ox-eye, 7 Extol, 10 Advertisement, 14 Rapid, 15 Feels, 17 Trying out, 18 Nightgown, 20 Lemur, 21 Medoc, 24 Snap, 25 Okra.

52 _____
ACROSS: 1 Well content, 9 Stand firm, 10 Natty, 11 Onegin, 12 In demand, 13 Tip-off, 15 Lollipop, 18 Billycan, 19 Ponder, 21 Casement, 23 Sarong, 26 Laden, 27 Inclement, 28 Right as rain.
DOWN: 1 Wash-out, 2 Leave, 3 Caddis- y, 4 Naif, 5 Edmonton, 6 Tense, 7 Keyed up, 8 Strapped, 14 Palisade, 16 Look a mess, 17 Haunting, 18 Backlog, 20 Right on, 22 Miner, 24 Opera, 25 Scut.

53 _____
ACROSS: 5 Pumice, 8 Took note, 9 Pencils, 10 Rider, 11 Miserable, 13 Draw near, 14 Cleave, 17 Ice, 19 Tee, 20 Tomato, 23 Redeemed, 26 Bartender, 28 Latin, 29 Siberia, 30 Stand out, 31 Nettle.
DOWN: 1 Stored, 2 Cordial, 3 In transit, 4 Stigma, 5 Pretence, 6 Mocha, 7 Calf-love, 12 Ire, 15 Levelling, 16 For a time, 18 Coincide, 21 Ere, 22 Emotion, 24 Errata, 25 Denote, 27 Treat.

54 _____
ACROSS: 1 Call out, 5 Earshot, 9 Modesty, 10 Albania, 11 Overtones, 12 Nylon, 13 Fused, 15 Off course, 17 Look after, 19 Draft, 22 Sepia, 23 Cut it fine, 25 Replace, 26 Testate, 27 Worsted, 28 Pay back.
DOWN: 1 Come off, 2 Ladders, 3 Onset, 4 Trying out, 5 Exams, 6 Robin hood, 7 Handler, 8 Trainee, 14 Draw apart, 16 First step, 17 Last row, 18 On paper, 20 Ali baba, 21 The beak, 23 Creed, 24 Testy.

55 _____
ACROSS: 1 Solicit, 5 Zebu, 9 Definite article, 10 Avid, 11 Bigot, 12 Snap, 15 Mugging, 16 Seafood, 17 Refusal, 19 Wrestle, 21 Dyne, 22 Toxin, 23 Zest, 26 Electronic brain, 27 Salt, 28 Gilbert.
DOWN: 1 Sidearm, 2 Lifting a finger, 3 Cone, 4 Tithing, 5 Zealous, 6 Bute, 7 Whelped, 8 Icing on the cake, 13 Tipsy, 14 Wales, 17 Redress, 18 Look-out, 19 Whiting, 20 Extinct, 24 Stoa, 25 Abel.

56 _____
ACROSS: 1 Bath chap, 6 Enigma, 9 Primer, 10 Rest-cure, 11 Main line, 12 Slight, 13 Negotiations, 16 Labour-saving, 19 Almond, 21 Sing sing, 23 Canister, 24 Enamel, 25 Sketch, 26 Not at all.
DOWN: 2 Abroad, 3 Hymen, 4 Harbinger, 5 Portent, 6 Eases, 7 Inclining, 8 Merchant, 13 Neologist, 14 Alignment, 15 Fall back, 17 Also-ran, 18 Unwell, 20 Ditch, 22 Scant.

57 _____
ACROSS: 1 Detrimental, 9 Pole-vault, 10 Liner, 11 Retort, 12 Crackpot, 13 Summit, 15 Daydream, 18 Ravenous, 19 Ardent, 21 Template, 23 Obtuse, 26 Tonic, 27 Mustachio, 28 Surrendered.
DOWN: 1 Deports, 2 To let, 3 Inversion, 4 Etui, 5 Tutorial, 6 Lilac, 7 Stratum, 8 One-piece, 14 Movement, 16 Dart-board, 17 Customer, 18 Rotator, 20 Toehold, 22 Locus, 24 Uther, 25 Isle.

58 _____
ACROSS: 1 Cuban, 4 Attribute, 8 Rheum, 9 Out with it, 11 Sikh, 12 Weird, 13 Fray, 16 Work with a will, 19 Paying the bill, 20 Tool, 22 Let on, 23 Onus, 26 Pressed on, 27 Petra, 28 Character, 29 Range.
DOWN: 1 Card-sharp, 2 Break away, 3 Name, 4 At one's wits end, 5 Ibis, 6 Usher, 7 Entry, 10 Turn the corner, 14 Prone, 15 Manic, 17 Islington, 18 Legislate, 20 Topic, 21 Omega, 24 Asia, 25 Spar.

59 _____
ACROSS: 1 Magistrate, 6 Gamp, 9 Retirement, 10 Blue, 13 Cedilla, 15 Apiary, 16 Evicts, 17 Dick Whittington, 18 Viewed, 20 Detour, 21 Deleted, 22 Late, 25 Life guards, 26 Earn, 27 Beanfeasts.
DOWN: 1 Mary, 2 Gate, 3 Surrey, 4 Remains to be seen, 5 Tangle, 7 Allocation, 8 Pleasantry, 11 Vaudeville, 12 Winchester, 13 Crowned, 14 Avenged, 19 Defile, 20 Delude, 23 Iris, 24 Isis.

60 _____
ACROSS: 1 Get out, 4 A fair cop, 9 Inland, 10 Big noise, 12 Gatt, 13 Crone, 14 Alms, 17 Full of spirit, 20 Ancien regime, 23 Abbe, 24 Egger, 25 Rear, 28 Pass it on, 29 Show up, 30 Sideline, 31 Crayon.
DOWN: 1 Going off, 2 Tall talk, 3 Ulna, 5 Friend in need, 6 Iona, 7 Chilli, 8 Please, 11 Dressing down, 15 Bound, 16 Mined, 18 Give away, 19 Terrapin, 21 Campus, 22 Abused, 26 Will, 27 Char.

61 ——

ACROSS: 1 Heavy punishment, 9 Germane, 10 Dottier, 11 Lope, 12 Buxom, 13 Dene, 16 Nostril, 17 Squeeze, 18 Cockpit, 21 Martini, 23 Smog, 24 Haunt, 25 Gina, 28 Umbrage, 29 Tornado, 30 Error of judgment.
DOWN: 1 Highland costume, 2 Apropos, 3 Yeah, 4 Unequal, 5 Indoors, 6 Hate, 7 Evil eye, 8 Three Men in a Boat, 14 Graph, 15 Lucre, 19 Crow-bar, 20 Tea-leaf, 21 Manitou, 22 Imitate, 26 Haar, 27 Prig.

62 ——

ACROSS: 1 Bare essentials, 9 Insolent, 10 Canon, 12 Oman, 13 Atmosphere, 15 Making up, 16 Meaner, 18 Napkin, 20 Blockade, 23 Lip-service, 24 Fiat, 26 Cilia, 27 Narrated, 28 Brief encounter.
DOWN: 2 Ransack, 3 Eton, 4 Spectrum, 5 Notion, 6 Incipience, 7 Lantern, 8 Endearments, 11 Commonplace, 14 Incinerate, 17 Electric, 19 Popular, 21 Aliment, 22 Avenue, 25 Tabu.

63 ——

ACROSS: 7 Minelayer, 8 Beast, 10 Rehearse, 11 Prefer, 12 Etna, 13 Validate, 15 Complex, 17 Hairpin, 20 Eggshell, 22 Reap, 25 School, 26 Archives, 27 Ashen, 28 Camembert.
DOWN: 1 Liner, 2 Defeat, 3 Marriage, 4 Reserve, 5 Defender, 6 Ascertain, 9 Opal, 14 Roughcast, 16 Passover, 18 Airscrew, 19 Almanac, 21 Eels, 23 Akimbo, 24 Beard.

64 ——

ACROSS: 1 Paced, 4 Aglitter, 10 Complex, 11 Trefoil, 12 Eros, 13 Media, 14 Tiny, 17 Operating table, 19 Charge the earth, 22 Race, 23 Stash, 24 Ewer, 27 Bestial, 28 Compere, 29 Nowadays, 30 Ruled.
DOWN: 1 Picked on, 2 Compote, 3 Dale, 5 Getting the sack, 6 Ilex, 7 Took ill, 8 Rally, 9 Experimentally, 15 Cairn, 16 Haver, 18 Sharp end, 20 Hacksaw, 21 Raw deal, 22 Rub in, 25 Hind, 26 Omar.

65 ——

ACROSS: 1 Opening words, 9 Refrain, 10 Accuser, 11 Vies, 12 Abrim, 13 Aide, 16 Article, 17 Reports, 18 Annuals, 21 Finnish, 23 Gain, 24 Total, 25 Spew, 28 Ironing, 29 Tea-gown, 30 Retaining fee.
DOWN: 1 Offbeat, 2 Elan, 3 Ignoble, 4 Glacier, 5 Once, 6 Dossier, 7 Drive a bargain, 8 Free as the wind, 14 Scrap, 15 Spent, 19 Noisome, 20 Shotgun, 21 Flatten, 22 Implore, 26 Aida, 27 Calf.

66 ——

ACROSS: 1 Right off, 5 Open up, 9 War years, 10 Clothe, 12 Relay race, 13 Aroma, 14 Cafe, 16 One love, 19 Lead off, 21 Bide, 24 Caned, 25 Still wine, 27 Issues, 28 Constant, 29 Arable, 30 Stood out.
DOWN: 1 Reward, 2 Garble, 3 Teeny, 4 Forgave, 6 Pull ahead, 7 Not so hot, 8 Prepared, 11 Memo, 15 A good deal, 17 Old china, 18 Magnesia, 20 Fist, 21 Bail out, 22 Virago, 23 Beat it, 26 Lasso.

67 ——

ACROSS: 1 Hard-heartedness, 9 Gladiator, 10 Elena, 11 Elegiac, 12 Limited, 13 Hue, 14 Expense, 17 Turn off, 19 Unnamed, 22 Pompeii, 24 Rue, 25 Antenna, 26 Retouch, 28 Islet, 29 Inebriate, 30 Near-sightedness.
DOWN: 1 Higher education, 2 Reade, 3 Haitian, 4 Attache, 5 Tartlet, 6 Dreamer, 7 Electrode, 8 Stand-offishness, 15 Panatella, 16 Sue, 18 Ufo, 20 Minutes, 21 Drawing, 22 Perfect, 23 Matured, 27 Usage.

68 ——

ACROSS: 6 Distracted, 8 Sash, 9 Bagatelle, 11 Abet, 12 Par, 13 Relations, 16 Cuba, 17 Catcher, 18 Seminar, 20 Pair, 21 Champagne, 23 Ash, 24 Stet, 25 Amaryllis, 29 Bred, 30 Toleration.
DOWN: 1 Limb, 2 Stag, 3 Fast, 4 Stilton, 5 Assemblage, 7 Deep sleep, 8 Starching, 10 Ada, 13 Read a story, 14 Lacerated, 15 Trenchant, 19 Parable, 22 All, 26 York, 27 Lots, 28 Scot.

69 ——

ACROSS: 1 Molasses, 9 Neaptide, 10 Leda, 11 Draught-horse, 13 Manifest, 15 Coddle, 16 Ides, 17 Mouse, 18 Abed, 20 Malawi, 21 Tea-chest, 23 Divertimento, 26 Norm, 27 Sunburst, 28 Holidays.
DOWN: 2 Overpaid, 3 Aladdin's cave, 4 Scrape, 5 Snag, 6 Particle, 7 Pier, 8 Reverend, 12 Old-fashioned, 14 Trust, 16 Immodest, 17 Moisture, 19 Easterly, 22 Agnail, 24 Vend, 25 Myth.

70 ——

ACROSS: 1 Pastoral, 5 Abacus, 9 Strained, 10 Agenda, 12 On the dole, 13 Tired, 14 Lime, 16 Palaver, 19 Bramble, 21 Feed, 24 Token, 25 Retaliate, 27 Unreal, 28 Terminus, 29 Espied, 30 Attorney.
DOWN: 1 Pass on, 2 Sprite, 3 Opine, 4 Acetone, 6 Bagatelle, 7 Contrive, 8 Standard, 11 Heap, 15 In bondage, 17 Abstruse, 18 Backdrop, 20 Eyre, 21 Fitment, 22 Cannon, 23 Measly, 26 Limbo.

71 _____
ACROSS: 7 Coastline, 8 Plead, 10 Innuendo, 11 Darwin, 12 Polo, 13 Eye-liner, 15 Battery, 17 Frigate, 20 Knuckles, 22 Seen, 25 Static, 26 Restrain, 27 Adore, 28 Adventure.
DOWN: 1 Round, 2 Escudo, 3 Clangour, 4 Snooker, 5 Flirting, 6 Manifesto, 9 Edge, 14 Magnitude, 16 Taciturn, 18 Resisted, 19 Astride, 21 Lock, 23 Errata, 24 Mitre.

72 _____
ACROSS: 1 Stand fast, 8 Ruling passion, 11 Poop, 12 Had on, 13 Oran, 16 Rattled, 17 Twaddle, 18 Too fast, 20 Priests, 21 Rare, 22 Brand, 23 Asia, 26 As far as it goes, 27 Down under.
DOWN: 2 Twig, 3 Niggard, 4 Flat out, 5 So so, 6 Put out to grass, 7 Court disaster, 9 Spare tire, 10 Underseal, 14 Alban, 15 Fagin, 19 Terrain, 20 Pension, 24 Mayo, 25 Ague.

73 _____
ACROSS: 1 Proposed, 9 Redstart, 10 Undo, 11 Telegraphese, 13 Fragment, 15 Cogent, 16 Edda, 17 Found, 18 Pond, 20 Gopher, 21 Bachelor, 23 Heart-strings, 26 Unit, 27 Lop-sided, 28 Ebenezer.
DOWN: 2 Rendered, 3 Photographer, 4 Shelve, 5 Drag, 6 Advanced, 7 Fare, 8 Attested, 12 High pressure, 14 Thumb, 16 Eggshell, 17 Fireside, 19 Noontide, 22 Candle, 24 Alps, 25 Ryde.

74 _____
ACROSS: 7 Periscope, 8 Mason, 10 Aptitude, 11 Crease, 12 Beta, 13 Rosemary, 15 Ranches, 17 Transit, 20 Bear-skin, 22 Post, 25 Prayer, 26 Threaten, 27 Leant, 28 Unbending.
DOWN: 1 Tempo, 2 Simile, 3 Accurate, 4 Appears, 5 Salesmen, 6 Constrain, 9 Acts, 14 Sage-green, 16 Carrying, 18 Reported, 19 Instant, 21 Kerb, 23 Shandy, 24 Meant.

75 _____
ACROSS: 1 Object-ball, 6 Slip, 10 Lathe, 11 Ombudsman, 12 Stippler, 13 Pasta, 15 Overeat, 17 Leisure, 19 Nomadic, 21 Finesse, 22 Clean, 24 Backside, 27 Impresari, 28 Olive, 29 Nile, 30 Penny royal.
DOWN: 1 Owls, 2 Jet stream, 3 Cheap, 4 Booklet, 5 Liberal, 7 Limes, 8 Pentameter, 9 Adoption, 14 Connection, 16 Endanger, 18 Ups-a-daisy, 20 Cabbage, 21 Faction, 23 Expel, 25 Stour, 26 Well.

76 _____
ACROSS: 1 Lose one's balance, 9 Battler, 10 Astride, 11 Upon, 12 Put on, 13 Noon, 16 Rake-off, 17 Trivial, 18 Low-down, 21 Chopper, 23 Tory, 24 Smart, 25 Ha-ha, 28 Ovation, 29 Iceberg, 30 Seek one's fortune.
DOWN: 1 Labour relations, 2 Set book, 3 Only, 4 Earmuff, 5 Bear out, 6 Loth, 7 Nairobi, 8 Eternal triangle, 14 Colon, 15 Pivot, 19 Warfare, 20 Nominee, 21 Cardiff, 22 Plateau, 26 Vigo, 27 Peer.

77 _____
ACROSS: 1 Severe sentence, 9 Arrested, 10 Since, 12 Eton, 13 Vowel sound, 15 Absolute, 16 Patent, 18 Bisect, 20 Threaded, 23 Tea-planter, 24 Zero, 26 Lotto, 27 Primrose, 28 Dress rehearsal.
DOWN: 2 Various, 3 Reel, 4 Set forth, 5 Nodded, 6 Easy stages, 7 Consume, 8 Ready to drop, 11 Legal battle, 14 Black looks, 17 Sheepish, 19 Shatter, 21 Dresses, 22 Sniper, 25 Area.

78 _____
ACROSS: 1 Left   at, 5 Wind up, 9 The bible, 10 Stymie, 11 Fitted in, 12 Geisha, 14 Petty crime, 18 Turned upon, 22 Hold up, 23 Ignorant, 24 Bairns, 25 Tail back, 26 Rugger, 27 Iterated.
DOWN: 1 Let off, 2 Fiesta, 3 Foiled, 4 All mixed up, 6 In the act, 7 Domestic, 8 Prelates, 13 At long last, 15 At the bar, 16 Grilling, 17 Sequence, 19 Howler, 20 Vacant, 21 Staked.

79 _____
ACROSS: 1 Handicap, 6 Wither, 9 Voyeur, 10 Gauntlet, 11 Trespass, 12 Dulcet, 13 Redistribute, 16 Shivering fit, 19 Stolid, 21 Teething, 23 Malinger, 24 Trophy, 25 Adagio, 26 Ladybird.
DOWN: 2 Aboard, 3 Dress, 4 Coriander, 5 Pegasus, 6 Wound, 7 Tittlebat, 8 Eleventh, 13 Revolting, 14 Re ected, 15 Shetland, 17 Natural, 18 Anchor, 20 Doggo, 22 H-bomb.

80 _____
ACROSS: 1 Capitalism, 9 Foot, 10 Postmaster, 11 Cocoon, 12 Soothed, 15 Sea-room, 16 Drear, 17 Nips, 18 Miss, 19 Paint, 21 Mislead, 22 Taken in, 24 Retail, 27 Intonation, 28 Idol, 29 Goods-train.
DOWN: 2 Atom, 3 Intent, 4 Amassed, 5 Iota, 6 Marcher, 7 Locomotion, 8 Stonemason, 12 Sand-martin, 13 Opposition, 14 Dread, 15 Saint, 19 Palling, 20 Talents, 23 Editor, 25 Otto, 26 Gobi.

81 _____
ACROSS: 5 Tackle, 8 Coolabah, 9 Bizarre, 10 Up-end, 11 Education, 13 Parlance, 14 Empire, 17 Haw, 19 Era, 20 Debate, 23 Hercules, 26 Seventeen, 28 Lupin, 29 Overfed, 30 Open-cast, 31 Essene.
DOWN: 1 Scrump, 2 Bone-dry, 3 Sand-yacht, 4 Parsec, 5 Twitcher, 6 Coast, 7 Larboard, 12 Dew, 15 Masculine, 16 Reserves, 18 Aesthete, 21 She, 22 Slipway, 24 Enrapt, 25 Senate, 27 Eerie.

82 _____
ACROSS: 1 Dismal, 4 Immolate, 9 Aright, 10 Esoteric, 12 Loco, 13 Sneer, 14 Carp, 17 Shooting star, 20 Dissertation, 23 Axis, 24 Spike, 25 Bach, 28 De ated, 29 Repair, 30 Mindless, 31 Severe.
DOWN: 1 Dead loss, 2 Switch on, 3 Ache, 5 Master-stroke, 6 Onto, 7 Abroad, 8 Except, 11 On one's uppers, 15 Staid, 16 Paean, 18 Vicarage, 19 In charge, 21 Random, 22 Tiffin, 26 Hail, 27 Hebe.

83 _____
ACROSS: 1 Gambol, 4 Activate, 9 Abrade, 10 Amicable, 12 Note, 13 Smelt, 14 Drug, 17 Short circuit, 20 Covent garden, 23 Echo, 24 Stook, 25 Sago, 28 Crackpot, 29 Deacon, 30 Rehearse, 31 Pledge.
DOWN: 1 Gladness, 2 Marathon, 3 Odds, 5 Complication, 6 Inca, 7 Albert, 8 Emerge, 11 Ambidextrous, 15 Stood, 16 Divan, 18 Advanced, 19 Announce, 21 Fencer, 22 Thrash, 26 Skua, 27 Peel.

84 _____
ACROSS: 7 Thickhead, 8 Got on, 10 Clear out, 11 Parody, 12 Heat, 13 Forget it, 15 Stinker, 17 Spotter, 20 Diabetes, 22 Sock, 25 Nereid, 26 Raw boned, 27 Afire, 28 Old record.
DOWN: 1 Whole, 2 Ice age, 3 Throttle, 4 Cast off, 5 Four feet, 6 Good mixer, 9 Spur, 14 Strike off, 16 Noble art, 18 Password, 19 As a rule, 21 To do, 23 Choice, 24 Tears.

85 _____
ACROSS: 8 Lien, 9 Urn, 10 Even so, 11 Gideon, 12 Metrical, 13 Infernal regions, 15 Contest, 17 Abetter, 20 Delaying tactics, 23 Strangle, 25 Dreary, 26 Winner, 27 Sun, 28 Easy.
DOWN: 1 Minion, 2 Inherent, 3 Burn one's fingers, 4 Anomaly, 5 Weather-boarding, 6 Gemini, 7 Ossa, 14 Nee, 16 Ode, 18 Titterer, 19 Ogreish, 21 Avaunt, 22 Caress, 24 Trip.

86 _____
ACROSS: 1 Varnished, 9 Retort, 10 Starboard, 11 Athena, 12 Annoyance, 13 Spring, 17 Leg, 19 Coinage, 20 Average, 21 Ass, 23 Amerce, 27 Arrowhead, 28 Castle, 29 Colourist, 30 Egoism, 31 Astronomy.
DOWN: 2 Acting, 3 Narrow, 4 Slogan, 5 Earache, 6 Sextuplet, 7 Polemical, 8 Strangled, 14 Scratches, 15 Diversion, 16 Matchless, 17 Lea, 18 Gas, 22 Serious, 24 Honour, 25 Charon, 26 Hansom.

87 _____
ACROSS: 1 Classic, 5 Rock-tar, 9 Marconi, 10 Scowled, 11 Telephony, 12 Stake, 13 Cowes, 15 Apprehend, 17 Chocolate, 19 Magic, 22 Lisle, 23 Whodunits, 25 Portage, 26 Electra, 27 Overdue, 28 Assured.
DOWN: 1 Cometic, 2 Air‑ ow, 3 Sloop, 4 Chipolata, 5 Rusty, 6 Cross-beam, 7 Tillage, 8 Redhead, 14 Score-card, 16 Phenomena, 17 Calypso, 18 Observe, 20 Glitter, 21 Costard, 23 Where, 24 Users.

88 _____
ACROSS: 1 From age to age, 8 Overact, 9 Precise, 11 Impious, 12 Slanted, 13 Kitty, 14 In a corner, 16 Estranged, 19 Fifer, 21 In a mood, 23 Matelot, 24 Gauntry, 25 Noisome, 26 Leading light.
DOWN: 1 Flea-pit, 2 Oratory, 3 Attesting, 4 Expos, 5 Oregano, 6 Glisten, 7 Not in keeping, 10 Elder brother, 15 Abdominal, 17 Traduce, 18 Adopted, 19 Fitting, 20 Fill out, 22 Doyen.

89 _____
ACROSS: 1 Batting order, 9 Aliment, 10 Tobacco, 11 Hack, 12 On top, 13 Pray, 16 Needles, 17 Treason, 18 Biscuit, 21 Inherit, 23 Alto, 24 Wasps, 25 Wish, 28 Tillage, 29 Spooner, 30 Prison record.
DOWN: 1 Brioche, 2 Tier, 3 Intones, 4 Gets out, 5 Ruby, 6 Encores, 7 Bathing beauty, 8 Body snatchers, 14 Flour, 15 Lethe, 19 Settler, 20 Trade in, 21 Impasse, 22 Reigned, 26 Bass, 27 Solo.

90 _____
ACROSS: 6 See through one, 8 Corker, 9 Rent acts, 10 Twa, 11 Stanza, 12 Tranship, 14 In a stew, 16 Splayed, 20 Spare man, 23 Apache, 24 Cot, 25 Filagree, 26 Future, 27 Silent service.
DOWN: 1 Week ends, 2 Shortage, 3 Top rate, 4 Agenda, 5 Morass, 6 Shooting pains, 7 Eat like a horse, 13 Nil, 15 Toe, 17 Platform, 18 Abattoir, 19 Incense, 21 Really, 22 Merino.

91 _____

ACROSS: 1 Vatican, 5 Vibrant, 9 Reclaim, 10 Undress, 11 Interpret, 12 Evita, 13 Thyme, 15 Titillate, 17 Mouse-trap, 19 Witch, 22 Sting, 23 Quarterly, 25 Naivete, 26 Pompeii, 27 Cayenne, 28 Rhizome.
DOWN: 1 Verdict, 2 Tacitly, 3 Chair, 4 Numerator, 5 Vault, 6 Bedfellow, 7 America, 8 Testate, 14 Evergreen, 16 Top-hamper, 17 Masonic, 18 Utility, 20 Torpedo, 21 Haywire, 23 Queue, 24 Tempi.

92 _____

ACROSS: 1 Back door, 5 Safari, 9 Renovate, 10 Chaste, 11 Tipstaff, 12 Orwell, 14 Contenders, 18 Alteration, 22 Kinder, 23 Agitates, 24 Vainly, 25 Monorail, 26 Ragged, 27 Idolater.
DOWN: 1 Berets, 2 Canape, 3 Devote, 4 Out of sorts, 6 Adherent, 7 Answered, 8 Idealist, 13 Stronghold, 15 Talk over, 16 Standing, 17 True blue, 19 Stroll, 20 Strait, 21 Ostler.

93 _____

ACROSS: 1 Spacecraft, 9 Yoyo, 10 Metatarsus, 11 Swains, 12 Hide-out, 15 Bran-tub, 16 Revue, 17 Gash, 18 Bier, 19 Haunt, 21 Oarsman, 22 Truancy, 24 Easter, 27 Inadequate, 28 Erne, 29 Reputation.
DOWN: 2 Peek, 3 Chaste, 4 Clamour, 5 Also, 6 Tussore, 7 Corinthian, 8 Gooseberry, 12 Hygrometer, 13 Desert song, 14 Texan, 15 Burnt, 19 Harrier, 20 Trisect, 23 Abrupt, 25 Ramp, 26 Otto.

94 _____

ACROSS: 1 High birth rate, 10 Optical, 11 Inverse, 12 Dire, 13 Get on, 14 Wise, 17 Females, 18 Fervent, 19 Uptight, 22 Chelsea, 24 Beam, 25 Grand, 26 Serf, 29 Supremo, 30 Adapter, 31 Beneath notice.
DOWN: 2 Interim, 3 Hock, 4 Illness, 5 Tail off, 6 Rive, 7 Terrine, 8 Load of rubbish, 9 Desert warfare, 15 Flogs, 16 Creep, 20 Trample, 21 Turn out, 22 Contain, 23 Sceptic, 27 Mere, 28 Pact.

95 _____

ACROSS: 7 Sergeants, 8 Stool, 10 Streaked, 11 Trench, 12 Oslo, 13 Umbrella, 15 Disband, 17 William, 20 Federate, 22 Itch, 25 Mother, 26 Triangle, 27 Troll, 28 Tailboard.
DOWN: 1 Tenth, 2 Agrees, 3 Back down, 4 Stadium, 5 Ethereal, 6 Dog-collar, 9 Stub, 14 Sideboard, 16 Beer hall, 18 Initials, 19 Neutral, 21 Afro, 23 Cannot, 24 Alarm.

96 _____

ACROSS: 1 Rip off, 4 Scouting, 9 Nilgai, 10 Contused, 12 Heir, 13 Delta, 14 Idle, 17 Room at the Top, 20 Board of Trade, 23 Abut, 24 Stoke, 25 Shia, 28 The eet, 29 Weirdo, 30 Numerate, 31 Ingest.
DOWN: 1 Run short, 2 Pile it on, 3 Flap, 5 Cook the books, 6 Up to, 7 Inside, 8 Gadget, 11 Beat a retreat, 15 Major, 16 Volta, 18 War horse, 19 See about, 21 Batten, 22 Museum, 26 Slur, 27 Lean.

97 _____

ACROSS: 1 Je ne sais quoi, 8 Algeria, 9 Fritter, 11 Reigate, 12 Retread, 13 Fugue, 14 Albatross, 16 Recollect, 19 Virgo, 21 Callous, 23 Linkage, 24 Serving, 25 Hospice, 26 Stage romance.
DOWN: 1 Jogging, 2 Narrate, 3 Stalemate, 4 Infer, 5 Quintet, 6 On the go, 7 Pair of braces, 10 Rediscovered, 15 Bethlehem, 17 Culprit, 18 Looming, 19 Venison, 20 Realise, 22 Sugar.

98 _____

ACROSS: 1 Marginal, 5 Vacant, 9 Listener, 10 Cast up, 12 Completed, 13 Calls, 14 Feed, 16 Skipper, 19 Contend, 21 Same, 24 Moist, 25 Scratched, 27 Ibadan, 28 Sentence, 29 Greens, 30 Stampede.
DOWN: 1 Malice, 2 Resume, 3 Ideal, 4 Abetted, 6 Anarchism, 7 Antelope, 8 Tapestry, 11 Odds, 15 Eye-strain, 17 Scamping, 18 Intimate, 20 Dash, 21 Serpent, 22 Change, 23 Adhere, 26 Totem.

99 _____

ACROSS: 1 Two-faced, 6 Albion, 9 Pelota, 10 Springer, 11 Disagree, 12 Lining, 13 Plain-clothes, 16 Self-hypnosis, 19 Aboard, 21 Triplane, 23 Londoner, 24 Uneven, 25 Hearty, 26 Elephant.
DOWN: 2 Weevil, 3 Flora, 4 Chairlady, 5 Discern, 6 April, 7 Banknotes, 8 Oleander, 13 Puff-adder, 14 Lassitude, 15 Pembroke, 17 Nut-tree, 18 Intern, 20 Dandy, 22 Leech.

100 _____

ACROSS: 7 Chump chop, 8 Lotus, 10 Aswan dam, 11 Odd job, 12 True, 13 Take a tip, 15 Off duty, 17 Wide boy, 20 Flat rate, 22 Fuss, 25 Beacon, 26 Imitated, 27 Screw, 28 Forgiving.
DOWN: 1 Chose, 2 Impair, 3 Acid test, 4 Con moto, 5 Bold face, 6 Autopilot, 9 Book, 14 Af uence, 16 Detached, 18 Infringe, 19 Venison, 21 Arno, 23 Starve, 24 Means.

101

ACROSS: 1 Blast-off, 5 Errand, 9 Resprays, 10 Avoids, 11 Get along, 12 Freeze, 14 Abstracted, 18 In hot water, 22 Pepper, 23 Acquires, 24 Slacks, 25 Hothouse, 26 Denude, 27 Stands up.

DOWN: 1 Borage, 2 Assets, 3 Turtle, 4 Flying boat, 6 Reversal, 7 Anisette, 8 Descends, 13 Stretch out, 15 Disposed, 16 Chaplain, 17 Streaked, 19 Rush in, 20 Argues, 21 Asleep.

102

ACROSS: 5 Dugout, 8 Early man, 9 Canards, 10 Often, 11 Open heart, 13 Tiny tots, 14 Unseat, 17 Spa, 19 Ate, 20 Canter, 23 After all, 26 Heavy fine, 28 Malay, 29 Correct, 30 Turn down, 31 Afters.

DOWN: 1 See out, 2 Crating, 3 Hypnotise, 4 Maggot, 5 Drawn out, 6 Grace, 7 Under way, 12 Psi, 15 Never mind, 16 Takes off, 18 Prefaces, 21 Van, 22 Calls on, 24 Feet up, 25 Laying, 27 Verne.

103

ACROSS: 6 Quick-tempered, 8 Latest, 9 Linesman, 10 Tic, 11 Stroll, 12 Antennae, 14 Brigade, 16 Traffic, 20 Passport, 23 Isobar, 24 Awn, 25 Starling, 26 Caddis, 27 Refrigeration.

DOWN: 1 Livelong, 2 Skittled, 3 Hell-cat, 4 Spinet, 5 Prison, 6 Quartermaster, 7 Dramatisation, 13 Eva, 15 Alp, 17 Raincoat, 18 Floodlit, 19 Stagger, 21 Scruff, 22 Origin.

104

ACROSS: 5 Assail, 8 Co-option, 9 Operate, 10 Relic, 11 Testament, 13 Reporter, 14 Teasel, 17 Ore, 19 Her, 20 Volume, 23 Deposing, 26 Container, 28 Exeat, 29 Neptune, 30 Osculate, 31 Ostend.

DOWN: 1 Scorer, 2 Collops, 3 Stockroom, 4 Donate, 5 Appetite, 6 Scram, 7 Intended, 12 Ere, 15 Erroneous, 16 Coroners, 18 Resigned, 21 Ode, 22 Sidecar, 24 Ernest, 25 Gather, 27 Title.

105

ACROSS: 8 Wide, 9 Spa, 10 Reason, 11 Adagio, 12 River-bed, 13 Gentlemanliness, 15 Gainsay, 17 Citadel, 20 Vegetable garden, 23 Arethusa, 25 Inside, 26 String, 27 Fah, 28 Iowa.

DOWN: 1 Riddle, 2 Heighten, 3 As sober as a judge, 4 Fairway, 5 Travelling light, 6 Warren, 7 Coke, 14 She, 16 Ace, 18 Acrostic, 19 Alfalfa, 21 Entail, 22 Endows, 24 Ruth.

106

ACROSS: 1 Black stockings, 9 Reactor, 10 Lactose, 11 Heat, 12 Periodical, 14 Retort, 15 Pennines, 17 Far apart, 18 Career, 21 Informally, 22 Stag, 24 Chalice, 25 Iron out, 26 Stands to reason.

DOWN: 1 Burgher, 2 As a matter of fact, 3 Kite, 4 Tureen, 5 Calliper, 6 Incidental, 7 Good connections, 8 Cellos, 13 Proportion, 16 Breakers, 17 Flitch, 19 Right on, 20 Albino, 23 Dole.

107

ACROSS: 1 Guide dogs, 9 En route, 10 Shovels, 11 Tunisia, 12 In any case, 14 Medieval, 15 Re-edit, 17 Leisure, 20 Eating, 23 Instance, 25 Addressed, 26 In a mess, 27 Titanic, 28 Nicosia, 29 Long reign.

DOWN: 2 Unhinge, 3 Divined, 4 Delicate, 5 Settee, 6 Wrong idea, 7 Cursive, 8 Befalling, 13 Smashed, 15 Resilient, 16 Ill at ease, 18 Rearming, 19 Askance, 21 Testate, 22 Needing, 24 Casual.

108

ACROSS: 1 Put to rights, 9 Done thing, 10 At one, 11 Loafer, 12 Step it up, 13 Dust up, 15 Impaired, 18 Chain-saw, 19 Friend, 21 The idiot, 23 Scamps, 26 Acute, 27 In a corner, 28 Late husband.

DOWN: 1 Puddled, 2 Tonga, 3 On the turn, 4 Isis, 5 High time, 6 Sharp, 7 Steeped, 8 Post free, 14 Stake out, 16 Atrocious, 17 Canoeist, 18 Cut back, 20 Desired, 22 Dwell, 24 Mensa, 25 Dash.

109

ACROSS: 1 Veteran, 5 Peasant, 9 Lying, 10 Get-at-able, 11 Estimation, 12 Scut, 14 In the long run, 18 Carpenter-bee, 21 Ulna, 22 Chivalrous, 25 Betrothed, 26 Nyasa, 27 Rockery, 28 Oddment.

DOWN: 1 Velvet, 2 Thirty, 3 Regimented, 4 Night, 5 Pot-boiler, 6 Asti, 7 Albacore, 8 Treating, 13 Underlined, 15 Hit the hay, 16 Scrubber, 17 Frenetic, 19 Morale, 20 Aslant, 23 Video, 24 Move.

110

ACROSS: 6 Corrigenda, 8 Real, 9 Steadfast, 11 Pill, 12 Ear, 13 Depositor, 16 Etch, 17 Macabre, 18 Somehow, 20 Last, 21 Dominates, 23 End, 24 Tier, 25 Insolence, 29 Stud, 30 Green light.

DOWN: 1 Boss, 2 Erse, 3 Aged, 4 Andante, 5 Fallacious, 7 Afternoon, 8 Represent, 10 Ago, 13 Dramatists, 14 Plastered, 15 Shredding, 19 Smashed, 22 Ale, 26 Long, 27 Nail, 28 Echo.

111_____

ACROSS: 1 Enterprising, 8 Plateau, 9 Samovar, 11 Leeward, 12 Solicit, 13 Busby, 14 Moderator, 16 Oil-paints, 19 Ascot, 21 Sublime, 23 Masonic, 24 Malaise, 25 Anglice, 26 Palette-knife.
DOWN: 1 Enamels, 2 Therapy, 3 Roundsman, 4 Risks, 5 Sampler, 6 Navy-cut, 7 Apple-blossom, 10 Return ticket, 15 Disembark, 17 Lobelia, 18 Asinine, 19 Assegai, 20 Connive, 22 Erect.

112_____

ACROSS: 1 Regress, 5 Bold, 9 Pressed for space, 10 Oust, 11 Acton, 12 Abut, 15 Flogged, 16 Tetanus, 17 Sleeper, 19 For love, 21 Tape, 22 Atlas, 23 Doer, 26 All along the line, 27 Byte, 28 Convent.
DOWN: 1 Reproof, 2 Grease one's palm, 3 Else, 4 Seduced, 5 Blow-out, 6 Last, 7 Creates, 8 Carbon monoxide, 13 Agape, 14 Start, 17 Set sail, 18 Retinue, 19 Frantic, 20 Earnest, 24 Ally, 25 Wean.

113_____

ACROSS: 7 Open-ended, 8 Aegis, 10 Measured, 11 Agency, 12 Anon, 13 Flurried, 15 Exposed, 17 Raiment, 20 Creditor, 22 Dope, 25 Ideals, 26 Meekness, 27 Stock, 28 Practised.
DOWN: 1 Upper, 2 Unison, 3 Entrance, 4 Send off, 5 Telegram, 6 Miscreant, 9 Tabu, 14 Extradite, 16 Ordnance, 18 Audience, 19 Primary, 21 Task, 23 Pencil, 24 Ashes.

114_____

ACROSS: 1 Bad blood, 5 Botham, 9 No longer, 10 Stills, 12 On the line, 13 Froze, 14 Twee, 16 Trireme, 19 Hold out, 21 Hyde, 24 Waste, 25 Last ing, 27 Varlet, 28 Big noise, 29 Rustle, 30 Send word.
DOWN: 1 Bunion, 2 Dilate, 3 Lance, 4 One time, 6 Out of mind, 7 Hold over, 8 Mastered, 11 Zest, 15 Wholemeal, 17 Chew over, 18 All-sorts, 20 Till, 21 Hostile, 22 Libido, 23 Agreed, 26 Fined.

115_____

ACROSS: 1 Problem children, 9 Eldest son, 10 Befit, 11 Earlier, 12 Relievo, 13 Ace, 14 Relight, 17 Drachma, 19 Doubter, 22 Catarrh, 24 Ado, 25 Husband, 26 Rorqual, 28 Reata, 29 Alienated, 30 Seaside landlady.
DOWN: 1 Preferred shares, 2 Order, 3 Lasting, 4 Musk-rat, 5 Hundred, 6 Lobelia, 7 Refresher, 8 National holiday, 15 Louisiana, 16 Hie, 18 Ria, 20 Trapani, 21 Radiate, 22 Corsica, 23 Throned, 27 Ultra.

116_____

ACROSS: 1 Restart, 5 Codicil, 9 Shallow, 10 Eastern, 11 Tap-dancer, 12 Haste, 13 Eider, 15 Important, 17 Conspires, 19 Eagre, 22 Set to, 23 Otherwise, 25 Animato, 26 Stomach, 27 Egghead, 28 Everest.
DOWN: 1 Rosette, 2 Slapped, 3 Alloa, 4 Town-crier, 5 Clear, 6 Discharge, 7 Chelsea, 8 Lenient, 14 Reprobate, 16 Posthaste, 17 Cascade, 18 Nothing, 20 Grimace, 21 Eyeshot, 23 Ovoid, 24 Rhone.

117_____

ACROSS: 8 Sinecure, 9 Erotic, 10 Low, 11 Pastoral, 12 Caress, 13 Comprehensively, 15 Versify, 18 Slurped, 21 Misconstruction, 24 Dermal, 25 Pairs off, 26 Ice, 27 Scorns, 28 Needless.
DOWN: 1 Virago, 2 Pent-up, 3 Quarter finalist, 4 Bellmen, 5 Newcastle United, 6 Co-driver, 7 Dissolve, 14 Mar, 16 Eminence, 17 Sycamore, 19 Phi, 20 Stipend, 22 Tussle, 23 Oafish.

118_____

ACROSS: 1 Nightingale, 10 Tunis, 11 Stop short, 12 Carried on, 13 Issue, 14 Impost, 16 Emigrant, 18 Gardener, 20 Garner, 23 Ousel, 24 Roundhead, 26 Notepaper, 27 Miser, 28 Kept counsel.
DOWN: 2 Inner, 3 His nibs, 4 Inside, 5 Good name, 6 Listing, 7 Sticking point, 8 Coxswain, 9 Street traders, 15 Parasite, 17 Decrepit, 19 Eclipse, 21 Abdomen, 22 Quarto, 25 Ensue.

119_____

ACROSS: 1 Might as well, 9 Phenomena, 10 Given, 11 Extras, 12 Went free, 13 Sedate, 15 Blackout, 18 Well-read, 19 Stakes, 21 Lying low, 23 Senora, 26 Clean, 27 Stationed, 28 Royal pardon.
DOWN: 1 Moppets, 2 Great, 3 Took after, 4 Shed, 5 Elatedly, 6 Light, 7 Content, 8 Overlook, 14 Dulcimer, 16 Catherina, 17 Famously, 18 Wildcat, 20 Stand-in, 22 Goner, 24 Owned, 25 Hail.

120_____

ACROSS: 1 Proms, 4 Bad spirit, 8 On top, 9 Separable, 11 Cues, 12 Adman, 13 Stem, 16 All for nothing, 19 Hold the record, 20 Lock, 22 Neath, 23 Pass, 26 Firm offer, 27 Outdo, 28 Royal arms, 29 Drake.
DOWN: 1 Poor catch, 2 On the nail, 3 Saps, 4 Beside oneself, 5 Parr, 6 Rebut, 7 Therm, 10 Plain features, 14 Plate, 15 Stook, 17 Indian tea, 18 Good score, 20 Lifer, 21 Carry, 24 Foil, 25 Ford.

121

ACROSS: 1 Bangladesh, 6 Verb, 9 Madagascar, 10 Scot, 12 Settle, 13 Purchase, 15 Adders tongue, 18 Meaningfully, 21 Travesty, 22 Optima, 24 Trip, 25 Celebrated, 26 Dame, 27 Assessment.
DOWN: 1 Bemuse, 2 Nudity, 3 Legal adviser, 4 Disk, 5 Statuesque, 7 Exchange, 8 Buttered, 11 School sports, 14 Weightless, 16 Imitated, 17 Paradigm, 19 Virtue, 20 Bandit, 23 Bede.

122

ACROSS: 1 Alarmist, 5 Abacus, 9 Offender, 10 Otters, 11 Largesse, 12 Praise, 14 Scrapbooks, 18 Collateral, 22 Regale, 23 Creature, 24 Intend, 25 Concrete, 26 Gadget, 27 Asserted.
DOWN: 1 Apollo, 2 Afford, 3 Manger, 4 Seersucker, 6 Bath-robe, 7 Creditor, 8 Suspense, 13 Paratroops, 15 Scorning, 16 Plighted, 17 Parlance, 19 Gauche, 20 Rudest, 21 Legend.

123

ACROSS: 1 Rerun, 4 Hurricane, 9 Apparel, 11 Ideally, 12 Shop, 13 Guise, 14 Writ, 17 Deforestation, 19 Protuberances, 21 Bury, 22 Utter, 23 Omar, 26 Steamer, 27 Tragedy, 28 Mid-stream, 29 Peter.
DOWN: 1 Rhapsodic, 2 Reproof, 3 Nary, 5 Reinstatement, 6 Ives, 7 Aileron, 8 Egypt, 10 Louis quatorze, 15 Brook, 16 Midas, 18 Destroyer, 19 Portend, 20 Comment, 21 Bosom, 24 Emit, 25 Ramp.

124

ACROSS: 1 Set screw, 5 Appear, 9 Overrate, 10 Cartel, 12 Distemper, 13 Nanny, 14 Chic, 16 Britain, 19 Out ow, 21 Cafe, 24 Staff, 25 Immediate, 27 Notary, 28 Collects, 29 Punchy, 30 Strategy.
DOWN: 1 Shoddy, 2 Theism, 3 Carve, 4 Ectopic, 6 Plaintiff, 7 Estonian, 8 Rallying, 11 Grub, 15 Hold forth, 17 Loosen up, 18 Straiten, 20 Whim, 21 Come out, 22 Gauche, 23 Measly, 26 Delta.

125

ACROSS: 7 Scrambled, 8 Nepal, 10 Frequent, 11 Raisin, 12 Bent, 13 Libretto, 15 Bayonet, 17 Polygon, 20 Finds out, 22 Norm, 25 Alsace, 26 Families, 27 Stick, 28 Beanstalk.
DOWN: 1 Acorn, 2 Basque, 3 Absentee, 4 Lentils, 5 Delivery, 6 Variation, 9 Crib, 14 Vacillate, 16 Ordnance, 18 Ornament, 19 Stiffen, 21 Odes, 23 Relate, 24 Wells.

126

ACROSS: 1 Hanover, 5 Liftoff, 9 Louvres, 10 Spectre, 11 Irradiate, 12 Wears, 13 Halts, 15 Orchestra, 17 Portrayer, 19 Local, 22 Alibi, 23 Discourse, 25 Tompion, 26 Rubbish, 27 Reneges, 28 Wattles.
DOWN: 1 Hellish, 2 Neutral, 3 Virid, 4 Raspatory, 5 Lisle, 6 Freewheel, 7 Outlast, 8 Freesia, 14 Straining, 16 Corkscrew, 17 Psalter, 18 Railman, 20 Cordial, 21 Leeches, 23 Dunes, 24 Orbit.

127

ACROSS: 1 Three-farthings, 9 Scissors, 10 Clean, 12 Laud, 13 Ritardando, 15 Prepared, 16 Entrap, 18 Nought, 20 Macaroni, 23 Talentless, 24 Tern, 26 Prang, 27 Tropical, 28 Channel swimmer.
DOWN: 2 Recluse, 3 East, 4 Agonised, 5 Tuscan, 6 Incidental, 7 Gleaner, 8 Uncompliant, 11 Sloping type, 14 Machine-gun, 17 Nauseous, 19 Unleash, 21 Overarm, 22 Clothe, 25 Hi-fi.

128

ACROSS: 1 Adolescents, 9 Treatment, 10 Inner, 11 Eleven, 12 Slighted, 13 Sister, 15 Announce, 18 Aversion, 19 Afters, 21 Intimate, 23 Concur, 26 Overt, 27 Anatomist, 28 Out of breath.
DOWN: 1 Actress, 2 Ox-eye, 3 Entremets, 4 Crew, 5 Nettling, 6 Sling, 7 Abridge, 8 Instance, 14 Spectres, 16 Off-colour, 17 Contract, 18 Adipose, 20 Stretch, 22 Motto, 24 China, 25 Calf.

129

ACROSS: 1 Panorama, 5 Albert, 9 Megapode, 10 Ignore, 11 Clear-cut, 12 Impart, 14 Pretension, 18 Quarter-day, 22 Appals, 23 Face-card, 24 Iceman, 25 Lemonade, 26 Twenty, 27 Escapade.
DOWN: 1 Pumice, 2 Nugget, 3 Report, 4 Medium rare, 6 Ligament, 7 Egomania, 8 Treating, 13 Stratagems, 15 Aquatint, 16 Ear-piece, 17 Stalwart, 19 Fedora, 20 Banana, 21 Adhere.

130

ACROSS: 1 Ticket collector, 9 Keep mum, 10 Chianti, 11 Inns, 12 Jiffy, 13 Ruse, 16 Topside, 17 Refresh, 18 Address, 21 Forties, 23 Clad, 24 Gluck, 25 Scab, 28 Uniform, 29 Idolise, 30 Tighten one's belt.
DOWN: 1 Take into account, 2 Clean up, 3 Elmo, 4 Combine, 5 Lucifer, 6 Evil, 7 Tonsure, 8 Raise the subject, 14 Siren, 15 Afore, 19 Dealing, 20 Solomon, 21 Faction, 22 Incline, 26 Go at, 27 Bows.

131

ACROSS: 5 Decamp, 8 Recalled, 9 Comport, 10 Dirge, 11 Cambridge, 13 Elevator, 14 Lounge, 17 Ebb, 19 Ill, 20 Course, 23 Plum-duff, 26 Celebrate, 28 Solve, 29 Lagoons, 30 Deserted, 31 Severs.

DOWN: 1 Bridge, 2 Scarlet, 3 Alienates, 4 Mexico, 5 Doorbell, 6 Capri, 7 Mortgage, 12 Ark, 15 Old master, 16 Coverage, 18 Bearings, 21 Apt, 22 Quality, 24 Leader, 25 Fiends, 27 Elope.

132

ACROSS: 1 Barrister, 8 Turn on the heat, 11 Pace, 12 Dogma, 13 Item, 16 Latch on, 17 Spinner, 18 Chicken, 20 Classic, 21 Rake, 22 Strip, 23 Iron, 26 Intimate terms, 27 Under arms.

DOWN: 2 Anna, 3 Run down, 4 Schemes, 5 Echo, 6 Quick thinking, 7 Past one's prime, 9 Applecart, 10 Americans, 14 Choke, 15 Pilau, 19 Nutcase, 20 Chimera, 24 Sign, 25 Seem.

133

ACROSS: 1 Accelerator, 10 Omaha, 11 Over to you, 12 Night life, 13 Feast, 14 Solace, 16 Writes up, 18 Revision, 20 Avidly, 23 Igloo, 24 Tropology, 26 Haversack, 27 Allow, 28 Seventeenth.

DOWN: 2 Clang, 3 Elastic, 4 Exotic, 5 Ale-berry, 6 Out of it, 7 Going straight, 8 Bypassed, 9 Multiply by two, 15 Lava-lava, 17 Port vale, 19 Scourge, 21 Violate, 22 Pocket, 25 Owlet.

134

ACROSS: 1 Contract, 5 Spread, 9 Spurious, 10 Stress, 11 Elements, 12 Whiter, 14 Drawbridge, 18 Confiscate, 22 Events, 23 Thinking, 24 Intend, 25 Adherent, 26 Garnet, 27 Enormous.

DOWN: 1 Cashes, 2 Nausea, 3 Railed, 4 Counteract, 6 Potsherd, 7 Eventide, 8 Disorder, 13 Switched on, 15 Screwing, 16 Investor, 17 Distance, 19 Endear, 20 Cicero, 21 Agates.

135

ACROSS: 1 Philanthropist, 9 Evaluate, 10 Loyal, 12 Iona, 13 Alimentary, 15 Hostelry, 16 Broken, 18 Fiesta, 20 Dramatic, 23 Stagecoach, 24 Hair, 26 Extra, 27 Stealthy, 28 Traffic-signals.

DOWN: 2 Invents, 3 Able, 4 Trailers, 5 Rheumy, 6 Palindrome, 7 Skylark, 8 Playing-card, 11 Tightfisted, 14 Centre-half, 17 Crackers, 19 Enactor, 21 Trachea, 22 Bonsai, 25 Flog.

136

ACROSS: 1 Bustle, 4 Accoutre, 9 Louvre, 10 Improved, 12 Yoga, 13 Sedan, 14 Free, 17 Forest of Dean, 20 Fiddlesticks, 23 Haul, 24 Dotty, 25 Adze, 28 Rotation, 29 Vacant, 30 Expiates, 31 Downed.

DOWN: 1 Bully off, 2 Sluggard, 3 Lord, 5 Commandments, 6 Okra, 7 Tavern, 8 Eddied, 11 Second to none, 15 Astir, 16 Party, 18 Acid rain, 19 Assented, 21 Charge, 22 Bust-up, 26 Stoa, 27 Halo.

137

ACROSS: 1 Kingfisher, 9 Fine, 10 Laryngitis, 11 Talent, 12 Fall out, 15 Beeline, 16 Error, 17 Move, 18 Mete, 19 Fused, 21 Lea et, 22 Ring out, 24 Fuhrer, 27 Invocation, 28 Rank, 29 Side-street.

DOWN: 2 Iran, 3 Glycol, 4 Ingenue, 5 Hate, 6 Rustler, 7 Give rise to, 8 Settlement, 12 Family firm, 13 Leviathans, 14 Trout, 15 Boxer, 19 Ferries, 20 Directs, 23 Gutter, 25 Avid, 26 Cope.

138

ACROSS: 1 Best form, 5 Fold up, 9 Hard case, 10 Stay up, 12 Long drive, 13 Egypt, 14 Blue, 16 Stowage, 19 Let drop, 21 Cult, 24 Theme, 25 Set a watch, 27 Embryo, 28 Hands out, 29 Target, 30 Elder son.

DOWN: 1 Beheld, 2 Shrink, 3 Faced, 4 Restive, 6 On the boil, 7 Day by day, 8 Pipettes, 11 Hews, 15 Large type, 17 Flat feet, 18 Steel bar, 20 Push, 21 Catcall, 22 Strops, 23 Photon, 26 Wedge.

139

ACROSS: 8 Sombrero, 9 Rhymed, 10 Ago, 11 Endeared, 12 Coxing, 13 Bowling analysis, 15 Airless, 18 Studded, 21 Stickit minister, 24 Re-edit, 25 Detailed, 26 Log, 27 Mettle, 28 Eloquent.

DOWN: 1 Borneo, 2 Abseil, 3 Beer and skittles, 4 Road-map, 5 Procrastination, 6 Lynx-eyed, 7 Meantime, 14 War, 16 In the red, 17 Lucidity, 19 Dot, 20 Smidgen, 22 Slip up, 23 Exeunt.

140

ACROSS: 1 Speedwell, 9 Allured, 10 Save-all, 11 Because, 12 Signboard, 14 Oarlocks, 15 Charge, 17 Erasing, 20 Osprey, 23 Cashmere, 25 Education, 26 Uplands, 27 Villain, 28 Sceptre, 29 Disgraced.

DOWN: 2 Planish, 3 Eleanor, 4 Walkover, 5 Lambda, 6 Blacklegs, 7 Trounce, 8 Adversity, 13 Roosted, 15 Concourse, 16 Germinate, 18 Notching, 19 Psalter, 21 Patella, 22 Emotive, 24 Rested.

141 ___
ACROSS: 1 Lake-dwelling, 9 Outside, 10 Gagster, 11 Thou, 12 Manor, 13 Fish, 16 Infield, 17 Smuggle, 18 Exploit, 21 Wagtail, 23 Seth, 24 Spots, 25 Thug, 28 Inferno, 29 Hatless, 30 Slip-carriage.
DOWN: 1 Lets off, 2 Knit, 3 Die-hard, 4 Engross, 5 Lugs, 6 Netting, 7 Container ship, 8 Archaeologist, 14 Felon, 15 Surge, 19 Pitiful, 20 Tapioca, 21 Watcher, 22 Athlete, 26 Grip, 27 Etna.

142 ___
ACROSS: 1 Short commons, 8 Lay bare, 9 Exactor, 11 Slip out, 12 Douglas, 13 Every, 14 East ender, 16 Barrister, 19 Tessa, 21 Armband, 23 Tripoli, 24 Deadpan, 25 Halogen, 26 Standardised.
DOWN: 1 Stylite, 2 Oratory, 3 Treatment, 4 Oread, 5 Measure, 6 Nettled, 7 Plasterboard, 10 Reservations, 15 Scratched, 17 Rampart, 18 In a spin, 19 Tri es, 20 Slogged, 22 Donna.

143 ___
ACROSS: 1 Sick as a parrot, 10 Despoil, 11 Chicago, 12 Ivan, 13 Angle, 14 Hind, 17 Intrude, 18 Distaff, 19 Tie-clip, 22 Tornado, 24 Argo, 25 Brass, 26 Beam, 29 Element, 30 Unicorn, 31 Rolling stones.
DOWN: 2 Instant, 3 Knob, 4 Silence, 5 Pickled, 6 Rain, 7 Ocarina, 8 Administrates, 9 Word of command, 15 Bully, 16 Usury, 20 El greco, 21 Puritan, 22 Tissues, 23 Anemone, 27 Tell, 28 Lido.

144 ___
ACROSS: 1 Hellcat, 5 Settler, 9 Niobium, 10 Upright, 11 Overproof, 12 Guilt, 13 Tasks, 15 In the lead, 17 Grave news, 19 Not in, 22 Tamil, 23 Cha-cha-cha, 25 Inroads, 26 Issuing, 27 Diluted, 28 Eastern.
DOWN: 1 Hang-out, 2 Lioness, 3 Chimp, 4 Temporise, 5 Stuff, 6 Turn green, 7 Log fire, 8 Rotated, 14 Steal past, 16 Toss aside, 17 Get wind, 18 Admiral, 20 Tactile, 21 Neat gin, 23 Cased, 24 Hosts.

145 ___
ACROSS: 1 Knave of diamonds, 9 Evanesced, 10 Mitre, 11 Ontario, 12 Lentisk, 13 Rag, 14 Fairway, 17 Erosion, 19 Hepatic, 22 Respect, 24 One, 25 Gremlin, 26 Plateau, 28 Ataxy, 29 Overtrump, 30 Ship of the desert.
DOWN: 1 Keep off the grass, 2 Apart, 3 Eyebrow, 4 Factory, 5 Indulge, 6 Memento, 7 Nutritive, 8 Speaking-trumpet, 15 Impresari, 16 Ali, 18 Roe, 20 Tally-ho, 21 Contort, 22 Replete, 23 Startle, 27 Elude.

146 ___
ACROSS: 5 Sparse, 8 Reporter, 9 Ordinal, 10 Proud, 11 Recession, 13 Landseer, 14 Notary, 17 Apt, 19 Asp, 20 Regina, 23 Dear dear, 26 Precisian, 28 Tress, 29 Picador, 30 Becoming, 31 Egoist.
DOWN: 1 Propel, 2 Appoint, 3 Tradesman, 4 Meagre, 5 Surgeons, 6 Amiss, 7 Seaboard, 12 Err, 15 Operation, 16 Learning, 18 Passport, 21 Ada, 22 Demerit, 24 Envied, 25 Resign, 27 Coati.

147 ___
ACROSS: 1 Dodge, 4 Loose-leaf, 9 Alcohol, 11 Elderly, 12 Hymn, 13 Angst, 14 Tier, 17 Roller-coaster, 19 Indispensable, 21 Daft, 22 Aches, 23 Slip, 26 Morocco, 27 Tessera, 28 Shoemaker, 29 Sleek.
DOWN: 1 Dray-horse, 2 Decimal, 3 Echo, 5 Overstatement, 6 Ends, 7 Earlier, 8 Foyer, 10 Longcase clock, 15 Bends, 16 Stash, 18 Cheapjack, 19 Inferno, 20 Believe, 21 Demos, 24 Scum, 25 Uses.

148 ___
ACROSS: 1 Firedamp, 5 Chopin, 9 Doldrums, 10 Insane, 11 Long shot, 12 Brutal, 14 Submission, 18 Prayer-book, 22 Crease, 23 Live down, 24 On a job, 25 Wish-wash, 26 Salter, 27 Animator.
DOWN: 1 Fiddle, 2 Relent, 3 Duress, 4 Mumbo-jumbo, 6 Huntress, 7 Plantain, 8 Needling, 13 Imposition, 15 Specious, 16 Baseball, 17 Keystone, 19 Newham, 20 Hobart, 21 Anchor.

149 ___
ACROSS: 1 Transaction, 9 Tear, 10 Supervision, 11 Idle, 14 Hearten, 16 Andante, 17 Sound, 18 Nods, 19 Oral, 20 Lever, 22 Heedful, 23 Romanic, 24 Lute, 28 Bill-sticker, 29 Arch, 30 Beyond doubt.
DOWN: 2 Roue, 3 Need, 4 Advises, 5 Test, 6 Orotund, 7 Wedding ring, 8 Breeze block, 12 Chinchillas, 13 Candlestick, 15 Novel, 16 Anger, 20 Luddite, 21 Roosted, 25 Alto, 26 Echo, 27 Kerb.

150 ___
ACROSS: 7 Have it out, 8 Not on, 10 Good deal, 11 Canada, 12 Spam, 13 Feel hurt, 15 Pasture, 17 Tipping, 20 Back yard, 22 Tamp, 25 Pounce, 26 A new leaf, 27 Sniff, 28 Black suit.
DOWN: 1 Capon, 2 Held up, 3 Streamer, 4 Qualify, 5 Township, 6 Cold front, 9 Acre, 14 Paramount, 16 Taken off, 18 In the act, 19 Ideally, 21 Alex, 23 Molest, 24 Way in.

151_____
ACROSS: 1 Chamberlain, **10** Relax, **11** Traveller, **12** Prejudice, **13** Rheum, **14** Rigged, **16** Hear, hear, **18** Delusion, **20** Call up, **23** Oscar, **24** Volunteer, **26** Cautioned, **27** Slime, **28** Degenerated.
DOWN: 2 Halle, **3** Mixture, **4** Entail, **5** Leavened, **6** In error, **7** Prepared to act, **8** Bluebell, **9** Crime reporter, **15** Golf-club, **17** Convince, **19** Service, **21** Amnesia, **22** Pledge, **25** Emile.

152_____
ACROSS: 1 Spill the beans, **10** Ireland, **11** Instant, **12** Tied, **13** Hoard, **14** Deep, **17** Rat race, **18** Moisten, **19** Lash out, **22** Chianti, **24** Stab, **25** Skill, **26** Gnar, **29** Ontario, **30** Interne, **31** Penny-farthing.
DOWN: 2 Present, **3** Leas, **4** Tadpole, **5** Epigram, **6** Easy, **7** Neatest, **8** History lesson, **9** Stipendiaries, **15** Bacon, **16** Mimic, **20** Startle, **21** Take off, **22** Collier, **23** Non-iron, **27** Erin, **28** Itch.

153_____
ACROSS: 1 Fall over, **5** Strand, **9** Loch ness, **10** Recoil, **11** In shreds, **12** Make it, **14** Best seller, **18** Aston villa, **22** Scarab, **23** At a price, **24** Denial, **25** Ambrosia, **26** Porker, **27** Assessed.
DOWN: 1 Fall in, **2** Locust, **3** Owners, **4** Easy does it, **6** The dales, **7** Above all, **8** Dilatory, **13** At all times, **15** Passed up, **16** Strainer, **17** On parade, **19** Sparse, **20** Misses, **21** Remand.

154_____
ACROSS: 1 Pop the question, **9** Satsuma, **10** Aniseed, **11** Urns, **12** Behind bars, **14** Exhale, **15** Get a loan, **17** Siphoned, **18** Strait, **21** Occasional, **22** Rook, **24** Glucose, **25** Heigh-ho, **26** Get the better of.
DOWN: 1 Posture, **2** Put in the picture, **3** Haul, **4** Quaker, **5** Examiner, **6** Third party, **7** One way or another, **8** Adds on, **13** Blood sport, **16** Kerosene, **17** Slough, **19** Take off, **20** Mashie, **23** Lift.

155_____
ACROSS: 7 Hairbrush, **8** Vicar, **10** Particle, **11** Entomb, **12** Free, **13** Malinger, **15** Oculist, **17** Absence, **20** Apple pie, **22** Ruts, **25** Ageing, **26** Unamused, **27 & 28** Day of reckoning.
DOWN: 1 Kayak, **2** Grater, **3** Crackers, **4** Esteems, **5** Distance, **6** Palm beach, **9** Heel, **14** Scapegoat, **16** Lollipop, **18** Barracks, **19** Refugee, **21** Page, **23** Truant, **24** Feint.

156_____
ACROSS: 1 Toddy, **4** Stand fast, **9** Instant, **11** Low dive, **12** Knot, **13** Skied, **14** Lead, **17** Electric light, **19** Chilling tales, **21** Scud, **22** Cut in, **23** List, **26** Halyard, **27** Got down, **28** Bit player, **29** Ri e.
DOWN: 1 Thickhead, **2** Disrobe, **3** Year, **5** Allied landing, **6** Dawn, **7** Aliment, **8** Tweed, **10** Take in laundry, **15** Strip, **16** Agate, **18** Past tense, **19** Couplet, **20** Laid off, **21** Sahib, **24** Fall, **25** Stir.

157_____
ACROSS: 1 Storm signal, **9** Ghee, **10** Solar energy, **11** Spat, **14** Everton, **16** Closure, **17** Nosey, **18** Spey, **19** Vlei, **20** Fatal, **22** Codicil, **23** Refresh, **24** Nipa, **28** Pigheadedly, **29** Sett, **30** Shepherdess.
DOWN: 2 Thou, **3** Roan, **4** Stepson, **5** Glee, **6** Angrily, **7** Shipbuilder, **8** See the light, **12** Seasickness, **13** Serendipity, **15** Nopal, **16** Cedar, **20** Finnish, **21** Leakage, **25** Shap, **26** Seed, **27** Plus.

158_____
ACROSS: 1 Capital charge, **10** Revenue, **11** Toccata, **12** Acne, **13** Nomad, **14** Logo, **17** Iterate, **18** Kindred, **19** Get over, **22** Cutlass, **24** Obey, **25** Agape, **26** Cols, **29** Natural, **30** Aconite, **31** Better oneself.
DOWN: 2 Advance, **3** Iona, **4** Acetone, **5** Cut back, **6** Arch, **7** Glamour, **8** Breaking point, **9** Major disaster, **15** Salve, **16** Unity, **20** Theatre, **21** Regular, **22** Captain, **23** Asocial, **27** Grit, **28** Boss.

159_____
ACROSS: 1 Cambric, **5** Instant, **9** Opinion, **10** Strides, **11** Economist, **12** Norma, **13** Press, **15** Ambulance, **17** Impatient, **19** Races, **22** Trier, **23** Residence, **25** Nothing, **26** Legless, **27** Earnest, **28** Spartan.
DOWN: 1 Close-up, **2** Moidore, **3** Rhino, **4** Candidate, **5** Inset, **6** Strangler, **7** Andiron, **8** Testate, **14** Saturnine, **16** Bath salts, **17** Intense, **18** Pointer, **20** Convert, **21** Stetson, **23** Right, **24** Dogma.

160_____
ACROSS: 7 Bad habits, **8** Rabid, **10** Slattern, **11** Uniate, **12** Chit, **13** Brown owl, **15** Hitched, **17** Cholera, **20** Stranger, **22** Rail, **25** Global, **26** Face-pack, **27** Genre, **28** Close call.
DOWN: 1 Sally, **2** Thatch, **3** Absentee, **4** Stand-by, **5** Rational, **6** Dirty work, **9** Auto, **14** Distiller, **16** Chambers, **18** Hard cash, **19** Profile, **21** Gall, **23** Impact, **24** Scale.

161

ACROSS: 1 Scatty, 4 Discover, 9 Orpine, 10 Marginal, 11 Talent, 12 Signpost, 14 Need a break, 18 Bellringer, 22 Religion, 23 Anonym, 24 Found out, 25 Egests, 26 Spearmen, 27 Stodge.
DOWN: 1 Spouting, 2 Appalled, 3 Tenon saw, 5 Imaginable, 6 Cogent, 7 Vendor, 8 Relate, 13 Irresolute, 15 Midnight, 16 Agonised, 17 Promisee, 19 Grafts, 20 Blouse, 21 Agadir.

162

ACROSS: 8 Coca, 9 Nap, 10 Eyelet, 11 Bow tie, 12 Look over, 13 Below the surface, 15 Banshee, 17 Pimento, 20 Cabinet minister, 23 Polestar, 25 Ratbag, 26 Intake, 27 Cue, 28 Mien.
DOWN: 1 Nodose, 2 Cast lots, 3 Under the weather, 4 Applies, 5 Revolutionaries, 6 Let off, 7 Were, 14 Cut, 16 Aga, 18 Easy time, 19 America, 21 Icecap, 22 Elated, 24 Owns.

163

ACROSS: 1 Neuralgia, 8 & 11 Night out on the tiles, 12 Crewe, 13 Sneak, 16 Enough, 17 Risque, 18 Aorta, 19 Narrow, 20 Altair, 21 Loyal, 24 Repel, 26 Ostia, 27 Get the picture, 28 Excluding.
DOWN: 2 Ethos, 3 Reopen, 4 Latvia, 5 Ionic, 6 Bibliographer, 7 Three-quarters, 9 St bernard, 10 Rehearsal, 13 Shawl, 14 Early, 15 Kraal, 22 Orwell, 23 Allied, 25 Latex, 26 Often.

164

ACROSS: 1 Contract, 5 Assess, 9 Entering, 10 Hatter, 12 Smoulders, 13 Chess, 14 Spot, 16 Improve, 19 Adverse, 21 Rush, 24 Scram, 25 Adventure, 27 Odious, 28 Irritate, 29 Donate, 30 Tenement.
DOWN: 1 Crease, 2 Nation, 3 Rural, 4 Contest, 6 Seascapes, 7 Entresol, 8 Stressed, 11 Asti, 15 Paramount, 17 Password, 18 Aversion, 20 Edam, 21 Reverse, 22 Humane, 23 Repent, 26 Noise.

165

ACROSS: 1 Hogmanay, 9 Ornament, 10 Isis, 11 Cabbage white, 13 Well bred, 15 Tirana, 16 Mesa, 17 Femur, 18 Ease, 20 Rapier, 21 Sustains, 23 Milton Keynes, 26 Halo, 27 Assassin, 28 Salopian.
DOWN: 2 Obsolete, 3 Miscellanist, 4 Number, 5 Yoga, 6 Ancestor, 7 Semi, 8 Steerage, 12 Horsemanship, 14 Dumas, 16 Marimbas, 17 Firmness, 19 Sand- ea, 22 Sinful, 24 Last, 25 Eons.

166

ACROSS: 1 Scarlet, 5 Comb, 9 Out of commission, 10 Hemp, 11 Hit on, 12 Scot, 15 Retinue, 16 Fancier, 17 Lucifer, 19 Auction, 21 Gait, 22 Ideal, 23 Bags, 26 Troubleshooting, 27 Beds, 28 Decency.
DOWN: 1 Smother, 2 Automatic pilot, 3 Left, 4 Two-time, 5 Come off, 6 Must, 7 Monitor, 8 Discrimination, 13 Snuff, 14 On ice, 17 Legatee, 18 Redress, 19 Abashed, 20 Nosegay, 24 Able, 25 Torc.

167

ACROSS: 1 Thither, 5 Nostril, 9 Tallies, 10 Spectra, 11 Easy terms, 12 Reign, 13 Sisal, 15 Increased, 17 Ptarmigan, 19 Scrub, 22 Easel, 23 First rate, 25 Illegal, 26 Lottery, 27 Reentry, 28 Osmosis.
DOWN: 1 Totters, 2 Ill uses, 3 Hoist, 4 Reserving, 5 Noses, 6 Sheerness, 7 Retains, 8 Learned, 14 Limelight, 16 Contralto, 17 Premier, 18 Absolve, 20 Readers, 21 Bye-byes, 23 Folly, 24 Totem.

168

ACROSS: 1 Converse, 5 Set off, 9 Cotton on, 10 Comedo, 11 Evaluate, 12 Used up, 14 Spell it out, 18 Shoot a line, 22 Fencer, 23 Well to do, 24 Rookie, 25 Pay a call, 26 Tweeny, 27 Grey mare.
DOWN: 1 Cocker, 2 Not bad, 3 Exodus, 4 Short spell, 6 Eton suit, 7 Open door, 8 Footpath, 13 Blonde hair, 15 Ask for it, 16 Round one, 17 Athenian, 19 Bleary, 20 Sonata, 21 Coolie.

169

ACROSS: 6 Bridge problem, 8 Fidget, 9 Nicotine, 10 Ain, 11 Adrift, 12 Eased off, 14 Cathode, 16 Wastrel, 20 Aspirant, 23 Sprawl, 24 Aft, 25 Gunpoint, 26 Resort, 27 Flight of steps.
DOWN: 1 Kingfish, 2 Agitated, 3 Spinner, 4 Coccus, 5 Slated, 6 Blindman's buff, 7 Man of few words, 13 Ens, 15 Oer, 17 Abstruse, 18 Thrashed, 19 Station, 21 Impair, 22 Alight.

170

ACROSS: 1 Stock-still, 9 Oslo, 10 Astringent, 11 Torrid, 12 Dulling, 15 Scarlet, 16 Grace, 17 Side, 18 Agra, 19 Stand, 21 Anglice, 22 Sad-iron, 24 Medusa, 27 Termitaria, 28 Navy, 29 Heaven-sent.
DOWN: 2 Task, 3 Corral, 4 Sinking, 5 Item, 6 Lattice, 7 Astrologer, 8 Goods-train, 12 Disbarment, 13 Lady Godiva, 14 Grate, 15 Scans, 19 Scratch, 20 Daytime, 23 Ideals, 25 Area, 26 Mien.

171
ACROSS: 1 Funfair, 5 Schools, 9 Oatmeal, 10 Tsarina, 11 Gainsayer, 12 Tramp, 13 Dwell, 15 Addiction, 17 Brainless, 19 El Cid, 22 Tilth, 23 Hyphenate, 25 Mercury, 26 Elation, 27 Nankeen, 28 Ratings.
DOWN: 1 Flogged, 2 Nitride, 3 Abets, 4 Relay-race, 5 Sitar, 6 Heartache, 7 Origami, 8 Sharpen, 14 Long house, 16 Disappear, 17 Bitumen, 18 Aileron, 20 Clarion, 21 Duennas, 23 , 24 Enact.

172
ACROSS: 1 Rider haggard, 9 Numbers, 10 At issue, 11 Rout, 12 Prime, 13 Mini, 16 Pastime, 17 Diocese, 18 Rake-off, 21 Mansion, 23 Tame, 24 Angst, 25 Mass, 28 On and on, 29 Initial, 30 Laissez faire.
DOWN: 1 Rumours, 2 Does, 3 Reserve, 4 Alarmed, 5 Grim, 6 Respite, 7 In preparation, 8 Beside oneself, 14 Widow, 15 Pound, 19 Kampala, 20 Finance, 21 Mastiff, 22 Imagine, 26 Odds, 27 Kiwi.

173
ACROSS: 1 Boarding school, 9 Croquet, 10 Curator, 11 Site, 12 Horoscopes, 14 Poorer, 15 Green y, 17 Miseries, 18 Esther, 21 Consecrate, 22 Awls, 24 Italics, 25 Pierrot, 26 As fit as a fiddle.
DOWN: 1 Backs up, 2 A month of Sundays, 3 Drum, 4 Notion, 5 Succours, 6 Hard cheese, 7 On top of the world, 8 Trusty, 13 Decree nisi, 16 Nebraska, 17 Muck in, 19 Rosette, 20 Utopia, 23 Peri.

174
ACROSS: 7 Lose heart, 8 Borax, 10 Dinosaur, 11 Opener, 12 Lear, 13 Schnapps, 15 Therapy, 17 At heart, 20 Space age, 22 Kite, 25 Cousin, 26 Anabolic, 27 Oscan, 28 Break it up.
DOWN: 1 Not in, 2 Begone, 3 Set a trap, 4 Arm rest, 5 Love game, 6 Take apart, 9 Gosh, 14 Chop house, 16 Rich seam, 18 Take away, 19 Megaera, 21 Acne, 23 Took in, 24 Lit up.

175
ACROSS: 1 Water, 4 Steamship, 8 Ingot, 9 Unspotted, 11 Tote, 12 Adore, 13 Tyke, 16 Perfect number, 19 Eat like a horse, 20 Lump, 22 Overt, 23 Beth, 26 Cineraria, 27 Match, 28 Turnstone, 29 Herod.
DOWN: 1 Waistline, 2 Tight spot, 3 Rate, 4 Sound receiver, 5 Moor, 6 Hotly, 7 Padre, 10 Stretcher case, 14 Grail, 15 Curry, 17 Beefeater, 18 Rough-shod, 20 Licit, 21 Manor, 24 Eros, 25 Umph.

176
ACROSS: 1 Idealists, 9 Galosh, 10 Imposture, 11 Adroit, 12 Constrain, 13 Chaise, 17 Sea, 19 Lignite, 20 Carouse, 21 Tit, 23 Scraps, 27 Assertion, 28 Magnet, 29 Balefully, 30 Tattoo, 31 Streaking.
DOWN: 2 Damson, 3 Arouse, 4 Intern, 5 Termite, 6 Card-sharp, 7 Notorious, 8 Shattered, 14 Classmate, 15 Aggregate, 16 Simpleton, 17 Set, 18 Act, 22 Instant, 24 Recede, 25 Struck, 26 Goblin.

177
ACROSS: 1 Dogma, 4 Incurious, 9 Pronoun, 11 Oil-well, 12 Erse, 13 Ogres, 14 Eddy, 17 Sophisticated, 19 Extraordinary, 21 Bout, 22 Scout, 23 Area, 26 Synonym, 27 Tin-tack, 28 Hexagonal, 29 Theft.
DOWN: 1 Depressed, 2 Glossop, 3 Amok, 5 Closed circuit, 6 Rule, 7 Overdid, 8 Sulky, 10 Nightwatchman, 15 Wilts, 16 Staid, 18 Pay-packet, 19 Equinox, 20 Aureate, 21 Bosch, 24 Snag, 25 Knut.

178
ACROSS: 1 Cliff-hanger, 10 Oscar, 11 Advertise, 12 Gold medal, 13 Iliad, 14 Erring, 16 Fair game, 18 Squatter, 20 Bartok, 23 Other, 24 Isolation, 26 Anglicise, 27 Drawn, 28 Change a note.
DOWN: 2 Local, 3 Foreman, 4 Hoards, 5 Novellas, 6 Earlier, 7 Congressional, 8 Militant, 9 Dead reckoning, 15 Roughage, 17 Sedition, 19 Tarnish, 21 Abandon, 22 Cohere, 25 Inapt.

179
ACROSS: 1 Observation, 9 Mete, 10 Sudden death, 11 Hues, 14 Hold-all, 16 Massage, 17 Aaron, 18 Reef, 19 Bind, 20 Theta, 22 Yew-tree, 23 Ordinal, 24 Toll, 28 Barrack room, 29 Noel, 30 Deferential.
DOWN: 2 Blue, 3 Ends, 4 Vanilla, 5 Ties, 6 Ottoman, 7 Regulations, 8 Wensleydale, 12 Cherry-stone, 13 Sleepwalker, 15 Lathe, 16 Motto, 20 Testate, 21 Article, 25 Free, 26 Fret, 27 Iota.

180
ACROSS: 1 Close to death, 9 Rattles, 10 Lucerne, 11 Abed, 12 Douse, 13 Call, 16 Old salt, 17 Noisome, 18 Eat dirt, 21 Catch on, 23 Ward, 24 To wit, 25 Blot, 28 Rooting, 29 Primate, 30 After the ball.
DOWN: 1 Cut dead, 2 Orly, 3 Ease out, 4 Only son, 5 Etch, 6 Tornado, 7 Break one's word, 8 Tell me another, 14 Fagin, 15 Dirty, 19 Turn off, 20 Thought, 21 Clippie, 22 Holdall, 26 Bite, 27 Diva.

181

ACROSS: 1 Vacillate, 8 Four-poster bed, 11 Mogul, 12 Extra, 13 Acrid, 16 Liebig, 17 Opened, 18 Oaten, 19 Answer, 20 Outwit, 21 Asher, 24 Aroma, 26 Serif, 27 Family quarrel, 28 Middleman.
DOWN: 2 Avril, 3 Ironic, 4 Litchi, 5 Three, 6 Congresswoman, 7 Getting warmer, 9 Smell a rat, 10 Candytuft, 13 Agora, 14 Ratch, 15 Donor, 22 Stayed, 23 Exhume, 25 Alibi, 26 Syria.

182

ACROSS: 1 Backhander, 6 Ahem, 10 Tenet, 11 Sidelines, 12 Cashmere, 13 Naive, 15 Concoct, 17 Satchel, 19 Torment, 21 Minutes, 22 Award, 24 Redeemed, 27 Ginger ale, 28 Addle, 29 Ewes, 30 News-vendor.
DOWN: 1 Bath, 2 Container, 3 Hitch, 4 Nascent, 5 Endless, 7 Hindi, 8 Masterless, 9 Plankton, 14 Acute angle, 16 Overdrew, 18 Hotheaded, 20 Terrace, 21 Madness, 23 Annie, 25 Erase, 26 Beer.

183

ACROSS: 1 Cabbage, 5 Bath, 9 Eton Boating Song, 10 Obey, 11 Midas, 12 Scot, 15 Terrain, 16 Dresser, 17 Padlock, 19 Teeming, 21 Rats, 22 Pearl, 23 Anna, 26 Procrastinating, 27 Smut, 28 Inbreed.
DOWN: 1 Cheroot, 2 Biodegradation, 3 Ambo, 4 Elation, 5 Brigand, 6 Toga, 7 Dogstar, 8 Concessionaire, 13 Manor, 14 Seven, 17 Parapet, 18 Knesset, 19 Termini, 20 Goat-god, 24 Drum, 25 Garb.

184

ACROSS: 1 Benchmark, 8 Up to the minute, 11 Lied, 12 Obeli, 13 Free, 16 Compact, 17 Decorum, 18 Heroism, 20 Explain, 21 Ache, 22 End up, 23 Amen, 26 In great demand, 27 Celebrity.
DOWN: 2 Eton, 3 Cohabit, 4 Mumbled, 5 Rank, 6 Speed merchant, 7 Star treatment, 9 Blockhead, 10 Permanent, 14 Maxim, 15 Scope, 19 Mandate, 20 Ecuador, 24 Cree, 25 Smut.

185

ACROSS: 1 Sweetmeats, 9 Over, 10 Close match, 11 Euclid, 12 Secedes, 15 Relapse, 16 Spear, 17 Anna, 18 Trio, 19 Romeo, 21 Gherkin, 22 Name-tag, 24 Trance, 27 Nom de plume, 28 Rack, 29 Desolation.
DOWN: 2 Wall, 3 Ensure, 4 Mummies, 5 Alto, 6 Schemer, 7 Evil spirit, 8 Cradle song, 12 Slaughters, 13 Conveyance, 14 Spoon, 15 Raven, 19 Ripened, 20 Oatmeal, 23 Eyelet, 25 Imps, 26 Ammo.

186

ACROSS: 1 Gored, 4 Put on show, 8 On top, 9 Abstainer, 11 Chin, 12 Senna, 13 Mint, 16 Initial letter, 19 Right to strike, 20 Cush, 22 Educe, 23 Mead, 26 Plane tree, 27 Agate, 28 Dinosaurs, 29 Speed.
DOWN: 1 Good cheer, 2 Retailing, 3 Dope, 4 Placed in order, 5 Noah, 6 Hindi, 7 Worst, 10 Single tickets, 14 Width, 15 Let in, 17 The senate, 18 Roundhead, 20 Cupid, 21 Spawn, 24 Keys, 25 Bass.

187

ACROSS: 6 Close quarters, 8 Mouser, 9 Upstairs, 10 Ice, 11 Active, 12 Underarm, 14 Heckled, 16 Dispose, 20 Mistral, 23 Motive, 24 Ado, 25 Reporter, 26 Thirst, 27 Separationist.
DOWN: 1 Joy-stick, 2 Retrieve, 3 Queue up, 4 Erased, 5 Repair, 6 Crotchetiness, 7 Surprise visit, 13 Ess, 15 Lar, 17 In motion, 18 Patricia, 19 Clarity, 21 Troupe, 22 In turn.

188

ACROSS: 1 Plastic, 5 Clapper, 9 Portion, 10 Earnest, 11 Exposures, 12 Greta, 13 Sisal, 15 Lorgnette, 17 Crossword, 19 Eater, 22 Ensue, 23 Landslide, 25 Sirloin, 26 Approve, 27 Theatre, 28 Tardier.
DOWN: 1 Peppers, 2 Apropos, 3 Twins, 4 Contralto, 5 Chess, 6 Arrogance, 7 Present, 8 Retrace, 14 Lashed out, 16 Redundant, 17 Cresset, 18 Observe, 20 Tripoli, 21 Roe-deer, 23 Lance, 24 Super.

189

ACROSS: 1 Furnace, 5 Epistle, 9 Amble, 10 Tide-gauge, 11 Breadcrumb, 12 Topi, 14 Stock-raising, 18 Telegraphist, 21 Rock, 22 Abnormally, 25 Blow-torch, 26 North, 27 Estuary, 28 Emanate.
DOWN: 1 Flabby, 2 Ribbed, 3 Anecdotage, 4 Eater, 5 Endomorph, 6 Inga, 7 Teutonic, 8 Evenings, 13 Dipsomania, 15 Cranberry, 16 Storable, 17 Blackout, 19 Gloria, 20 Lychee, 23 Ochre, 24 Stoa.

190

ACROSS: 1 Switch on, 9 Opposite, 10 Stye, 11 Apprehension, 13 Play fair, 15 Stroke, 16 Doff, 17 Owned, 18 Aunt, 20 To boot, 21 Warranty, 23 Come a cropper, 26 Ovid, 27 Emigrate, 28 Spending.
DOWN: 2 Waterloo, 3 Treaty of rome, 4 Hoop-la, 5 Note, 6 Appeased, 7 Midi, 8 Be in debt, 12 Spread abroad, 14 Renew, 16 Detached, 17 Optician, 19 Notation, 22 Repose, 24 Maid, 25 Odes.

191_____
ACROSS: 7 Recapture, 8 Ashes, 10 Bulls-eye, 11 Harems, 12 Idea, 13 Left bank, 15 Pitcher, 17 Obesity, 20 Reindeer, 22 Safe, 25 Groove, 26 Shutters, 27 Scene, 28 Lightship.
DOWN: 1 Genus, 2 Sailed, 3 Steerage, 4 Brie y, 5 Ascribes, 6 Terminate, 9 Chef, 14 Wisecrack, 16 Confound, 18 Besought, 19 Brassie, 21 Eyed, 23 Fetish, 24 Drain.

192_____
ACROSS: 1 Pack it in, 5 Haul up, 9 Typecast, 10 Blotto, 11 Fair skin, 12 Stress, 14 Act the hero, 18 Chew the fat, 22 Double, 23 Well, well, 24 Muscat, 25 Pile it on, 26 Cutter, 27 Attempts.
DOWN: 1 Put off, 2 Capsid, 3 In case, 4 In stitches, 6 All at sea, 7 Let me see, 8 Poor show, 13 Strategist, 15 Academic, 16 Get upset, 17 Stellate, 19 Allege, 20 Belt up, 21 Clones.

193_____
ACROSS: 1 Prototype, 9 Cobalt, 10 Blossomed, 11 Spinet, 12 Ecologist, 13 Unreal, 17 Ode, 19 Battle of Flowers, 20 Mot, 21 Ermine, 25 Embracing, 26 To date, 27 Entourage, 28 Votary, 29 Aylesbury.
DOWN: 2 Relict, 3 Tussle, 4 Though, 5 Pressed for money, 6 Companion, 7 Laundered, 8 Stateless, 14 Objective, 15 Stamp-duty, 16 Planetary, 17 Oom, 18 Eft, 22 Groove, 23 Scarab, 24 Onager.

194_____
ACROSS: 6 Prioresses, 8 Side, 9 Ballerina, 11 Avid, 12 Rat, 13 Continent, 16 Eric, 17 Stowage, 18 Lineate, 20 Also, 21 Navigator, 23 Rye, 24 Ague, 25 Rendering, 29 List, 30 Lone ranger.
DOWN: 1 Grub, 2 Pool, 3 Mere, 4 Aspires, 5 Administer, 7 Startling, 8 Statement, 10 Lot, 13 Cattle-grid, 14 New forest, 15 In general, 19 Evening, 22 Air, 26 Ears, 27 Iona, 28 Glee.

195_____
ACROSS: 1 Reliance, 5 Isaiah, 9 Magnolia, 10 Dapper, 12 Dumbarton, 13 Eased, 14 Scar, 16 Whatnot, 19 Retreat, 21 Cues, 24 Chess, 25 Wimbledon, 27 Pagoda, 28 Quickset, 29 Tehran, 30 Leadenly.
DOWN: 1 Remedy, 2 Legume, 3 Agora, 4 Critter, 6 Stalemate, 7 Imposing, 8 Heredity, 11 Snow, 15 Clepsydra, 17 Crackpot, 18 Strength, 20 Town, 21 Commune, 22 Edison, 23 Knotty, 26 Lucid.

196_____
ACROSS: 1 On the rocks, 6 Plug, 10 Tokay, 11 Top-secret, 12 Spitfire, 13 Adorn, 15 Fragile, 17 Silesia, 19 Leeward, 21 Bad name, 22 Cower, 24 Strapped, 27 Noviciate, 28 Rhone, 29 Errs, 30 Belladonna.
DOWN: 1 Oath, 2 Take place, 3 Egypt, 4 Outside, 5 Kippers, 7 Largo, 8 Got engaged, 9 Derailed, 14 Off-licence, 16 In a trice, 18 Shakedown, 20 Disease, 21 Barbell, 23 Waver, 25 Pared, 26 Hera.

197_____
ACROSS: 1 Human sacrifice, 9 Look out, 10 Learner, 11 Till, 12 Relay races, 14 Regard, 15 Tea-chest, 17 Integral, 18 Edicts, 21 Pro igate, 22 Emma, 24 Amateur, 25 Taken up, 26 Easy come, easy go.
DOWN: 1 Holster, 2 Moonlight sonata, 3 Neon, 4 Antler, 5 Released, 6 Fratricide, 7 Conscience money, 8 Prosit, 13 Art gallery, 16 Kangaroo, 17 In play, 19 Shampoo, 20 Statue, 23 Skua.

198_____
ACROSS: 7 Well set up, 8 Whoop, 10 Get ahead, 11 Abroad, 12 Bear, 13 Wild card, 15 Fishnet, 17 Chateau, 20 China tea, 22 Life, 25 In form, 26 Embraces, 27 Fusee, 28 Cracked up.
DOWN: 1 Lever, 2 Cleave, 3 Rehearse, 4 Put-down, 5 Short cut, 6 Royal road, 9 Tail, 14 His honour, 16 Hangover, 18 Hold back, 19 Madeira, 21 Tome, 23 Flamen, 24 Pep up.

199_____
ACROSS: 1 Possess, 5 Annelid, 9 Silver medallist, 10 Hiss, 11 Ad lib, 12 Shoe, 15 Loftily, 16 Geology, 17 Stirrup, 19 Celebes, 21 Dail, 22 Truro, 23 Ezra, 26 Conference pears, 27 Stylist, 28 Exordia.
DOWN: 1 Paschal, 2 Self-sufficiency, 3 Ewer, 4 Someday, 5 Addling, 6 Nile, 7 Leighton buzzard, 8 Dithery, 13 Fiery, 14 Jolly, 17 Seduces, 18 Perfect, 19 Coracle, 20 Swansea, 24 Demi, 25 Up to.

200_____
ACROSS: 5 Settle, 8 Procures, 9 Trimmer, 10 Radii, 11 Abandoned, 13 Seaborne, 14 Leaser, 17 Ida, 19 Pen, 20 Tartar, 23 Adherent, 26 Discourse, 28 Roger, 29 Earache, 30 Standard, 31 Vestas.
DOWN: 1 Spares, 2 Cordial, 3 Auditoria, 4 Replan, 5 Strangle, 6 Tempo, 7 Liege men, 12 Bed, 15 Endearing, 16 Badinage, 18 Draughts, 21 Was, 22 Belgian, 24 Dearth, 25 Tirade, 27 Coast.

201 ——
ACROSS: 1 Candour, 5 Durable, 9 Awake, 10 Discourse, 11 Subscriber, 12 Stoa, 14 Callisthenic, 18 Trigger-happy, 21 Orly, 22 Diagnostic, 25 Limousine, 26 Learn, 27 Retinue, 28 Tidings.
DOWN: 1 Classy, 2 Nearby, 3 Overcharge, 4 Radii, 5 Dyspepsia, 6 Root, 7 Baritone, 8 Elegance, 13 Shopsoiled, 15 Larvicide, 16 Stroller, 17 Diplomat, 19 Attain, 20 Scones, 23 Greet, 24 Burn.

202 ——
ACROSS: 1 Macon, 4 Godfather, 9 Derange, 11 Rambled, 12 Rays, 13 Stock, 14 Moor, 17 Tongue in cheek, 19 Disheartening, 21 Mace, 22 Chief, 23 Cain, 26 Trimmer, 27 Tacitus, 28 Halloween, 29 Mowed.
DOWN: 1 Moderated, 2 Carry on, 3 Nuns, 5 Direct current, 6 Army, 7 Hillock, 8 Radar, 10 Eat like a horse, 15 Hussy, 16 Beget, 18 Organised, 19 Decrial, 20 In a stew, 21 Match, 24 Umbo, 25 Scum.

203 ——
ACROSS: 1 Regime, 4 Aperture, 9 Seldom, 10 Death-bed, 12 Unit, 13 Siren, 14 Snow, 17 Cheap edition, 20 Street corner, 23 Ahab, 24 Stoop, 25 Mint, 28 Half inch, 29 Sultan, 30 Mistrust, 31 Bridge.
DOWN: 1 Resource, 2 Gulliver, 3 Mood, 5 Presentation, 6 Rate, 7 Unbent, 8 Endows, 11 Fiddlesticks, 15 Spots, 16 Cocoa, 18 Indicted, 19 Pretence, 21 Mayhem, 22 Naples, 26 Pier, 27 Purr.

204 ——
ACROSS: 1 Wilts, 4 Easy catch, 8 Sewer, 9 Tipped off, 11 Earl, 12 Lay on, 13 Play, 16 Anticlockwise, 19 The common herd, 20 Magi, 22 Index, 23 Knot, 26 Prototype, 27 Scuba, 28 Dished out, 29 Swede.
DOWN: 1 Washed out, 2 Lower case, 3 Spry, 4 Entrance money, 5 Coed, 6 Troll, 7 Hefty, 10 Pronouncement, 14 Stood, 15 Skied, 17 Indenture, 18 Exact fare, 20 Moped, 21 Gloss, 24 Core, 25 Uses.

205 ——
ACROSS: 1 Betting slip, 9 Negligent, 10 Thing, 11 Astray, 12 Kilowatt, 13 Echoic, 15 Fenestra, 18 Beginner, 19 Offcut, 21 Injected, 23 Acedia, 26 Timid, 27 Tradition, 28 Torch-bearer.
DOWN: 1 Bandage, 2 Tight, 3 Imitation, 4 Glen, 5 Latticed, 6 Patio, 7 Regatta, 8 Gigantic, 14 High jump, 16 Effective, 17 Detector, 18 Bristol, 20 Trainer, 22 Cadet, 24 Drier, 25 Bath.

206 ——
ACROSS: 1 Separate, 5 Legend, 9 Threaten, 10 Tenths, 12 Redresser, 13 Tuner, 14 Mien, 16 Average, 19 Artisan, 21 Rush, 24 Taper, 25 Oast-house, 27 Calmed, 28 Tow-paths, 29 Errata, 30 Headsmen.
DOWN: 1 Satire, 2 Parody, 3 Reade, 4 Treason, 6 Electress, 7 Estonian, 8 Disorder, 11 Area, 15 Insurgent, 17 Particle, 18 Stippler, 20 Nook, 21 Restore, 22 Custom, 23 Reason, 26 Hoped.

207 ——
ACROSS: 1 Homer, 4 Traverse, 10 Rustler, 11 Notable, 12 Pray, 13 Fishy, 14 Stay, 17 Pre-arrangement, 19 Monkey business, 22 Tope, 23 Recto, 24 Pier, 27 Theorem, 28 Emotion, 29 Resident, 30 Lithe.
DOWN: 1 Hornpipe, 2 Mistake, 3 Rile, 5 Run the gauntlet, 6 Veto, 7 Ribston, 8 Every, 9 Ordinary seaman, 15 Brake, 16 Ambit, 18 Estrange, 20 Oppress, 21 Elitist, 22 Tutor, 25 Grid, 26 Foil.

208 ——
ACROSS: 1 Boredom, 5 Accused, 9 Choicer, 10 Stirrup, 11 Reinstate, 12 Jacks, 13 Magus, 15 Spit it out, 17 Abandoned, 19 Truer, 22 Lovat, 23 Dressed up, 25 Abstain, 26 Innards, 27 Striker, 28 Epitome.
DOWN: 1 Buckram, 2 Rooting, 3 Ducks, 4 Mortal sin, 5 Aisle, 6 Clip-joint, 7 Sirocco, 8 Deposit, 14 Sidetrack, 16 In due time, 17 All ears, 18 Advisor, 20 Undergo, 21 Riposte, 23 Donor, 24 Sunni.

209 ——
ACROSS: 5 Speech, 8 Dummy run, 9 Smashed, 10 Set-to, 11 Aftermath, 13 Above all, 14 Employ, 17 Nip, 19 Ado, 20 Nudism, 23 Sentinel, 26 Acropolis, 28 Lauds, 29 Cabinet, 30 Irrigate, 31 Flight.
DOWN: 1 Odessa, 2 Emotion, 3 By no means, 4 Mutual, 5 Simmered, 6 Epsom, 7 Creation, 12 Fly, 15 Mortal sin, 16 Pub crawl, 18 Immodest, 21 PSI, 22 Angular, 24 Escort, 25 Lashes, 27 Owing.

210 ——
ACROSS: 1 Sit up, 4 Local call, 9 Vamoose, 11 Mingled, 12 Lias, 13 Adman, 14 Avon, 17 Reign of terror, 19 Watch one's step, 21 Fort, 22 Swarm, 23 Tiny, 26 Another, 27 Shingle, 28 Hot headed, 29 Sidon.
DOWN: 1 Savile row, 2 Timpani, 3 Plot, 5 Comrade in arms, 6 Land, 7 All over, 8 Laden, 10 End of the world, 15 Unity, 16 Arise, 18 Happy mean, 19 Work out, 20 Twigged, 21 Flash, 24 Thee, 25 Hiss.

211
ACROSS: 1 Before one's time, 9 Marimba, 10 Spartan, 11 Asti, 12 Cheapskate, 14 Tundra, 15 Hillside, 17 Tahitian, 18 Enosis, 21 In question, 22 Drop, 24 Open out, 25 Science, 26 Self-employment.
DOWN: 1 Bombast, 2 First in the queue, 3 Ramp, 4 Orache, 5 Ecstatic, 6 Transplant, 7 Mutual insurance, 8 Sneeze, 13 Written-off, 16 Factotum, 17 Tailor, 19 Sapient, 20 Consul, 23 Tidy.

212
ACROSS: 1 Bricabrac, 9 Avarice, 10 Pasture, 11 Manatee, 12 Miniature, 14 Endanger, 15 Repton, 17 Veteran, 20 Island, 23 Mattress, 25 Headstone, 26 Riptide, 27 Fielder, 28 Leashed, 29 Sea-strand.
DOWN: 2 Realise, 3 Catmint, 4 Baritone, 5 Carmen, 6 Maintains, 7 Vintage, 8 Rehearsed, 13 Release, 15 Rigmarole, 16 Oversight, 18 Air-dries, 19 Stop-gap, 21 Littler, 22 Nankeen, 24 Sherds.

213
ACROSS: 1 Cubit, 4 Sand- ea, 10 Bittern, 11 Radical, 12 Land, 13 Timon, 14 Grow, 17 Recommendation, 19 Electrotherapy, 22 Sets, 23 Ascot, 24 Cave, 27 Biretta, 28 Effendi, 29 Relegate, 30 Acted.
DOWN: 1 Cobblers, 2 Botanic, 3 Teem, 5 Air-conditioner, 6 Dodo, 7 Locarno, 8 Allow, 9 Antidepressant, 15 Smock, 16 Steep, 18 Lyre-bird, 20 Literal, 21 Against, 22 Sober, 25 Stag, 26 Offa.

214
ACROSS: 1 Nurseryman, 6 Anil, 9 Short spell, 10 Gala, 12 Odious, 13 Chairman, 15 Object-lesson, 18 House-warming, 21 Cardinal, 22 Fleece, 24 Omit, 25 Comic verse, 26 Tang, 27 Typewriter.
DOWN: 1 Nestor, 2 Rookie, 3 Eat humble pie, 4 Yaps, 5 All the time, 7 Near miss, 8 Learning, 11 Live in clover, 14 Defamatory, 16 Checkout, 17 Guardian, 19 Regret, 20 Veneer, 23 Bile.

215
ACROSS: 1 Casualties, 9 Puma, 10 Wellington, 11 Toddle, 12 Raiders, 15 Sultana, 16 Slept, 17 Gape, 18 Aged, 19 Toxic, 21 Tide-rip, 22 Galleon, 24 Nimble, 27 Lock and key, 28 Land, 29 Getting off.
DOWN: 2 Anew, 3 Unload, 4 Lancers, 5 Iota, 6 Sent out, 7 Quadrangle, 8 Gamewarden, 12 Right angle, 13 Impediment, 14 Sloop, 15 Sprig, 19 Time-lag, 20 Campari, 23 Lap-dog, 25 Scot, 26 Beef.

216
ACROSS: 1 Highlighted, 9 Neurology, 10 Usher, 11 Oxtail, 12 Archives, 13 Trough, 15 Ciphered, 18 Creepers, 19 Stadia, 21 Refusing, 23 Handle, 26 Arrow, 27 On draught, 28 Deferred pay.
DOWN: 1 Hang out, 2 Gaunt, 3 Looking up, 4 Go on, 5 Toy train, 6 Dough, 7 Perused, 8 Shivered, 14 Open fire, 16 Hit parade, 17 Bring off, 18 Carcase, 20 Alertly, 22 Sawed, 24 Dig up, 25 Oder.

217
ACROSS: 1 Tell-tale sign, 8 Harbour, 9 Groaner, 11 Kinesis, 12 Perhaps, 13 Thyme, 14 Implement, 16 Enrolment, 19 Limit, 21 Encoded, 23 Ingenue, 24 Driving, 25 Ontario, 26 Regent street.
DOWN: 1 Tyranny, 2 Look-see, 3 Turnstile, 4 Leg-up, 5 Scourge, 6 Gunwale, 7 Shake the head, 10 Rose to the top, 15 Petticoat, 17 Recline, 18 Luddite, 19 Legatee, 20 Minaret, 22 Digit.

218
ACROSS: 1 Dental surgeon, 10 Hoppers, 11 Potable, 12 Need, 13 Board, 14 Stun, 17 Inspect, 18 Shallot, 19 Glitter, 22 Pageant, 24 Left, 25 Bloom, 26 Adam, 29 Upright, 30 Aspirin, 31 Condescending.
DOWN: 2 Express, 3 Then, 4 Last out, 5 Umpires, 6 Gate, 7 Orbital, 8 Thinking aloud, 9 Reinstatement, 15 Set to, 16 Largo, 20 Inferno, 21 Relates, 22 Probate, 23 Andiron, 27 Egad, 28 Aped.

219
ACROSS: 8 Chin-chin, 9 Precis, 10 Tie, 11 Envisage, 12 Notice, 13 Potential danger, 15 Careful, 18 English, 21 Alfred Hitchcock, 24 Roused, 25 Loose-box, 26 Goo, 27 Innate, 28 Canoeist.
DOWN: 1 Shinto, 2 Endive, 3 The Artful Dodger, 4 Enteral, 5 Opened an account, 6 Sentinel, 7 Ditchers, 14 Tor, 16 All-found, 17 Eurasian, 19 Ido, 20 Airlock, 22 Clever, 23 Choose.

220
ACROSS: 1 Havering, 6 Recall, 9 Corona, 10 On the way, 11 Farewell, 12 Repeat, 13 Imperishable, 16 Mandarin duck, 19 Damsel, 21 Set about, 23 Armature, 24 Random, 25 Madras, 26 Tide over.
DOWN: 2 Amoral, 3 Erode, 4 In a temper, 5 Growler, 6 Rotor, 7 Cheapjack, 8 Leasable, 13 In despair, 14 Shuttered, 15 Calabria, 17 Nascent, 18 Furore, 20 Louis, 22 Bingo.

221

ACROSS: **7** Elongates, **8** Began, **10** Runs into, **11** Checks, **12** Undo, **13** Prestige, **15** Charade, **17** Refrain, **20** Brandish, **22** Tick, **25** Screen, **26** Believes, **27** Seven, **28** Made haste.
DOWN: **1** Aloud, **2** Unison, **3** Main road, **4** Recoups, **5** Repeater, **6** Back again, **9** Ache, **14** Character, **16** Rendered, **18** Extolled, **19** She-bear, **21** Iona, **23** Cretan, **24** Teeth.

222

ACROSS: **1** Fillip, **4** One's word, **9** Lesson, **10** Ecstatic, **12** Type, **13** Often, **14** Sind, **17** Lost interest, **20** Three of a kind, **23** Oxon, **24** Seven, **25** Perm, **28** Do the lot, **29** Go down, **30** Put aside, **31** Shandy.
DOWN: **1** Full tilt, **2** Last post, **3** Iron, **5** Nuclear power, **6** Site, **7** Outfit, **8** Decode, **11** Off the record, **15** Dishy, **16** Assam, **18** Live down, **19** Odd money, **21** Hold up, **22** Foot it, **26** Keys, **27** Doth.

223

ACROSS: **1** Anemone, **5** Decided, **9** Built, **10** Sometimes, **11** Unmuf ing, **12** User, **14** Short-circuit, **18** Sheepishness, **21** Ante, **22** Originated, **25** Liverpool, **26** Decor, **27** All-star, **28** Pay-load.
DOWN: **1** Arbour, **2** Enigma, **3** Out of shape, **4** Easel, **5** Dominican, **6** City, **7** Damascus, **8** Discrete, **13** Present-day, **15** Reservoir, **16** Ismailia, **17** Festival, **19** Stucco, **20** Adored, **23** Galop, **24** Fret.

224

ACROSS: **1** Atonement, **9** Hooters, **10** Cocaine, **11** Nicosia, **12** Unbarring, **14** Osculate, **15** Remark, **17** Aerials, **20** Eerily, **23** Province, **25** Admission, **26** Nibbler, **27** Valerie, **28** Elapses, **29** Seventeen.
DOWN: **2** Trounce, **3** Niagara, **4** Mandrake, **5** Things, **6** Concourse, **7** Hessian, **8** Ashamedly, **13** Noticed, **15** Responder, **16** Racialist, **18** Levitate, **19** Forbear, **21** Respect, **22** Leonine, **24** Caress.

225

ACROSS: **1** Prunella, **9** Milliner, **10** Stir, **11** Semi-detached, **13** Alfresco, **15** Peseta, **16** Oder, **17** Chess, **18** Race, **20** Enzyme, **21** Dowagers, **23** Homesickness, **26** Trot, **27** Nineteen, **28** Tolerant.
DOWN: **2** Retailed, **3** Nursery rhyme, **4** Litmus, **5** Amid, **6** Platypus, **7** Inch, **8** Graduate, **12** Cash register, **14** Oread, **16** Overhang, **17** Credited, **19** Careworn, **22** Weevil, **24** Mind, **25** Kent.

226

ACROSS: **1** Ambivalence, **9** Order-form, **10** Usage, **11** Heyday, **12** Step back, **13** Repair, **15** Bear down, **18** Leave out, **19** Unites, **21** Cast away, **23** Trivia, **26** Elfin, **27** Impounded, **28** Dressed down.
DOWN: **1** Another, **2** Buddy, **3** Verbalise, **4** Loop, **5** No matter, **6** Equip, **7** Break-in, **8** Gadabout, **14** Play safe, **16** Run around, **17** Curative, **18** Lychees, **20** Stand-in, **22** Awned, **24** Video, **25** Opus.

227

ACROSS: **1** Kicked back, **6** Abel, **9** Theatrical, **10** Rung, **13** Tackles, **15** Thomas, **16** Sorbet, **17** Pestle and mortar, **18** Apache, **20** Collie, **21** Ottoman, **22** Hole, **25** Institutes, **26** Rase, **27** Scoreboard.
DOWN: **1** Kate, **2** Crew, **3** Extras, **4** Bricks and mortar, **5** Coaxes, **7** Bluebottle, **8** Lightermen, **11** Stepfather, **12** Constables, **13** Tally-ho, **14** Solomon, **19** Ethnic, **20** Cantab, **23** Etna, **24** Used.

228

ACROSS: **7** Well ahead, **8** Dogma, **10** Hear hear, **11** Chilli, **12** Edge, **13** Abrogate, **15** Despite, **17** Strolls, **20** Speak out, **22** Reel, **25** Stable, **26** Clear out, **27** Slick, **28** Put in hand.
DOWN: **1** Jewel, **2** Flared, **3** Cheese it, **4** Fairway, **5** Coming to, **6** Small talk, **9** Acer, **14** Keep still, **16** Play back, **18** Turned in, **19** Stuck up, **21** Oder, **23** Earthy, **24** Sunni.

229

ACROSS: **1** Anemometer, **6** Waif, **9** Conversion, **10** Wail, **12** Insect, **13** Dear dear, **15** Spiritualist, **18** Staff-officer, **21** Hysteria, **22** Astral, **24** Dove, **25** Daydreamer, **26** Lark, **27** Settlement.
DOWN: **1** Arctic, **2** Ernest, **3** One's cup of tea, **4** Erst, **5** Egocentric, **7** Academic, **8** Filtrate, **11** Create a scene, **14** Pro igate, **16** Asphodel, **17** Passover, **19** Gramme, **20** Claret, **23** Adit.

230

ACROSS: **1** Sediment, **5** Adrift, **9** Alienate, **10** Slip-up, **12** Constable, **13** Idles, **14** Ache, **16** Senator, **19** Adoring, **21** Meet, **24** Heron, **25** Abominate, **27** Ladder, **28** Pleasant, **29** Reeves, **30** Steerage.
DOWN: **1** Scarce, **2** Deigns, **3** Monet, **4** Notable, **6** Dalliance, **7** Impolite, **8** Tapestry, **11** Less, **15** Clientele, **17** Bachelor, **18** Porridge, **20** Glad, **21** Moonlit, **22** Malaya, **23** Gentle, **26** Irate.

231
ACROSS: 1 Doomsday, 6 Marble, 9 Stores, 10 Road sign, 11 Side-drum, 12 Stunts, 13 Flying doctor, 16 Hairdressers, 19 Player, 21 Lustrous, 23 Ignition, 24 Ulster, 25 Stress, 26 Estonian.
DOWN: 2 Oxtail, 3 Morse, 4 Destroyer, 5 Yardman, 6 Means, 7 Resources, 8 Legation, 13 Forty-five, 14 Dress-suit, 15 Gaslight, 17 Silence, 18 Eureka, 20 Ruins, 22 Rosin.

232
ACROSS: 1 Give-away price, 10 Letters, 11 Explain, 12 Yank, 13 Daddy, 14 Fire, 17 Andante, 18 Doing up, 19 Discard, 22 Charmer, 24 Orbs, 25 Prime, 26 Eyot, 29 Elation, 30 Oregano, 31 Change of heart.
DOWN: 2 Intoned, 3 Even, 4 Wastage, 5 Yielded, 6 Rape, 7 Craving, 8 Play hard to get, 9 In desperation, 15 Unbar, 16 Vital, 20 Sabbath, 21 Derange, 22 Come off, 23 Mayfair, 27 Lien, 28 Here.

233
ACROSS: 1 Impale, 4 Clarinet, 9 Sundae, 10 Agnostic, 12 Read, 13 Rolls, 14 Acre, 17 Balance sheet, 20 Insurrection, 23 Heir, 24 Ivies, 25 Ogre, 28 Positive, 29 Denote, 30 Ladybird, 31 Desert.
DOWN: 1 Inscribe, 2 Pentacle, 3 Loaf, 5 Legal charges, 6 Rood, 7 Notice, 8 Ticket, 11 Sole survivor, 15 Inane, 16 Teach, 18 Diagnose, 19 Interest, 21 Chapel, 22 Missed, 26 Stab, 27 Mete.

234
ACROSS: 6 Military staff, 8 Minute, 9 Leathery, 10 Twa, 11 Octave, 12 Made up to, 14 Caveman, 16 Check in, 20 Tap dance, 23 With it, 24 Ass, 25 Stroller, 26 Took in, 27 Reincarnation.
DOWN: 1 Ill usage, 2 Et cetera, 3 Arc lamp, 4 Island, 5 Cachou, 6 Main character, 7 First division, 13 Exe, 15 Moa, 17 Hows that, 18 Catholic, 19 Bearers, 21 Drop in, 22 No luck.

235
ACROSS: 1 Pins and needles, 9 Unnerve, 10 Hunters, 11 Burr, 12 Brigantine, 14 Reform, 15 Tarragon, 17 Castaway, 18 Borrow, 21 Primordial, 22 Amid, 24 Line-out, 25 Sucrose, 26 Plastic surgeon.
DOWN: 1 Plumber, 2 Non-professional, 3 Airy, 4 Dreary, 5 Echogram, 6 Dining-room, 7 Evening primrose, 8 Astern, 13 Treasonous, 16 Banditti, 17 Cupola, 19 Widgeon, 20 Tarsus, 23 Acer.

236
ACROSS: 1 Toleration, 6 Gala, 10 Spurn, 11 Reformers, 12 Adoption, 13 Eater, 15 Evening, 17 Epigram, 19 Suspend, 21 Pullman, 22 Excel, 24 Aperitif, 27 Damascene, 28 Sedan, 29 Rill, 30 Adventurer.
DOWN: 1 Task, 2 Laundress, 3 Ran up, 4 Terming, 5 Offence, 7 Avert, 8 Assortment, 9 Free will, 14 News-vendor, 16 Idealist, 18 Remainder, 20 Dead-end, 21 Precede, 23 Camel, 25 Inset, 26 Knar.

237
ACROSS: 1 Agglomerate, 8 Hibernating, 11 Abet, 12 Garb, 13 Seducer, 15 Morello, 16 Debar, 17 Nous, 18 Vlei, 19 Bifid, 21 Entreat, 22 Arcadia, 23 Tent, 26 Hell, 27 Gatecrasher, 28 Pseudograph.
DOWN: 2 Grit, 3 Lie-a-bed, 4 Many, 5 Rotator, 6 Tang, 7 Maisonnette, 8 Headhunting, 9 Gall bladder, 10 Abdominally, 14 Remit, 15 Maria, 19 Bandeau, 20 Dresser, 24 Taps, 25 Trio, 26 Help.

238
ACROSS: 1 Long shot, 5 Crimea, 9 Sagacity, 10 Larvae, 11 Exegeses, 12 Fairer, 14 Republican, 18 Give credit, 22 Send on, 23 Boastful, 24 Loofah, 25 Adherent, 26 Digger, 27 Grandson.
DOWN: 1 Listed, 2 Nugget, 3 Sicken, 4 On the level, 6 Readable, 7 Maverick, 8 Aberrant, 13 Put in order, 15 Egg salad, 16 Evensong, 17 Accolade, 19 Astern, 20 Afters, 21 Gluten.

239
ACROSS: 1 Looks through, 9 Bloater, 10 Leg-pull, 11 Ease, 12 Lento, 13 Comb, 16 Topless, 17 Retreat, 18 Forward, 21 Cheerio, 23 Iota, 24 Comma, 25 Butt, 28 Turns up, 29 Smasher, 30 Spider monkey.
DOWN: 1 Looks up, 2 Otto, 3 Screens, 4 Holster, 5 Olga, 6 Glucose, 7 Object of mirth, 8 Globe-trotters, 14 Decay, 15 Other, 19 Rat-trap, 20 Dropper, 21 Comes to, 22 Roughly, 26 Used, 27 Back.

240
ACROSS: 1 Put off, 4 A good way, 9 Lie low, 10 Comedian, 12 Butt, 13 Fresh, 14 Fete, 17 Current issue, 20 Pitch and toss, 23 Arid, 24 Mid on, 25 Bema, 28 Good nick, 29 Decays, 30 Prompter, 31 Broken.
DOWN: 1 Pull back, 2 The stars, 3 Flog, 5 Grouse season, 6 Oyez, 7 Waiver, 8 Yonder, 11 Arctic Circle, 15 Get it, 16 Ruddy, 18 Come back, 19 Assassin, 21 Hang up, 22 Kimono, 26 Snip, 27 Gear.

www.ingramcontent.com/pod-product-compliance
Ingram Content Group UK Ltd.
Pitfield, Milton Keynes, MK11 3LW, UK
UKHW040640280225
455688UK00002B/40